THE VOICE
OF PSALMS

PSALMS RETOLD BY THE FRIENDS OF

ECCLESIA BIBLE SOCIETY

WITH REFLECTIONS FROM THE PSALMS

WRITTEN BY KAREN MOORE AND JAMES F. COUCH, JR.

THOMAS NELSON
Since 1798

NASHVILLE   DALLAS   MEXICO CITY   RIO DE JANEIRO   BEIJING

Friends of Ecclesia Bible Society

Contributors to the Psalms

Contributing Writers

ny Allen, Lee Allen, Isaac Anderson, Eric Bryant, David B. Capes, Don Chaffer, Lori Chaffer, a Leigh Cobble, Greg Garrett, Christena Graves, Sara Groves, Charlie Hall, Kelly Hall, tin Hyde, Greg LaFollette, Katie Lerch, Paul Littleton, Todd Littleton, Christian McCabe, e Morell, Damien O'Farrell, Sean Palmer, Jonathan Hal Reynolds, Matthew Ronan, Chris Seay, bie Seay, Allison Smythe, Matthew Paul Turner, Seth Woods, Dieter Zander

Biblical Scholars

id B. Capes, PhD; Brett Dutton, PhD; Sheri Klouda, PhD; Creig Marlowe, PhD; Chuck Pitts, PhD; n Russell, PhD; Felisi Sorgwe, PhD; Kristin Swenson, PhD; Nancy de Claissé Walford, PhD

Editorial Review By:

eah Bell, James F. Couch, Jr., Marilyn Duncan, Amanda Haley, Kelly Hall, Merrie Noland

TABLE OF CONTENTS

PREFACE

literary project reflects the age in which it is written. **The Voice** is created for and by a church
reat transition. Throughout the body of Christ, extensive discussions are ongoing about a variety
ssues including style of worship, how we separate culture from our theology, what it means to
the gospel, and how we faithfully communicate the essential truth of historic Christianity. At the
ter of this discussion is the role of Scripture. Instead of furthering the division over culture and
ology, it is time to bring the body of Christ together again around the Bible. Thomas Nelson Publishers
Ecclesia Bible Society together are developing Scripture products that foster spiritual growth and
ological exploration out of a heart for worship and mission. We have dedicated ourselves to hearing
proclaiming God's voice through this project.

Previously most Bibles and biblical reference works were produced by professional scholars writing
cademic settings. **The Voice** uniquely represents collaboration among scholars, pastors, writers,
sicians, poets, and other artists. The goal is to create the finest Bible products to help believers
erience the joy and wonder of God's revelation. Four key words describe the vision of this project:

- holistic   considers heart, soul, and mind
- beautiful   achieves literary and artistic excellence
- sensitive   respects cultural shifts and the need for accuracy
- balanced   includes theologically diverse writers and scholars

iqueness of *The Voice*

ut 40 different human authors are believed to have been inspired by God to write the Scriptures. **The**
ce retains the unique literary perspective of the human writers. Most English translations attempt
ven out the styles of the different authors in sentence structure and vocabulary. Instead, **The Voice**
nguishes the uniqueness of each author. The heart of the project is retelling the story of the Bible
form as fluid as modern literary works yet remaining painstakingly true to the original manuscripts.
omplished writers and biblical scholars are teamed up to create an English rendering that, while
reat artistic value, is carefully aligned with the original texts. Attention is paid to the use of idioms,
stic elements, confusion of pronouns, repetition of conjunctions, modern sentence structure, and the
lic reading of the passage. In the process, the writer or scholar may adjust the arrangement of words
xpand the phrasing to create an English equivalent.

To help the reader understand how the new rendering of a passage compares to the original
uscripts, **italic type** indicates words not directly tied to a dynamic translation of the original
uage. These words or sentences in italics may contain information meant to help the reader better
erstand the text without having to stop and read footnotes or a study guide.

Throughout **The Voice,** other language devices improve readability. We follow the standard
ventions used in most translations regarding textual evidence. **The Voice** is based on the earliest

and best manuscripts from the original Hebrew. When significant variations influence a reading, follow the publishing standard by bracketing the passage and placing a note at the bottom of the p while maintaining the traditional chapter and verse divisions. The footnotes reference quoted mate and help the reader understand the translation for a particular word. For clarity, some pronouns replaced with their antecedents. Word order and parts of speech are sometimes altered to help reader understand the original passage.

Our purpose in using these literary devices is to enhance the beauty of the Scriptures and to as the reader in clearly and quickly understanding the meaning of the text. We are constrained to faithful to these ancient texts while giving the present reader a respectful and moving experience the Word of God.

—Ecclesia Bible Soc

ABOUT *THE VOICE* PROJECT

As retold, edited, and illustrated by a gifted team
of writers, scholars, poets, and storytellers

New Way to Process Ideas

is Seay's (president of Ecclesia Bible Society) vision for *The Voice* goes back 20 years to his early mpts to teach the whole biblical narrative as the story of God's redemptive work in the Liberating g. As Western culture has moved into what is now referred to as postmodernism, Chris has observed : the way a new generation processes ideas and information raises obstacles to traditional methods aching biblical content. His desire has grown to present the Bible in ways that overcome these tacles to people coming to faith. Instead of adhering to propositional-based thought patterns, people ay are more likely to interact with events and individuals through complex observations involving otions, cognitive processes, tactile experiences, and spiritual awareness. Much as in the parables of us and in the metaphors of the prophets, narrative communication touches the whole person.

e Timeless Narrative

* *Voice* is a fresh expression of the timeless narrative known as the Bible. Stories of God's goodness : were told to each generation by their grandparents and tribal leaders were recorded and assembled orm the Christian Scriptures. Too often, the passion, grit, humor, and beauty have been lost in the slation process. *The Voice* seeks to recapture what was lost.

From these early explorations by Chris and others has come *The Voice:* a Scripture project to scover the story of the Bible. Thomas Nelson Publishers and Ecclesia Bible Society have joined ether to stimulate unique creative experiences and to develop Scripture products and resources oster spiritual growth and theological exploration out of a heart for the mission of the church and ship of God.

ditional Translations

ing the Bible into the language of modern readers has too often been a painstaking process of elating the biblical languages to the English vernacular. The Bible is filled with passages intended spire, captivate, and depict beauty. The old school of translation most often fails at attempts to municate beauty, poetry, and story. *The Voice* is a collage of compelling narratives, poetry, song, , and wisdom. *The Voice* will call you to enter into the whole story of God with your heart, soul, mind.

New Retelling

* *Voice* is at heart a retelling of the story of God's love and redemption of creation. The "retelling" lves translation and elaboration, but mostly entering into the story of the Scriptures and recreating event for our culture and time. It doesn't ignore the role of scholars, but it also values the role of ers, poets, songwriters, and artists. In this work, a team of scholars partners with the writers to blend

the mood and voice of the original author with an accurate rendering of the words of the text in Engl **The Voice** is unique in this collaboration. Its goal is to create the finest Bible products to help believ experience the joy and wonder of God's revelation.

To accomplish the objectives of **The Voice** project and to facilitate the various products envisio within it, the Bible text is being translated. We trust that this retelling will be a helpful contribution fresh engagement with Scripture. **The Voice** brings the biblical text to life and reads more like a gr novel than the traditional versions of the Bible that are seldom opened in contemporary culture.

Readable and Enjoyable

A careful process is being followed to assure that the spiritual, emotional, and artistic goals of project are met. First, the retelling of the Bible has been designed to be readable and enjoyable emphasizing the narrative nature of Scripture. Beyond simply providing a set of accurately transla individual words, phrases, and sentences, our teams were charged to render the biblical texts w sensitivity to the flow of the unfolding story. We asked them to see themselves not only as guardian the sacred text, but also as storytellers, because we believe that the Bible has always been intende be heard as the sacred story of the people of God.

Personal and Diverse

Second, as a consequence of this team approach, **The Voice** is both personal and diverse. God u several instruments to communicate His message in Psalms, and each one has a unique voice literary style. Standard translations tend to flatten these individual styles so that each book reads m or less like the others—with a kind of impersonal textbook-style prose. Some versions have more attention to literary style—but again, the literary style of one writer, no matter how gifted, unintentionally obscure the diversity of the original voices. To address these problems, we asked teams to try to feel and convey the diverse literary styles of the original authors.

Faithful

Third, we have taken care that **The Voice** is faithful and that it avoids prejudice. Anyone who has wor with translation knows that there is no such thing as a completely unbiased or objective translation. while we do not pretend to be purely objective, we asked our teams to seek to be as faithful as poss to the biblical message as they understood it together. In addition, as we partnered biblical scho and theologians with our writers, we intentionally built teams that did not share any single theolog tradition. Their diversity has helped each of them not to be trapped within his or her own indivic preconceptions, resulting in a faithful and fresh rendering of the Bible.

Stimulating and Creative

Fourth, we have worked hard to make **The Voice** both stimulating and creative. As we engaged biblical text, we realized again and again that certain terms have conventional associations for moc readers that would not have been present for the original readers—and that the original readers w have been struck by certain things that remain invisible or opaque to modern readers. Even more, realized that modern readers from different religious or cultural traditions would hear the same wc

erently. We want the next generation of Bible readers—whatever their background—to have the
st opportunity possible to hear God's message the way the first generation of Bible readers heard it.

ansformative

ally, we desire that this translation will be useful and transformative. It is all too common in many
our Protestant churches to have only a few verses of biblical text read in a service, and then that
ection too often becomes a jumping-off point for a sermon that is at best peripherally related to,
ch less rooted in, the Bible itself. The goal of *The Voice* is to promote the public reading of longer
tions of Scripture—followed by thoughtful engagement with the biblical narrative in its richness and
ness and dramatic flow. We believe the Bible itself, in all its diversity and energy and dynamism, is
message.

her products available with *The Voice*

- *The Last Eyewitness: The Final Week*—the final week of the life of Jesus on earth.
- *The Dust Off Their Feet: Lessons from the First Church*—Book of Acts.
- *The Voice of Matthew*—the Gospel of Matthew.
- *The Voice of Luke: Not Even Sandals*—the Gospel of Luke.
- *The Voice from on High*—from 19 Old and New Testament books the story of the Liberating King.
- *The Voice Revealed*—the full Gospel of John in a compact edition.
- *The Voice of Hebrews: The Mystery of Melchizedek*—the Book of Hebrews.
- *The Voice of Mark: Let Them Listen*—the Gospel of Mark.
- *The Voice of Romans: The Gospel According to Paul*—Romans.
- *The Voice New Testament*

e Team

team writing *The Voice of Psalms* brings unprecedented gifts to this unique project. An award-
ning fiction writer, an acclaimed poet, a pastor renowned for using art and narrative in his preaching
teaching, Hebrew authorities, and biblical scholars are all coming together to capture the beauty
diversity of God's Word. So far, the community of talent that has created *The Voice's* publications
the result of the extraordinary contributions of 11 New Testament writers, 15 Old Testament writers,
New Testament scholars, 40 Old Testament scholars, and 35 other contributors to music, art, Web
design, and articles.

A Word from Ecclesia Bible Society

I speak for every artist, musician, editor, writer, and scholar involved in this retelling of the Book
Psalms in saying it has been an honor to have labored, studied, fasted, and prayed over the work th
we believe God has placed before us. We have not taken the task lightly, and through the process
have been changed. We are thrilled to see the ways that God uses His Word to speak to His people a
reveal Himself to those who had never heard His voice clearly.

As you engage with the poetry and drama of the Psalms, may you find a renewed sense of what i
like to be in the presence of God. Psalms is much more than a collection of hymns; it is the interacti
of God's people in the midst of turmoil and victory, of brokenness and blessing, of fear and joy with
source of all they are and hope to be. This is the story of the enduring trust of dedicated believers a
their God's discipline of them and His mercy in their time of need. We experience the precarious life th
had between their enemies and their rock, the Eternal One of Israel. The emotion is raw and very re

We believe that as you read you will be able to experience God taking the broken pieces of yc
life and making you whole; your anger and resentment will be replaced with hope and grace; you
imagine a new way to live as a participant in God's redemptive work in this world.

I invite you to listen to **The Voice of Psalms** with an open heart. You will hear God as He whispe
of His love to His people of Israel and now to you.

Chris Seay
President, Ecclesia Bible Society

A Twenty-Eight-Day Reading Plan
for the Season of Advent

celebrate during the four weeks of Advent, read the quote below and then the selection from
lms.

One:　　　　Before Anything—There Was God　　　　Reading—Psalm 104:1-13

fore time itself was measured, the Voice was speaking. The Voice was and is God. This *celestial* Voice
nained ever present with the Creator; His speech shaped the entire cosmos. *Immersed in the practice
reating,* all things that exist were birthed in Him. His breath filled all things with a living, breathing
nt. John 1:1-4

Two:　　　　God—Always in Control　　　　Reading—Psalm 99:1-5

rnal God *(to the serpent):* What you have done carries great consequences. Now you are cursed more
han cattle or other beasts. You will writhe on your belly forever, consuming the dust out *of which man
was made.* I will make you and your brood enemies of the woman and all her children; the woman's
hild will stomp your head, and you will bite his heel. Genesis 3:14-15

Three:　　　　God's Love Is Immense　　　　Reading—Psalm 36:5-12

　　He said *clearly* to me, "You are My son.
　　　　Today I have become your Father." Psalm 2:7

Four:　　　　High in Our Hearts　　　　Reading—Psalm113:1-9

t *yourself.* The Lord will give you a proof-sign, a pledge, anyway: See, a young maiden will conceive.
e will give birth to a son and name Him Immanuel, *that is, "God with us."* Isaiah 7:14

Five:　　　　His Ways Are Wondrous　　　　Reading—Psalm 111:1-10

here, *finally,* is the story of the Liberator's birth *(it is quite a remarkable story):*
　　Mary was engaged to marry Joseph, *son of David.* They hadn't married. And yet, some time well
ore their wedding date, Mary learned that she was pregnant by the Holy Spirit. Joseph, because he
s kind and upstanding and honorable, wanted to spare Mary shame. He did not wish to cause her
re embarrassment than necessary. Matthew 1:18-19

Six:　　　　Offer Thanks—Feel His Joy　　　　Reading—Psalm 105:1-5

　　Now when Joseph had decided to act on his instincts, a messenger of the Lord came to him in a
am.

ssenger of the Lord: Joseph, son of David, do not be afraid to wed Mary *and bring her into your home
nd family* as your wife. *She did not sneak off and sleep with someone else*—rather, she conceived the
aby she now carries through the miraculous wonderworking of the Holy Spirit. She will have a son,
nd you will name Him Jesus, *which means "the Lord saves,"* because this Jesus is the person who will
ave all of His people from sin. Matthew 1:20-21

Seven:　　　　Clothed in Majesty　　　　Reading—Psalm 93:1-5

The Eternal One will be, really be, among us.
　　The radiant glory *of the Lord* will be revealed.
　　All flesh together will take it in.
　　Believe it. None other than God, the Eternal One has spoken. Isaiah 40:5

Day Eight: Declare—Salvation from God Reading—Psalm 96:1-13

Joseph woke up from his dream and did exactly what the messenger had told him to do: he married Mary and brought her into his home as his wife (though he did not consummate their marriage until after her son was born). *And when the baby was born*, Joseph named Him Jesus, *Savior*. Matthew 1:24

Day Nine: He Is Coming Reading—Psalm 98:1-9

But from you, Bethlehem of Ephrathah,
    in the land of Judah, are no poor relation—
From your people will come a Ruler
    who will be the shepherd of My people, Israel,
Whose origins date back to the distant past,
    to the ancient days. Micah 5:2

Day Ten: Sing with Great Affection Reading—Psalm 108:1-4

Nearby, in the fields outside of Bethlehem, a group of shepherds were guarding their flocks *from predators* in the darkness of night. Suddenly a messenger of the Lord stood in front of them, and the darkness was replaced by a glorious light—the shining light of God's glory. They were terrified!

Messenger: Don't be afraid! Listen! I bring good news, news of great joy, news that will affect all peopl[e] everywhere. Today, in the city of David, a Liberator has been born for you! He is the promised Liberating King, the Supreme Authority! You will know you have found Him when you see a baby, wrapped in a blanket, lying in a feeding trough. Luke 2:8-12

Day Eleven: The Glorious King Comes Reading—Psalm 24:1-10

Hope of all hopes, dream of our dreams,
    a child has been born, *sweet-breathed*, a son is given to us: a living gift.
And even now, with tiny features and dewy hair,
    He is great. The power of leadership
    and the weight of authority will rest on His shoulders.
His name? His name *we'll know in many ways*—
    He will be called Wonderful Counselor, *wise beyond belief*, the Great God,
Dear Father everlasting, ever-present never-failing,
    Master of wholeness, SarShalom (*which means* "Prince of peace").
His leadership will bring such prosperity *as you've never seen before*—
    sustainable in its integrity, peace for all time.
    This child will keep alive God's promise to David—
A throne forever, *right here among us.*
    He will restore sound leadership that will not, that cannot be perverted or shaken. Isaiah 9:6-7

Day Twelve: You Who Serve—Lift Your Praise Reading—Psalm 134:1-3

Jesus was born in the town of Bethlehem, in the province of Judea, at the time when King Herod reigned. *Not long after Jesus was born,* magi, wise men or seers from the East, *understood that the One w[ho] would save His people from sin had been born, so they set off to find the baby Savior.* Making their way fro[m] the East to Jerusalem, these wise men made inquiries.

Wise Men: Where is this newborn, who is the King of the Jews? When we were far away in the East we saw His star, and we have followed its glisten and gleam all this way to worship Him. Matthew 2:1-2

Day Thirteen: Erupt with Joy Reading—Psalm 66:1-7

The wise men *left Herod's chambers* and went on their way. The star they had first seen in the East reappeared—a miracle that, of course, overjoyed and enraptured the wise men. The star led them to the house where Jesus lay; and as soon as the wise men arrived, they saw Him with His mother Mary, and they bowed down and worshiped Him. They unpacked their satchels and gave Jesus gifts of gold, frankincense, and myrrh. Matthew 2:9-11

Fourteen: We Witness His Great Deeds   Reading—Psalm 107:23-38

Raised up in the presence of all peoples.
He is the light who reveals Your message to the other nations,
      and He is the shining glory of Your *covenant* people, Israel. Luke 2:31-32

Fifteen   He Reigns over All Other Lords   Reading—Psalm 136:1-9

Behold! The time is near
      when I will raise up an *authentic*, righteous Branch of David,
      an heir of his royal line,
A King who will rule justly and act wisely
      and bring righteousness to the land. Jeremiah 23:5

Sixteen: His Throne Is in the Heavens   Reading—Psalm 103:19-22

us: I am. *One day* you will see the Son of Man "sitting at His right hand, *in the place of honor and* ower," and "coming in the clouds of heaven." Mark 14:62

Seventeen: The Great Shepherd   Reading—Psalm 23:1-6

rnal One: Watch carefully! I will personally judge between the fat sheep and the skinny sheep. Because ou bully the weak and push them around with your haunches, shoulders, and horns until they are cattered all over *the mountains*, I will step in and save them. *I will be their rescuer!* They will no longer e hunted and hassled. I will judge between one sheep and another. I will designate one shepherd over he entire flock: My *faithful* servant, David. He will *watch over them and* take care of them. He will be heir shepherd. Ezekiel 34:20-23

Eighteen: His Rule Is Forever   Reading—Psalm 145:8-21

O God, Your throne is eternal;
      You will rule your kingdom with a scepter of justice. Psalm 45:6

Nineteen: Celebrate His Love   Reading—Psalm 118:21-29

all be his Father, and he will be My son. I shall not take My favor from him as I took it from *Saul* o reigned before you. I shall establish him *and his descendants as My representatives* in My temple and My kingdom forever. His throne will last forever. 1 Chronicles 17:13-14

Twenty: He Hears My Call   Reading—Psalm 116:1-7

ses: Let's say I go to the people of Israel and tell them, "The True God of your fathers has sent me to escue you," and then they reply, "What is His name?" What should I tell them then?
: I AM WHO I AM. This is what you should tell the people of Israel: "I AM has sent me to rescue you." his is what you are to tell Israel's people: "The Eternal God of your fathers, the God of Abraham, the God of Isaac, and the God of Jacob is the One who has sent me to you." This is My name forevermore, nd this is the name by which all future generations shall remember Me. Exodus 3:13-15

Twenty-One: He Is Perfect   Reading—Psalm 19:1-10

The Eternal One has sworn an oath
      and cannot change His mind:
"You are a priest forever—
      in the *honored* order of Melchizedek." Psalm 110:4

Twenty-Two: Sing with All Your Strength   Reading—Psalm 149:1-5

He will feed His fold like a shepherd;
      God will assure that we are safe and content.
He will gather together His lambs, *the weak and the wobbly ones* into His arms,
      carrying them close to His bosom. Isaiah 40:11

Day Twenty-Three: Rescue the Flock: Israel   Reading—Psalm 80:1-3

Eternal One: I will personally go out searching for My sheep. I will find them wherever they are, *and I w look after them*. In the same way that a shepherd seeks after, *cares for, and watches over* his scattered flock, so will I be the guardian of My congregation. I will be their Rescuer! *No matter where they ha scattered, I will journey to find them*. I will bring them back from the places where they were scattere on that dark and cloudy day. *I will reach into hard-to-reach places; I will search out every secret pocket the earth in order to save them from the darkness*. Ezekiel 34:11-12

Day Twenty-Four: Celebrate—He's in Charge   Reading—Psalm 111:1-5

"From there I will make the strength of David's *kingdom* grow
        and prepare a lamp for My anointed one.
I will clothe his enemies with *a garment of* shame;
        but as for David's son, his crown will shine *brightly like the sun*." Psalm 132:17-18

Day Twenty-Five: Let No One Be Left Out   Reading—Psalm 150:1-6

Eternal One: Behold! I am sending My messenger,
        and he will clear the road ahead for Me.
The Lord you seek will suddenly arrive at His temple
        and the messenger of God's covenant, your soul's delight.
Watch! Because He too is coming.

Can anyone live through the day when He arrives?
        Will anyone be left standing when He appears?
He is a purifying fire;
        He is lye soap.
Like a refiner of silver,
        He will purify the descendants of Levi—
        until they are pure, unalloyed gold and silver.
Then they *will draw near to* the Eternal One,
        presenting offerings with righteous, *clean hands*. Malachi 3:1-3

Day Twenty-Six: His Chosen People   Reading—Psalm 114:1-7

Ah, how beautiful the feet of those on the mountain
        who declare the good news *of victory,*
        of peace and liberation.
The voice that calls to Zion, *that place of choice and God's promise people,*
        announcing to them, "Your God rules!" Isaiah 52:7

Day Twenty-Seven: The Heavens Praise Him   Reading—Psalm 148:1-6

Voice from Heaven: You are My Son, the Son I love, and in You I take great pleasure. Luke 3:22

Day Twenty-Eight: God's Glory   Reading—Psalm 8:1-9

You said, "I have made a covenant with My chosen one.
        I made My servant, David, this promise:
'I will establish your dynasty so that you and your descendants will always be secure.
        Your rule will continue for generations to come.'" Psalm 89:3-4

A FORTY-DAY READING PLAN
FOR THE SEASON OF LENT

a biblical meditation each day of Lent, read the quote below and then the selection from Psalms.

One: He Covered All Their Sins   **Reading—Psalm 85:1-13**

And on this child *from David's line*, the Spirit of the Eternal One will *alight and* rest.
> On this one, fresh and green,
> the spirit of wisdom and discernment *will shine like the dew.*
He will judge fairly and act courageously.
> Grounded in deep knowledge and reverence of the Eternal One,
> He will determine fairness and equity.
He will consider more than what meets the eye,
> and weigh in more than what he's told. Isaiah 11:2-3

Two: Foundation of Life—Trust Him   **Reading—Psalm 28:1-9**

The stone that the builders rejected
> has become the very stone that holds together the entire foundation. Psalm 118:22

Three: He Brought Back the Exiles to Zion   **Reading—Psalm 126:1-6**

So *be ready and* watch carefully. The time is approaching, coming ever so close when no one will any longer, "As the Eternal One lives, who freed the Israelites out of slavery in Egypt." Instead, they say, "As the Eternal One lives, who *ended our exile and* gathered the descendants of Israel out of the th and out of all other countries where He had scattered them." Then the Israelites will live in their n land. Jeremiah 23:7-8

Four: He Cherishes All That Is Upright   **Reading—Psalm 11:1-7**

nal One: I will personally go out searching for My sheep. I will find them wherever they are, *and I will ook after them.* In the same way that a shepherd seeks after, *cares for, and watches over* his scattered ock, so will I be the guardian of My congregation. I will be their Rescuer! *No matter where they have cattered, I will journey to find them.* I will bring them back from the places where they were scattered n that dark and cloudy day. *I will reach into hard-to-reach places; I will search out every secret pocket of he earth in order to save them from the darkness.* Ezekiel 34:11-12

Five: Don't Forget the Downtrodden   **Reading—Psalm 10:12-17**

Let every king *on earth* bow down before him
> and every nation be in his service.
For he will rescue the needy when they ask for help!
> *He will save* the burdened and *come to the aid of* those who have no other help.
He offers compassion to the weak and the poor;
> he will *help and* protect the lives of the needy! Psalm 72:11-13

Six: A Safe Place   **Reading—Psalm 18:1-19**

But God will reach into the grave and save my life from its power.
> He will fetch me *and take me into His eternal house.* Psalm 49:15

Seven: A Great Light   **Reading—Psalm 80:1-7**

Then, *such healing, such repair:* the eyes of the blind will be opened,
> the ears of the deaf will be clear *to hear the ring of music.*

The lame will leap like deer *excited*;
　they will run and jump tirelessly and gracefully.
The stutterer, the stammerer, and the tongue of the mute
　will sing out loud and strong, *clear as a new day.* Isaiah 35:5-6

Day Eight:　　Inhabitants of His Pasture　　Reading—Psalm 95:1-7

He will feed His fold like a shepherd;
　God will assure that we are safe and content.
He will gather together His lambs, *the weak and the wobbly ones* into His arms,
　carrying them close to His bosom.
And God tenderly leads those *burdened by caretaking*
　like a shepherd leads the mothers of her lambs. Isaiah 40:11

Day Nine:　　How Long Must I Agonize?　　Reading—Psalm 13:1-6

Eternal One: A voice rises from Ramah—
　weeping and mourning are heard *out loud all day and night.*
It is Rachel weeping for her children,
　who have been killed; *she weeps,*
　and she will not be comforted. Jeremiah 31:15

Day Ten:　　Attacked Since I Was Young　　Reading—Psalm 129:1-8

Out of what seemed like nothing, sterile and empty conditions,
　He came. Like a tender shoot from rock-hard ground.
He didn't look like anything or anyone of consequence—
　He had no physical beauty to attract attention.
So He was dismissed *at best* and sometimes abused.
　We didn't think much of Him,
　this man of constant suffering, grief's *patient* friend. Isaiah 53:2-3

Day Eleven:　　A Shelter for Those in Misery　　Reading—Psalm 9:9-20

But He hurt because of us; because of us, He suffered so.
　Our wrongdoing wounded and crushed Him.
He endured the breaking that made us whole.
　His injuries became our healing.
We had wandered off, like shepherdless sheep
　scattered by our aimless striving and endless pursuits. Isaiah 53:5-6

Day Twelve:　　He Set Me on a Rock　　Reading—Psalm 27:1-15

Though I treat them well, they answer me with evil;
　Though I give them love, they reply with *a gesture of* hatred.
Here's what they say: Find some evil scoundrel to go after him.
　Let's get some accuser *to level charges* against him. Psalm 109:5-6

Day Thirteen:　　Entrusting My Spirit into Your Hands　　Reading—Psalm 31:1-5

I will *watch over My sheep and* feed My flock. *Whenever they are tired*, they can lie down in the cool,
mountain grass and rest *for as long as they like.* When they are lost, I will look for them and bring back
every last stray. I will bind up the injured and strengthen the weak. Ezekiel 34:15-16

Day Fourteen:　　His Word Is Perfect and True　　Reading—Psalm 33:1-12

Jesus: I tell you the truth: Moses did not give you bread from heaven; it is My Father who offers you
bread from heaven. The bread of God comes down out of heaven and breathes life into the cosmos
John 6:32-33

y Fifteen: A Dry Land   Reading—Psalm 143:1-12

us: I am the bread that gives life. If you come to My table and eat, you will never go hungry. Believe n Me, and you will never go thirsty. Here I am standing in front of you, and still you don't believe. All that My Father gives to Me comes to Me. I will receive everyone; I will not send away anyone who comes to Me. John 6:35-37

y Sixteen: His Grace Lasts a Lifetime   Reading—Psalm 30:1-12

us: So if you want to know the will of the Father, know this: everyone who sees the Son and believes n Him will live eternally; and on the last day, I am the One who will resurrect him. John 6:40

y Seventeen: The Great Shepherd   Reading—Psalm 23:1-6

us: I am the good shepherd; I know My sheep, and My sheep know Me. As the Father knows Me, know the Father; I will give My life for the sheep. John 10:14-15

y Eighteen: Guide My Journey along Your Path   Reading—Psalm 17:1-5

us: I am the path, the truth, and the *energy of* life. No one comes to the Father except through Me. ohn 14:6

y Nineteen: My Constant Helper   Reading—Psalm 17:1-5

us: But the truth is that My departure will be a gift that will serve you well, because if I don't leave, the great Helper will not come to your aid. When I leave, I will send Him to you. John 16:7

y Twenty: Come to Rescue You   Reading—Psalm 20:1-9

    Cry out with joy, O daughter of Zion!
        Shout *jubilantly*, O daughter of Jerusalem!
    Look—your King is coming;
        He is righteous and able to save.
    He comes seated humbly on a donkey,
        on a colt, a foal of a donkey. Zechariah 9:9

y Twenty-One: Israel Didn't Obey   Reading—Psalm 81:1-13

us: Didn't the prophets write, "My house will be called a house of prayer, for all the people," you have made it into a "haven for thieves"? Mark 11:17

y Twenty-Two: He Never Rests or Sleeps   Reading—Psalm 121:1-8

    The Eternal One will liberate His servants;
        those who seek refuge in Him will never be condemned. Psalm 34:22

y Twenty-Three: My Companion   Reading—Psalm 55:1-14

    And Judas, the one who intended to betray Him, had said *to the elders and the chief priests* that he uld give them a sign.

as: *I'll greet Him with a kiss.* And you will know that the One I kiss is the One you should arrest. Matthew 26:48

y Twenty-Four: I Am All Alone   Reading—Psalm 88:8-18

us: This scene has come together just so, so that the prophecies in the sacred Scripture could be ulfilled.

d at that, all the disciples ran away and abandoned Him. Matthew 26:56

y Twenty-Five: God Knows How People Think   Reading—Psalm 94:1-11

    Everyone who sees me laughs at me;
        they whisper *to one another* I'm a loser; they sneer and mock me, saying,
    "He relies on the Eternal One; let the Eternal rescue
        and keep him safe because He is happy with him." Psalm 22:7-8

Day Twenty-Six: Strangers Rally against Me   Reading—Psalm 54:1-7
> False witnesses step forward;
>> they ask me *strange* questions for which I have no answers. Psalm 35:11

Day Twenty-Seven: Too Many Adversaries to Count   Reading—Psalm 3:1-8
> I'm surrounded by many tormentors;
>> like strong bulls of Bashan, they circle around me *with their taunts.*
> They open their mouths wide at me
>> like ravenous, roaring lions. Psalm 22:12-13

Day Twenty-Eight: I Will Judge Fairly   Reading—Psalm 75:1-10
Pilate: You presented this man to me as a rabble-rouser, but I examined Him in your presence and foun
> Him not guilty of the charges you have leveled against Him. Luke 23:14

Day Twenty-Nine: Let Their Devices Bring Ruin   Reading—Psalm 5:1-12
> Judas—the one who had betrayed Him *with a kiss for 30 pieces of silver*—saw that Jesus had been
condemned, and suddenly Judas regretted what he had done. He took the silver back to the chief pries
and elders *and tried to return it to them.* Matthew 27:3

Day Thirty: Why Have You Turned Your Back?   Reading—Psalm 74:1-3, 12-
> My God, my God, why have You turned Your back on me?
>> Your ears are deaf to my groans. Psalm 22:1

Day Thirty-One: Shield Me from Violent Men   Reading—Psalm 140:1-8
> My life is poured out like water,
>> and all my bones have slipped out of joint.
> My heart melts like wax inside me.
> My strength is gone, dried up like shards of pottery;
>> my *dry* tongue sticks to the roof of my mouth;
>> You lay me in the dust of death. Psalm 22:14-15

Day Thirty-Two: Has He Withdrawn His Compassion?   Reading—Psalm 77:1-9
> And me? I cry out to Him,
>> "Heal my soul, O Eternal One, and show mercy
>> because I have sinned against You!" Psalm 41:4

Day Thirty-Three: The Foolish Believes There Is No God   Reading—Psalm 14:1-4
The Roman Centurion, *the soldier in charge of the executions,* stood in front of Jesus, [heard His words
and saw the manner of His death.
Centurion: Surely this man was the Son of God! Mark 15:39

Day Thirty-Four: I Can't Worship if I'm Dead   Reading—Psalm 6:1-10
> And when He was dead, He was buried with disgrace
>> *in borrowed space* (among the rich)
> Even though He did no wrong deed
>> and no evil came from His mouth. Isaiah 53:9

Day Thirty-Five: We Thought of Zion   Reading—Psalm 137:1-6
> When You ascended the sacred mountain,
>> with Your prisoners in tow, Your captives *in chains,*
>> You *sat in triumph* receiving gifts from men,
> Even from those who rebel *against You,* so that *You,* the Eternal God,
>> might take up residence there. Psalm 68:18

A FORTY-DAY READING PLAN TO WORSHIP THE ETERNAL ONE WITH YOUR PRAISE

For a time of praise each day, read the entire psalm and the reflection that accompanies every other psalm listed below.

Day One:	Psalm 150	Day Twenty-One:	Psalm 34
Day Two:	Psalm 47	Day Twenty-Two:	Psalm 108
Day Three:	Psalm 27	Day Twenty-Three:	Psalm 23
Day Four:	Psalm 67	Day Twenty-Four:	Psalm 36
Day Five:	Psalm 96	Day Twenty-Five:	Psalm 138
Day Six:	Psalm 146	Day Twenty-Six:	Psalm 114
Day Seven:	Psalm 100	Day Twenty-Seven:	Psalm 147
Day Eight:	Psalm 148	Day Twenty-Eight:	Psalm 61
Day Nine:	Psalm 65	Day Twenty-Nine:	Psalm 84
Day Ten:	Psalm 43	Day Thirty:	Psalm 135
Day Eleven:	Psalm 19	Day Thirty-One:	Psalm 134
Day Twelve:	Psalm 97	Day Thirty-Two:	Psalm 48
Day Thirteen:	Psalm 113	Day Thirty-Three:	Psalm 91
Day Fourteen:	Psalm 29	Day Thirty-Four:	Psalm 66
Day Fifteen:	Psalm 93	Day Thirty-Five:	Psalm 104
Day Sixteen:	Psalm 117	Day Thirty-Six:	Psalm 133
Day Seventeen:	Psalm 57	Day Thirty-Seven:	Psalm 136
Day Eighteen:	Psalm 76	Day Thirty-Eight:	Psalm 99
Day Nineteen:	Psalm 98	Day Thirty-Nine:	Psalm 145
Day Twenty:	Psalm 92	Day Forty:	Psalm 24

A FORTY-DAY READING PLAN FOR SEEKING HELP FROM THE TRUE GOD

To assist you in a season dedicated to seeking God's help, read the entire psalm and the reflection that accompanies the majority of the psalms listed below.

Day One:	Psalm 1	Day Twenty-One:	Psalm 42
Day Two:	Psalm 31	Day Twenty-Two:	Psalm 85
Day Three:	Psalm 22	Day Twenty-Three:	Psalm 63
Day Four:	Psalm 17	Day Twenty-Four:	Psalm 46
Day Five:	Psalm 142	Day Twenty-Five:	Psalm 122
Day Six:	Psalm 18	Day Twenty-Six:	Psalm 123
Day Seven:	Psalm 4	Day Twenty-Seven:	Psalm 140
Day Eight:	Psalm 6	Day Twenty-Eight:	Psalm 55
Day Nine:	Psalm 50	Day Twenty-Nine:	Psalm 143
Day Ten:	Psalm 62	Day Thirty:	Psalm 86
Day Eleven:	Psalm 38	Day Thirty-One:	Psalm 103
Day Twelve:	Psalm 28	Day Thirty-Two:	Psalm 64
Day Thirteen:	Psalm 54	Day Thirty-Three:	Psalm 125
Day Fourteen:	Psalm 30	Day Thirty-Four:	Psalm 74
Day Fifteen:	Psalm 71	Day Thirty-Five:	Psalm 118
Day Sixteen:	Psalm 60	Day Thirty-Six:	Psalm 121
Day Seventeen:	Psalm 44	Day Thirty-Seven:	Psalm 59
Day Eighteen:	Psalm 56	Day Thirty-Eight:	Psalm 141
Day Nineteen:	Psalm 107	Day Thirty-Nine:	Psalm 13
Day Twenty:	Psalm 12	Day Forty:	Psalm 130

Psalm 1

[1]*God's* blessings follow you *and await you at every turn*:
> when you don't follow the advice of those who delight in wicked
> > schemes,
When you avoid sin's highway,
> when judgment and sarcasm beckon you, but you refuse.
[2]For you, the Eternal One's Word is your happiness.
> It is your focus—from dusk to dawn
And in the nights that separate the two—you are consumed with its message.
[3]You are like a tree,
> planted by *flowing, cool* streams of water *that never run dry.*
Your fruit ripens in its time;
> your leaves never fade or curl *in the summer sun.*
No matter what you do, you prosper.

[4]For those who focus on sin, the story is different.
> They are like the fallen husk of wheat, tossed by an open wind, *left*
> > *deserted and alone.*

PSALM 1 | **"Focus—from dusk to dawn."** The psalmist must be joking; we are being pulled one way and moments later find ourselves pulled in an altogether different direction. The world around us is demanding every ounce of focus we have. How can we focus on God's path when the pull of the world is presented in tempting packages everywhere we turn?

In the face of such conflict, we rebel at the very idea that we are to follow a path God has prepared when we are certain that only we know what is best. The emphasis in this psalm is on "the Eternal One's Word," which is followed immediately by the phrase "is your happiness." God wants us to stay centered on His unyielding love for us that brings us "happiness." With that in mind, what will we do? Will we be tossed by the winds of the world's demands, left deserted and alone, or will we follow the way of the Eternal One for our own happiness?

Focus: never take your eyes off the goal. The goal is happiness in the presence of the Eternal One, and the path is His Word to us. The distraction is the world and all it's attractions. Focus.

[5]In the end, the wicked will fall in judgment;
     the guilty will be separated from the innocent.
[6]Their road suddenly will end in death,
     yet the journey of the righteous has been charted by the Eternal One.

PSALM 2

[1]*You are wondering:* What has provoked the nations to embrace *anger and*
     *chaos?**
     Why are the people making plans to pursue their own vacant and
          empty greatness?
[2]Leaders of nations stand united;
     rulers put their heads together,
          plotting against the Eternal One and His Anointed *King,* trying to
               figure out
[3]How they can throw off the gentle reign of God's love,
     step out from under the restrictions of His claims *to advance their own*
          schemes.

[4]*At first,* the Power of heaven laughs *at their silliness.*
     The Eternal mocks their *ignorant selfishness.*
[5]But His laughter turns to rage, and He rebukes them.
     As God displays His *righteous* anger, they begin to know *the meaning*
          of fear. He says,

2:1 Greek manuscripts read "rage."

PSALM 2 | **"Be warned!"** Hey! Wait just one minute! Why am I being warned?
Is it because we are no different from those in Jesus' time who chose to save a
murderer from the cross instead of saving the Son of God? We often look right
past the reality God has set before us. Here we see "leaders of nations . . . plotting
against the Eternal One." Look what follows: "Trying to figure out how can they
throw off the gentle reign of God's love." God will not allow any of us to frustrate
His love. In the end, there will be two groups: those who side with God and "bow
down before God's Son" and those who "step out from under" the grace of God.

⁶"I am the One who appointed My king who reigns from Zion, My mount
of holiness.
He is the one in charge."

⁷I am telling *all of you the truth. I have heard* the Eternal One's decree.
He said *clearly* to me, "You are My son.
Today I have become your Father."
⁸*His offer to Me transcends generosity. He withholds nothing. He said,*
"The nations shall be yours for the asking,
and the entire earth will belong to you.
⁹They are yours to crush with an iron scepter,
yours to shatter like fragile, clay pots."

¹⁰So *leaders,* kings, and judges,
be wise, and be warned.
¹¹*There is only one God,* the Eternal One;
worship Him with respect and awe;
take delight in Him and tremble.
¹²Bow down before God's son.
If you don't, you will face His anger *and retribution,* and you won't stand
a chance.
For it doesn't take long to kindle *royal* wrath,

But blessings await all who *trust in Him.*
They will find God a *gentle* refuge.

So "be warned": believing in the Son means the difference between
experiencing God's gentle refuge and His anger! This is why our choice should
either fill us with hope or cause us to tremble in despair.

The Eternal One has put all things in the hands of His Son—the power to
crush and the opportunity to bless. We can indeed worship the Son with respect
and awe and receive all He desires to give us, or we can choose another way and
find ourselves unable to stand in the face of His anger. Here's the big question
then: With which group are you standing: with those on God's side or with those
against Him? Be warned.

PSALM 3

A SONG OF DAVID *COMPOSED* WHILE FLEEING FROM HIS SON ABSALOM.

¹Eternal One, my adversaries are many, too many to count.
   Now they have taken a stand against me!
²Right to my face they say,
   "God will not save you!"

[pause]*

³But You, Eternal One, wrap around me like an *impenetrable* shield.
   You give me glory and lift my eyes *up to the heavens.*
⁴I lift my voice to You, Eternal One,
   and You answer me from Your sacred heights.

[pause]

⁵I lay down *at night* and fall asleep.
   I awake in the morning—*healthy, strong, vibrant*—because the
      Eternal supports me.
⁶No longer will I fear my tens of thousands of enemies
   who have surrounded me!

⁷Rise up, O Eternal One!
   Rescue me, O God!
For You have dealt my enemies a strong blow to the jaw!
   You have shattered their teeth! *Do so again.*

⁸Liberation truly comes from the Eternal.
   Let Your blessings shower down upon Your people.

[pause]

3:2 Literally, selah, likely a musical direction from a Hebrew root meaning "to lift up"

PSALM 4

FOR THE WORSHIP LEADER. A SONG OF DAVID ACCOMPANIED
BY STRINGS.

[1]Answer my prayers, O True God, *the righteous,* who makes me right.
I was hopelessly surrounded, and You rescued me.
Once again hear me; hide me in Your favor;
bring victory in defeat and hope in hopelessness. Please.

[2]How long will you sons of Adam *steal my dignity,* reduce my glory to
shame?
Why pine for the fruitless and dream a delusion?

PSALM 4 | **A good night's rest** is something all of us long for. Getting one
can really be hard when all you can think about are those never-ending struggles
you face. What is your big struggle? Is it how others don't see your value, is it
your inability to get ahead, or is it an addiction, or is it a weakness in your personality
you can't conquer? When you settle down at night in the quiet with just your own
thoughts to keep you company, it seems your big struggle is all you can think
about. Or maybe you are like one of those in this psalm who say something like,
"Where is the good in the world?" Your concern, if it goes unchecked, will likely
grow deeper and darker until it affects your understanding of God and the world.
You may one day find yourself in the throes of full-blown depression—continually
irritable and tired all of the time.

So what is to be done? How can you avoid such negativity in your own life?
The psalmist here says his life is just the opposite, and it is "because I trust You,
You alone, O Eternal One." It seems too simple, but it is true. By remaining solidly
trusting of the Eternal One and asking Him to let His brilliant light shine upon you,
to be gracious to you, and to give you His peace, you can share in the joy of the
psalmist: you *can be* filled with His joy—feasting on God's presence and drinking
to your heart's content of the Spirit.

Can't rest? Tossing and turning? It is time to sleep peacefully, as those who
totally trust all of life to the Eternal One.

[pause]*

³Understand this: The Eternal One treats as special those like Him.
The Eternal will answer my prayers *and save me.*

⁴Think long; think hard. When you are angry, don't let it carry you
into sin.
When night comes, *in calm* be silent.

[pause]

⁵*From this day forward,* offer *to God* the *right* sacrifice from a heart made
right *by God.*
Entrust yourself to the Eternal One.

⁶Crowds *of disheartened people* ask, "Who can show us what is good?"
Let Your brilliant face shine upon us, O Eternal One, *that we may
know the undeniable answer.*
⁷You have filled me with joy, *and happiness has risen* in my heart, *great
delight and unrivaled joy,*
even more than when bread abounds and wine flows freely.
⁸*Tonight* I will sleep securely on a bed of peace
because I trust You, You alone, O Eternal One, will keep me safe.

Psalm 5

For the worship leader. A song of David accompanied
by flutes.*

¹Bend Your ear to me and listen to my words, O Eternal One;
hear the deep cry of my heart.
²Listen to my call *for help,*
my King, my True God;
to You *alone* I pray.

4:2 Literally, selah, likely a musical direction from a Hebrew root meaning "to lift up"
5:title Hebrew, nehiloth, meaning is uncertain. Only use of this word in the Old Testament.

³In the morning, O Eternal One, listen for my voice;
>   in the day's first light, I will offer my prayer to You and watch
>   expectantly *for Your answer.*

⁴You're not a God who smiles at sin;
>   You cannot abide with evil.
⁵The proud wither in Your presence;
>   You hate all who pervert and destroy what is good.
⁶You destroy those with lying lips;
>   the Eternal One detests those who murder and deceive.

⁷Yet I, by Your loving grace,
>   am welcomed into Your house;
>   I will turn my face toward Your holy place
>   and fall on my knees in reverence before You.
⁸O Eternal One, lead me in *the path of* Your righteousness
>   amidst those who wish me harm;
>   make Your way clear to me.

⁹Their words cannot be trusted;
>   they are destructive to their cores.
>   What comes out of their mouths is as foul as a rotting corpse;
>   their words stink of flattery.
¹⁰Find them guilty, O True God;
>   let their own devices bring them ruin.
>   Throw them out, *and let them drown* in the deluge of their sin,
>   for in revolt they *brazenly* spit in Your face.

¹¹But let those who run to You for safety be glad they did;
>   let them break out in joyful song.
>   May You keep them safe—
>   their love for You resounding in their hearts.
¹²You, O Eternal One, are the One who lays all good things in the laps of the
>   right-hearted.
>   Your blessings surround them like a shield.

PSALM 6

FOR THE WORSHIP LEADER. A SONG OF DAVID ACCOMPANIED
BY THE LYRE.*

¹O Eternal One, don't punish me in Your anger
   or harshly correct me.
²Show me grace, Eternal God. I am completely undone.
   Bring me back together, Eternal One. Mend my shattered bones.
³My soul is drowning in darkness.
   How long can You, the Eternal, let things go on like this?

6:title Hebrew, *sheminith,* perhaps an eight-stringed instrument from a root meaning "eight"

PSALM 6 | **"God, where are You?"** Have you ever been in complete darkness without a flashlight or a candle? If you were in a strange place, you were probably terrified. Sometimes it feels like God has turned out the light and simply gone away from us, leaving us to the ways of the world and to the schemings of our enemies. This is how David feels in this psalm. He says, "How long can You, the Eternal, let things go on like this?" Notice how David was not afraid to be completely honest with God; have you ever spoken to God with such candor? Sometimes we pray, we cry, we exhaust every effort we can imagine to get Him to hear us and to help us out of our weakened state one more time. But are we honest enough to shout out, "Come on, God! Where are You?"

But look at what David says next, "Come back, Eternal One, and lead me to Your saving light. Rescue me because I know You are truly compassionate." You see, David can be honest in his appeal because He knows that God is listening and that He has demonstrated in the past that He is there to rescue David.

Have you experienced the depth of despair and then, almost without realizing it, sensed that the Eternal One has been there with you the whole time? Your spirit rises and your viewpoint changes. David prays for God's light. Just a glimmer of His light—just a few moments at His feet—changes everything.

Rejoice, knowing that God does answer our prayers. The Light is brighter than ever, because He lets us experience what it means to be in the dark, away from Him.

⁴Come back, Eternal One, and lead me to Your saving light.
　　Rescue me because I know You are truly compassionate.
⁵*I'm alive for a reason*—I can't worship You if I'm dead.
　　If I'm six feet under, how can I thank You?

⁶I'm exhausted. *I cannot even speak,* my voice fading as sighs.
　　Every day ends *in the same place*—lying in bed, covered in tears,
　　my pillow wet with sorrow.
⁷My eyes burn, devoured with grief;
　　they grow weak as I constantly watch for my enemies.

⁸All who are evil, stay away from me
　　because the Eternal One hears my voice, listens as I cry.
⁹The Eternal God hears my simple prayers;
　　the Eternal receives my request.
¹⁰All who seek to destroy me will be humiliated;
　　they will turn away and suddenly crumble in shame.

PSALM 7

A SONG* OF DAVID TO THE ETERNAL ONE REGARDING CUSH,
THE BENJAMINITE.

¹O Eternal One, my God, in You I seek refuge.
　　Save me from those who are chasing me. Rescue me,
²Or else they will tear me to pieces as a lion *devours his prey*;
　　they will carry me off with no one to snatch me *from their jaws.*

³O Eternal One, my God, if I have done anything wrong *to deserve this,*
　　if there is blood on my hands,
⁴If I have mistreated a friend,
　　or if I have stolen from an adversary without *just* cause,
⁵Then let my enemy come after me and catch me,
　　stomping me into the ground, ending my life,
　　and grinding my honor into the dirt.

7:title Hebrew, *shiggaion,* meaning is uncertain.

[pause]*

⁶Arise, O Eternal One, inflamed by Your anger.
　　Come and counter the rage of my adversaries;
　　open Your eyes, my God; hear my plea for justice *once and for all.*

⁷Let the people gather around You.
　　Return to Your *rightful* place above them in the high *court.*
⁸The Eternal One will judge the nations.
　　Judge me now, Eternal One, according to my virtue and integrity.

⁹Please, bring the evil actions of these wicked, *wicked* people to an end!
　　But secure the righteous,
　For You, righteous God,
　　examine our hearts and minds.
¹⁰God is my defender;
　　He rescues those who have a pure heart.
¹¹God is a just judge;
　　He passes judgment daily *against the person who does evil.*

¹²If the wicked do not turn *from their evil deeds,* God will sharpen His
　　　sword;
　　He will bend His bow, stringing it *in readiness.*
¹³*Yes,* He has prepared His deadly weapons
　　with His arrows flaming hot.
¹⁴See, my enemies are fertile with evil.
　　They conceive trouble
　　and give birth to deception.
¹⁵They prepare a trap, digging a *deep* pit,
　　and fall into the snare they have made.
¹⁶The trouble they plan will return to punish them,
　　and their violent acts will come back to haunt them.

¹⁷*As a result,* I will thank the Eternal One for His justice
　　and sing praises in honor of the Eternal One, Most High.

7:5 Literally, selah, likely a musical direction from a Hebrew root meaning "to lift up"

PSALM 8

FOR THE WORSHIP LEADER: A SONG OF DAVID ACCOMPANIED
BY THE HARP.*

¹O Eternal One, our Lord,
   Your majestic name is heard throughout the earth;

Your magnificent glory shines far above the skies.
   ²From the mouths *and souls* of infants and toddlers, *the most innocent,*
You have decreed power to stop Your adversaries
   and quash those who seek revenge.

8:title Hebrew, *gittith,* a winepress or a musical instrument from Gath

PSALM 8 | **"Why do You care?"** Have you ever climbed a high mountain
and looked out over the valley far below? Remember how impressed you were
by the vastness of the landscape? Similarly can you recall lying on the ground
beneath a sky full of stars on a cloudless night, realizing what tiny specks we
are in comparison with everything that God has created? At one time or another,
each of us is confronted with the immensity of God's creation and our relative
insignificance to the whole.

Such moments of God-awareness lift us above personal concerns. They
remind us that we're part of a much grander scheme—an amazing and wonderful
framework, designed to sustain our lives in the midst of tremendous beauty.
Moments like these bring us closer to our Creator.

David asks the obvious question, "Why do You care about us mortals?" He
says we are "specks of dust floating about the cosmos." Some questions are just
too big for our little minds to answer. These questions form the backdrop that
makes God's love so amazing. Why would He care about us? As amazing as it
seems, God does care about our meager lives, and He has raised us up so that
with loud voices and clean hearts we can offer Him praise. Our praise should come
from wide-eyed wonder and truly grateful hearts. We are of value to such a great
Creator.

³When I gaze to the skies and meditate on Your creation—
    on the moon, stars, *and all* You have made,
⁴I can't help but wonder why You care about mortals—
    sons *and daughters* of men—
    specks of dust floating about the cosmos.

⁵But You placed the son of man just beneath God
    and honored him like royalty, crowning him with glory and honor.
⁶You ordained him to govern the works of Your hands,
    to nurture the offspring of Your divine imagination;
    You placed everything *on earth* beneath his feet:
⁷All kinds of domesticated animals,
    even the wild animals in the fields *and forests.*
⁸The birds of the sky and the fish of the sea,
    all *the multitudes of living things* that travel the currents of the oceans.

⁹O Eternal One, our Lord,
    Your majestic name is heard throughout the earth.

PSALM 9*

FOR THE WORSHIP LEADER. A SONG OF DAVID TO THE TUNE
"DEATH OF A SON."*

¹All my heart will give thanks to You, Eternal One.
    I will tell others about Your amazing works.
²I will be glad and celebrate You!
    I will praise You, O Most High!

³When my adversaries turned and fled,
    they fell and died right in front of You,
⁴For You supported my just cause.
    From Your throne, You have judged wisely.

Psalm 9 Psalms 9–10 were originally a single acrostic poem.
9:title Hebrew, *muth-labben,* perhaps the melody to which the song is sung

⁵You confronted the nations; You have destroyed the wicked.
  You have erased their names from history.
⁶The enemy is finished, their time is up;
  their cities will lay in ruin forever;
  all memory of them is gone.

⁷Still the Eternal One remains and will reign forever;
  He has taken His place on His throne for judgment.
⁸So He will judge the world rightly.
  He shall execute that judgment equally on all people.

⁹For the Eternal One will be a shelter for those who know misery,
  a refuge during troubling times.
¹⁰Those who know Your name will rely on You,
  for You, O Eternal One, have not abandoned those who search
    for You.

¹¹Praise the Eternal One who lives on Zion's holy hill.
  Tell *the story of* His great acts among the people!
¹²For He remembers the victims of violence and avenges their blood,
  He does not turn a deaf ear to the cry of the needy.

¹³Be gracious to me, O Eternal One.
  Notice the harm I have suffered because of my enemies,
  You who carries me safely away from death's door,
¹⁴So that I may rehearse Your deeds, declare Your praise,
  and rejoice in Your rescue
  when I take my stand in the gates of Zion.

¹⁵The nations have fallen into the pit they dug *for others*;
  their own feet caught, snared by the net they hid.
¹⁶The Eternal One is *well* known, *for He has taken action* and secured
    justice;
  He has trapped the wicked through the work of their own hands.

[pause with music]*

9:16 Hebrew, *higgaion selah,* meaning is uncertain, possibly a musical direction

¹⁷The wicked are headed for death and the grave;
    all the nations who forget the True God *will share a similar fate.*

¹⁸For those in need shall not always be forgotten,
    and the hope of the poor will never die.

¹⁹Eternal One, arise! Do not allow mere mortals to win the day.
    Judge the nations Yourself.
²⁰Put the fear *of God* in them, Eternal One!
    Remind the nations they are mere men, *not gods.*

[pause]*

PSALM 10*

¹Why, O Eternal One, are You so far away?
    Why can't You be found during troubling times?
²Mean and haughty people hunt down the poor.
    May they get caught up in their own wicked schemes.

³For the wicked celebrates the evil cravings of his heart
    as the greedy curses and rejects the Eternal One.
⁴The arrogance of the wicked one keeps him from seeking the True God.
    He truly thinks, "There is no God."

⁵His ways *seem* always to be successful;
    Your judgments, too, *seem* far beyond him, out of his reach.
    He looks down on all his enemies.
⁶In his heart he has decided, "Nothing will faze me.
    From generation to generation I will not face trouble."

⁷His mouth is full of curses, lies, and oppression.*
    Beneath his tongue lie trouble and wickedness.

9:20 Literally, selah, likely a musical direction from a Hebrew root meaning "to lift up"
Psalm 10 Psalms 9–10 were originally a single acrostic poem.
10:7 Romans 3:14

⁸He hides in the shadows of the villages,
    waiting to ambush and kill the innocent in dark corners.
He eyes the weak and the poor.

⁹*Ominously,* like a lion in its lair,
    he lurks in secret to waylay those who are downtrodden.
When he catches them, he draws them in and drags them off with his net.

¹⁰Quietly crouching, laying low,
    ready to overwhelm the next by his strength,
¹¹The wicked thinks in his heart, "God has forgotten us!
    He has covered His face and will never notice!"

¹²Arise, O Eternal One, *my* True God. Lift up Your hand.
    Do not forget the downtrodden.
¹³Why does the wicked revile the True God?
    He has decided, "He will not hold me responsible."

¹⁴But *wait!* You have seen, and You will consider the trouble and grief *he
        caused.*
    You will impose consequences for his actions.
The helpless, the orphans, commit themselves to You,
    and You have been their Helper.

¹⁵Break the arm of the one guilty of doing evil;
    investigate all his wicked acts;
    hold him responsible for every last one of them.
¹⁶The Eternal One will reign as King forever.
    The *other* nations will be swept off His land.

¹⁷O Eternal One, You have heard the longings of the poor and lowly.
    You will strengthen them; You *who are of heaven* will hear them,
¹⁸Vindicating the orphan and the oppressed
    so that men who are of the earth will terrify them no more.

PSALM 11

FOR THE WORSHIP LEADER. *A SONG* OF DAVID.

¹I am already in the soft embrace of the Eternal One,
    so why do you beckon me *to leave,* saying,
    "Fly like a bird to the mountains.
²Look! The wicked approach with bows bent,
    sneaking around in the shadows,
    setting their arrows against their bowstrings to pierce everyone whose
        heart is pure.
³If the foundations are crumbling,
    is there hope for the righteous?"

PSALM 11 | **Crumbling Foundations.** David gives us two strong images in this psalm: the first of being hunted by evil men moving from shadow to shadow, waiting to launch arrows from their hiding places. The second is of buildings crumbling from weak foundations. But God stands strong. He is not afraid, but sits squarely upon His throne: the ruler and judge of all. So where are we in all of this? Are we secure and sure of our position? If the foundations are crumbling around us because we've been laid off from our jobs, our debt load has broken our spirits, or our lives have taken a downward spiral, what can we do? Should we be looking behind us and peering into the shadows, afraid of evil people? Should we be trying to escape from our crumbling lives? No. We can look to the Eternal God, whose foundation is never shaken and who sits squarely on His throne. Our security is in Him.

We're reminded that God is steadfast and that He examines us, exploring the motives that emanate from our hearts. He is ever-faithful, ever-watchful, searching each of us: despising evil, valuing good.

We can either keep our eyes on those things that are falling down around us or we can focus our attention on the motivation of our own hearts and on the One who watches over us, who longs to see us face-to-face. Our security does not come from our situation. Security comes from the only One who stands above all the debris and is on His exalted throne.

⁴But the Eternal One *has not moved*; He remains in His holy temple.
  The Eternal sits *squarely* on His heavenly throne.
    He observes the sons of Adam *and daughters of Eve, examining us within and without,*
  exploring every fiber of our beings.
⁵The Eternal One searches the hearts of those who are good,
  but He despises all those who can't get enough of *perversion and* violence.
⁶If you are evil, He will rain hot lava over your head,
  will fill your cup with burning wind and *liquid* fire *to scorch your insides.*

⁷The Eternal One is right in all His ways;
He cherishes all that is upright.
  Those who do what is right in His eyes will see His face.

Psalm 12

FOR THE WORSHIP LEADER. A SONG OF DAVID ACCOMPANIED BY THE LYRE.*

¹Help me, O Eternal One, for I can't find anyone who follows You.
  The faithful have fallen out of sight.
²Everyone tells lies through sweet-talking lips
  and speaks from a hollow and deceptive heart.

³May the Eternal One silence all sweet-talking lips,
  stop all boasting tongues.
⁴Of those who say, "With our words we will win;
  our lips are our own. Who is the master of our souls?"

⁵"I will rise up," says the Eternal One,
  "because the poor are being trampled, and the needy groan *for My saving help.*
  I will lift them up to the safety they long for."

12:title Hebrew, *sheminith,* perhaps an eight-stringed instrument from a root meaning "eight"

⁶The promises of the Eternal One, *they are true,* they are pure—
>　like silver refined in a furnace,
>　purified seven times, *they will be without impurity.*

⁷You, O Eternal One, will be their protector.
>　You will keep them safe from those around them forever.
⁸All around those who are wicked parade, *proud and arrogant,*
>　and people applaud their emptiness.

PSALM 13

FOR THE WORSHIP LEADER. A SONG OF DAVID.

¹How long, O Eternal One? How long will You forget me? Forever?
>　How long will You look the other way?

²How long must I agonize,
>　grieving Your absence in my heart every day?
How long will You let my enemies win?

³Turn back; respond to me, O Eternal One, my True God!
>　Put the spark of life in my eyes, or I'm dead.

PSALM 14 | **Clueless.** You know how sometimes it is difficult to know if something is really true or if we are being fed a lie. We're all clueless at times, but when it comes to God, we cannot afford to remain that way. The clueless ones actually think they can live without God. They think they know what's going on. They think they can turn their backs and even make fun of people who have their faces turned toward Him. It shows how little they know about God. It is dangerous to ignore God or to try and fool Him. David provides us with a compelling visual image of God leaning over the arm of His throne in heaven and peering down on us.

[4]My enemies will boast they have beaten me;
    my foes will celebrate that I have stumbled.

[5]But I trust in Your faithful love;
    my heart leaps at the thought of imminent deliverance by You.
[6]I will sing to the Eternal One,
    for He is always generous with me.

PSALM 14

FOR THE WORSHIP LEADER. *A SONG* OF DAVID.

[1]A *wicked and* foolish man truly believes there is no God.
    They are vile; *their sinfulness nauseating to their Creator;*
    their actions are *soiled and* repulsive; *every deed is depraved;*
    not one of them does good.

[2]The Eternal One leans over from heaven to survey the sons of Adam.
    No one is missed, and no one can hide.
    He searches to see who understands *true wisdom,*
    who desires to know the True God.

As much as the evil deeds of violence and greed may sicken us, we can't begin to imagine what those acts do to the heart of the perfectly holy Eternal One. Because God by His very nature is nauseated with endless wickedness, we should know that He cares very much for those who choose to share His values.

God gives us clues about how He wants people to live. He leaves them everywhere. Those who deny God are avoiding the truth that stares us all in the face. No matter what the clueless think, the Eternal One will know who rejects Him—even when they hide behind closed doors; He gets to have the final say in how things turn out. He promises to restore hope to those who trust in Him. It isn't wise to remain clueless when it comes to God.

³They all turn *their backs,* walking their own roads; they are rancid, *leaving a trail of rotten footsteps behind them;*

not one of them does good,

not even one.

⁴Do the wicked have no clue *about what really matters?*

They devour my brothers and sisters the way a man eats his dinner.

They ignore the Eternal One *and don't call on Him, rejecting His reality and truth.*

⁵They shall *secretly* tremble *behind closed doors, hearts beating hard within their chests,*

knowing that God always avenges the upright.

⁶You laugh at the counsel of the poor, the needy, the troubled *who put their trust in God.*

You try to take away their only hope,

but the Eternal One is a strong shelter *in the heaviest storm.*

⁷May *a new day, a day of* deliverance come for Israel, starting with Zion.

When the Eternal One breaks the chains of His oppressed people,

the family of Jacob will rejoice, and Israel will be delighted.

PSALM 15

A SONG OF DAVID.

¹Eternal One, who is invited to stay in Your dwelling?

Who is granted passage to Your holy mountain?

²*Here is the answer:* The one who lives with integrity, does what is right,

and speaks *honestly* with truth from the heart.

³The one who doesn't speak evil against others

or wrong his neighbor,

or slander his friends.

⁴The one who loathes the loathsome,

honors those who fear the Eternal One,

And keeps all promises no matter the cost.
⁵The one who does not lend money with gain in mind
     and cannot be bought to harm an innocent name.

If you live this way, you will not be shaken *and will live together with the
     Eternal One.*

PSALM 16

A PRAYER* OF DAVID.

¹Protect me, God, for the only safety I know is found in the moments I
     seek You.
²I told You, Eternal One, "You are my Lord,
     for the only good I know in this world is found in You alone."

16:title Hebrew, *miktam,* meaning is uncertain.

PSALM 16 | **The One Who Is Our Oasis.** At the outset, David causes us
to think about certain moments of our lives, and in particular, those moments when
we actually feel safe. This idea strikes a deep chord in our hearts as we become
more painfully aware of the lack of safety in nearly every corner of the globe. It
may be a brutal uprising in a developing country, or a student accused of spying in
a backwater part of the world, or a natural disaster that takes us all by surprise.

At a loss for any kind of worldly security, our only real protection and our
only real truth come as we seek the company of our God. Do we deserve to have
a beautiful life with pleasures that are never-ending? Only in our dreams. We, like
everyone else, face uncertainty in how our lives will play out, but with a major
difference. We get the power to rise above it all. Even more, we get to experience
true joy and contentment no matter what the outcome.

In a culture that bombards our senses at every turn, making it nearly
impossible for us to find even a little peace, we're privileged to know the One who
is our oasis. We can go to God at any time and know that He is there with full
knowledge of our trials. The security He offers is a peace that stands above our
circumstances—a true peace because it works even in the truth of a hard life.

³The beauty of faith-filled people encompasses me.
    They are true, and my heart is thrilled beyond measure.
⁴*All the while* the despair of many, who abandoned Your goodness for *the*
    empty promises of false gods increases day by day.
    I refuse to pour out blood offerings,
    to utter their names from my lips.

⁵You, Eternal One, are my sustenance and my *life-giving* cup.
    In that cup, You hold my future and my eternal riches.
⁶My home is surrounded in beauty;
    You have gifted me with *abundance and* a rich legacy.

⁷I will bless the Eternal One, whose wise teaching orchestrates my days
    and centers my mind at night.
⁸The Eternal One is ever present with me;
    at all times He goes before me.
 I will not live in fear *or abandon my calling*
    because He stands at my right hand.

⁹*This is a good life*—my heart is glad, my soul is full of joy,
    and my body is at rest. *Who could want for more?*
¹⁰You will not abandon me to experience death and the grave
    or leave me to rot alone.

¹¹*Instead,* You direct me on the path that leads to *a beautiful* life.
    As I walk with You, the pleasures are never-ending,
    and I know true joy *and contentment.*

PSALM 17

A PRAYER OF DAVID.

¹Listen, O Eternal One, to my cry for justice.
    These words of mine are true—turn Your ear toward me.
²Announce that I am free of all the charges against me—*only You can see*
    into my heart to know that to be true.
    Treat me with fairness; look at me with justice.

³You have searched me—my heart *and soul*—awakened me *from dreaming*
  and tested me.
  You've found nothing against me.
  I have resolved not to sin in what I say.
⁴The path violent men have followed,
  I will not travel. Violence is not my way.
 Your ways and Your voice now guide my journey.
⁵*I will press on*—moving steadfastly forward along Your path.
  I will not look back. I will not stumble.

⁶I am crying aloud to You, O True God, for I long to know Your answer.
  Hear me, *O God.* Hear my plea. *Hear my prayer for help.*
⁷Put Your marvelous love on display *for all to see.*
  Liberator of those who long for shelter beside You,
  set them safely away from their enemies, *ever welcomed by grace.*

⁸Keep *close watch over* me as the apple of Your eye;
  shelter me in the shadow of Your wings.
⁹*Protect me* from the wicked who are poised to attack,
  from the enemies swarming around me *and closing in quickly.*
¹⁰*Like clay baking in the sun*, their hearts have hardened;
  arrogance spills from their mouths.
¹¹They've tracked me down *like quarry.* They're surrounding me
  and are poised to throw me down into the dirt.
¹²Like a lion—*crouching in the brush*—they are ready to tear *me apart.*
  Like young lions in their hiding places, they are poised to strike.

¹³Rise up and confront them, O Eternal One! Make them pay.
  By Your sword, set me free from my wicked enemies!
¹⁴*May Your rescue find me here.* By Your hand, save me from my enemies,
  Eternal One.
  Save me from men whose hopes are rooted in this world.
 But as for those You cherish, may they feast on all You have set aside
  for them;
  may their children never be in need;
  may they have enough so their children will inherit their wealth.

¹⁵But as for me, my hope is to see Your face.
>When I am vindicated, I will look upon the *holy* face of God,
>>and when I awake, *the longing of* my soul will be satisfied in *the glow of* Your presence.

PSALM 18

FOR THE WORSHIP LEADER. A SONG OF DAVID, THE ETERNAL ONE'S SERVANT, WHO ADDRESSED THESE WORDS TO THE ETERNAL AFTER HE HAD RESCUED HIM FROM SAUL AND HIS OTHER ENEMIES.

¹I love You, Eternal One, *source of* my power.
²The Eternal One is my rock, my fortress, and my salvation;
>He is my True God, the stronghold in which I hide,
>>my strong shield, the horn that calls forth help, and my tall-walled tower.
³I call out to the Eternal One, who is worthy to be praised—
>that's how I will be rescued from my enemies.

⁴The bonds of death encircled me;
>the currents of destruction tugged at me;
⁵The sorrows of the grave wrap around me;
>the traps of death lay in wait for me.

⁶In my time of need, I called to the Eternal One;
>I begged my True God for help.
He heard my voice echo up to His temple,
>and my cry came to His ears.

⁷Because of His great anger, the earth shook and staggered;
>the roots of the mountains shifted.
⁸Smoke poured out from His nose,
>and devouring fire burst from His mouth.
>Coals glowed from Him.

⁹He bent the heavens and descended;
    inky darkness was beneath His feet.
¹⁰He rode upon a heavenly creature,* flying;
    He was carried quickly on the wings of the wind.
¹¹He took darkness as His hiding place—
    both the dark waters *of the seas* and the dark clouds of the sky.
¹²Out from His brilliance
    hailstones and burning coals
    broke through the clouds.
¹³The Eternal One thundered in the heavens;
    the Highest spoke; His voice rumbled [in the midst of hail and
        lightning].*
¹⁴He shot forth His arrows and scattered the wicked;
    He flung forth His lightning and struck them.
¹⁵Then the deepest channels of the seas were visible,
    and the very foundations of the world were uncovered
  At Your rebuke, O Eternal One,
    at the blast of wind from Your nostrils.

¹⁶He reached down *His hand* from above me; He held me.
    He lifted me from the raging waters.
¹⁷He rescued me from my strongest enemy,
    from all those who sought my death,
    for they were too strong.
¹⁸They came for me in the day of my destruction,
    but the Eternal One was the support of my life.
¹⁹He set me down in a safe place;
    He saved me to His delight; *He took joy* in me.

²⁰The Eternal One responded to me according to my goodness;
    I kept my hands clean, and He blessed me.
²¹I kept the ways of the Eternal One
    and have not walked away from my True God in wickedness.

18:10 Hebrew, *cherub*
18:13 Greek manuscripts and some Hebrew manuscripts omit this portion.

²²All His laws were there before me,
  and I did not push His statutes away.
²³I was blameless before Him;
  I kept myself from guilt *and shame.*
²⁴That's why the Eternal One has rewarded me for my right living;
  He's rewarded me because He saw my hands were clean.

²⁵You are loyal to those who are loyal;
  with the innocent, You prove to be innocent;
²⁶With the clean, You prove to be clean;
  and with the twisted, You make Yourself contrary.
²⁷For You rescue humble people,
  but You bring the proud back in line.
²⁸You are the lamp who lights my way;
  the Eternal One, my God, lights up my darkness.
²⁹With Your help, I can conquer an army;
  I can leap over walls with a helping hand from You.
³⁰Everything God does is perfect;
  the promise of the Eternal One rings true;
  He stands as a shield for all who hide in Him.

³¹Who is the True God except the Eternal One?
  Who stands like a rock except our God?
³²The True God who encircled me with strength
  and made my pathway straight.
³³He made me sure-footed as a deer
  and placed me high up where I am safe.
³⁴He teaches me to fight
  so that my arms can bend a bronze bow.
³⁵You have shielded me with Your salvation,
  supporting me with Your *strong* right hand,
  and it makes me strong.
³⁶You taught me how to walk with care
  so my feet will not slip.

[37]I chased my enemies and caught them
  and did not stop until they were destroyed.
[38]I broke them and threw them down beneath my feet,
  and they could not rise up again.
[39]For You equipped me for battle,
  and You made my enemies fall beneath me.
[40]You made my enemies turn tail and run,
  and all who wanted my destruction, I destroyed.
[41]They looked everywhere, but no one came to rescue them;
  they asked the Eternal One, but He did not answer them.
[42]I beat them to sand, to dust that blows in the wind;
  I flung them away like trash in the gutters.

[43]You rescued me from conflict with the peoples;
  You raised me up to rule over nations.
  People who did not know me have come to serve me.
[44]Strangers come to me, afraid.
  As soon as they hear about me, they serve me;
[45]Strangers who have lost heart
  come fearfully *to me* from behind their high walls.

[46]The Eternal One is alive! My Rock is blessed,
  and exalted is the True God of my deliverance—
[47]The God who avenged me
  and placed the peoples under me,
[48]Who rescued me from all my foes.
  Truly, You raised me up above my enemies
  and saved me from the violent ones.

[49]For this I will praise You among the nations, O Eternal One,
  and sing praises to Your name.
[50]He is a tower of salvation for His king
  and shows His enduring love to His anointed,
  to David and his descendants forever.

Psalm 19

FOR THE WORSHIP LEADER. A SONG OF DAVID.

[1]The celestial realms announce God's glory;
    the skies testify of His hands' great work.
[2]Each day pours out more of their sayings;
    each night, more *to hear and more* to learn.
[3]Inaudible words are their manner of speech,
    and silence, their means to convey.
[4]Yet from here to the ends of the earth, their voices* have gone out;
    the whole world can hear what they say.*

  God stretched out in these heavens a tent for the sun,
[5]And the sun is like a groom who, after leaving his room, *arrives at the*
      wedding in splendor;
    he is the strong runner who, *favored to win in his race,* is eager to face
      his challenge.
[6]He rises at one end of the skies
    and runs in an arc overhead;
    nothing can hide from his heat, *from the swelter of his daily tread.*

[7]The Eternal One's law is perfect,
    turning lives around.
  His words are reliable and true,
    instilling wisdom to open minds.
[8]The Eternal One's directions are correct,
    giving satisfaction to the heart.
  God's commandments are clear,
    lending clarity to the eyes.
[9]The awe of the Eternal is clean,
    sustaining for all of eternity.
  The Eternal's decisions are sound;
    they are right through and through.

19:4 Hebrew manuscripts read "line."
19:4 Romans 10:18

¹⁰They are worth more than gold—
    even more than abundant, pure gold.
They are sweeter *to the tongue* than honey
    or the drippings of the honeycomb.

¹¹In addition *to all that has been said,* Your servant will find, *hidden in Your*
    commandments, both a strong warning
    and a great reward for keeping them.
¹²Who could possibly know all that he has done wrong?
    Forgive my hidden *and unknown* faults.
¹³As I am Your servant, protect me from *my bent toward* pride,
    and keep sin from ruling my life.
If You do this, I will be without blame,
    innocent of the great breach.

¹⁴May the words that come out of my mouth and the musings of my heart
    meet with Your gracious approval,
    O Eternal One, my Rock,
    O Eternal One, my Redeemer.

PSALM 19 | **Consider the place where you stand**—the place where you feel the most secure and the most powerful. David was a king, and yet he was aware that within himself, he had no power. He was not able to stand without the Eternal One, and neither are we. But then, why would we want to?

It isn't unusual for someone to look at creation and recognize the magnitude of God. David instead observes the depth of God's wisdom in the insightfulness of His words. You see, all religions have sacred texts, but our God has laid before us knowledge of the very character of people, pointing out their great weaknesses and providing healing for their greatest flaws and most troubling circumstances. The directions, commands, and decisions that David sees in the books of Moses bring him to his knees before the Eternal One. They are worth more than gold and purer than the finest honey. The words of God are a great gift. With them we know ourselves better and we gain the secrets of the ages.

The Eternal One doesn't tell David the choices will be easy, but He does help let him know that the rewards of listening intently to His will and His voice offer more security than anything this world can possibly provide. He is the only Rock that won't be shaken.

PSALM 20

¹May the Eternal One's answer find you, *come to rescue you,*
    when you desperately cling to the end of your rope.
May the name of the True God of Jacob be your shelter.
²May He extend *hope and* help to you from His *holy* sanctuary
    and support you from *His sacred city of* Zion.
³May He remember all that you have offered Him;
    May your burnt sacrifices serve as a prelude to His mercy.

[pause]*

⁴May He grant the dreams of your heart
    and see your plans through to the end.
⁵When you win, *we will not be silent!* We will shout
    and raise high our banners in the great name of our God!
May the Eternal One say yes to all your requests.

⁶*I don't fear;* I'm confident that help will come to the one anointed by the
    Eternal One:
    heaven will respond to his plea;
    His mighty right hand will win the battle.
⁷Many put their hope in chariots, others in horses,
    but we place our trust in the name of the Eternal One, our True God.
⁸Soon our enemies will collapse and fall, *never to return home;*
    all the while, we will rise and stand firm.

⁹Eternal One, grant victory to our king!
    Answer our plea *for help.*

20:3 Literally, selah, likely a musical direction from a Hebrew root meaning "to lift up"

PSALM 21

For the worship leader. A song of David.

¹The king is glad because You, O Eternal One, are strong.
    In *light of* Your salvation, he is singing Your name.
²You have given him all he could wish for.
    After hearing his prayer, You withheld nothing.

[pause]*

³True blessings You lavished upon the king;
    a crown of precious gold You placed upon his head.
⁴His prayer was to live *fully*. You responded with even more—
    a never-ending life to enjoy.
⁵With Your help, his fame and glory have grown;
    You raise him high and cover him in majesty.
⁶You shower him with blessings that last forever;
    he finds joy in knowing Your presence *and loving You*.
⁷For the king puts his trust in the Eternal One,
        so he will not be shaken because of the persistent love of the Most
            High God.

⁸*King,* your hand will reach for all your enemies;
    your right hand will seize all who hate you.
⁹When you arrive *at the battle's edge,*
    you will seem to them a furnace.
For the fire of the Eternal One's anger, the heat of His wrath
    will burn and consume them.
¹⁰You will cut off their children,
    lop off the branches of their family tree.
The earth will never know them,
    nor will they ever be numbered among Adam's kin.
¹¹When they scheme against you,
    when they conspire their mischief, such efforts will be in vain.

21:2 Literally, selah, likely a musical direction from a Hebrew root meaning "to lift up"

¹²At the sight of you, they will sound the retreat;
>   your bows, drawn back, will aim directly at their faces.

¹³Put Your strength, Eternal One, on display for all to see;
>   we will sing and make music of Your mighty power.

PSALM 22

FOR THE WORSHIP LEADER. A SONG OF DAVID TO *THE TUNE* "DEER OF
THE DAWN."*

¹My God, my God, why have You turned Your back on me?
>   Your ears are deaf to my groans.
²O my God, I cry all day and You are silent;
>   my tears in the night bring no relief.

³Still, You are holy;
>   You make Your home on the praises of Israel.
⁴Our *mothers and* fathers trusted in You;
>   they trusted, and You rescued them.
⁵They cried out to You *for help* and were spared;
>   they trusted in You and were vindicated.

⁶But I am a worm and not a human being,
>   a disgrace and an object of scorn.
⁷Everyone who sees me laughs at me;
>   they whisper *to one another* I'm a loser; they sneer and mock me,
>   saying,
⁸"He relies on the Eternal One; let the Eternal rescue
>   and keep him safe because He is happy with him."

⁹But You are the One who granted me life;
>   You endowed me with trust as I nursed at my mother's breast.
¹⁰I was dedicated to You at birth;
>   You've been my God from my mother's womb.

22:title Hebrew, *ayyeleth ha-shachar,* perhaps the melody to which the song is sung

¹¹Stay close to me—
    trouble is at my door;
    no one else can help me.

¹²I'm surrounded by many tormenters;
    like strong bulls of Bashan,* they circle around me *with their taunts.*
¹³They open their mouths wide at me
    like ravenous, roaring lions.

¹⁴My life is poured out like water,
    and all my bones have slipped out of joint.

22:12 A region east of the Sea of Galilee

PSALM 22 | **"You are silent."** Can you identify with David in this psalm? He voices a suffering and loneliness that foreshadowed what Jesus the Messiah would later endure on the cross. David's words are truly amazing. They offer one of the greatest proofs of the truth of God's Word. A thousand years before these words were literally fulfilled at the end of the Savior's life on this earth, David experiences them in part in his own life. These words hit home with us also because we, too, can identify in a small way with the pain when bullies shout their insults, mock our beliefs, and try to weaken our connection with the Eternal One.

In trying times, perhaps we struggle most with what we perceive to be God's silence. Those who would laugh at our desire to follow after God can sound louder than the One in whom we've placed our trust. But think of what Jesus experienced on His cross for us: "I cry . . . and You are silent. . . . I am a worm . . . a disgrace . . . an object of scorn. . . . They sneer and mock me. . . . My life is poured out like water . . . all my bones have slipped out of joint. My heart melts like wax . . . my dry tongue sticks to the roof of my mouth . . . they pierced my hands . . . my feet. People gawk and stare at me. They made a game of dividing my clothes." All of these words were literally, exactly fulfilled with Jesus on the cross. What David felt and what we may for a brief moment experience, Jesus literally agonized through for us. Can there be any unbelief in the face of these words?

The encouraging news is that, although enemies killed Jesus and chased David, God is an ever-faithful strength for us. He has already made note of the winners. He already knows the bullies will be silenced. We have an amazing God on our side.

My heart melts like wax inside me.
¹⁵My strength is gone, dried up like shards of pottery;

> my *dry* tongue sticks to the roof of my mouth;
> You lay me in the dust of death.

¹⁶A throng of evil ones has surrounded me

> like *a pack of wild* dogs;

They* pierced my hands and *ripped a hole in* my feet.
¹⁷I count all my bones;

People gawk and stare at me.
¹⁸They *made a game out of* dividing my clothes among themselves;

> they cast lots for the clothes on my back.

¹⁹But You, O Eternal One, stay close;

> O You, my help, hurry to my side.

²⁰Save my life from violence,

> my *sweet* life from the teeth of the wild dog.

²¹Rescue me from the mouth of the lion.

> From the horns of the wild oxen, You responded to my plea.

²²I will speak Your Name to my brothers and sisters

> when I praise You in the midst of the community.

²³You who revere the Eternal One, praise Him—

> descendants of Jacob, worship Him;
> be struck with wonder before Him, all you children of Israel.

²⁴He's not put off

> by the suffering of the suffering one;

He doesn't pretend He hasn't seen him;

> when he pleaded for help, He listened.

²⁵You stir my praise in the great assembly;

> I will fulfill my vows before those who humble their hearts
> before Him.

22:16 Most Hebrew manuscripts read "like the lion."

²⁶Those who are suffering will eat and be nourished;

    those who seek Him will praise the Eternal One.

    May your hearts beat strong forever!

²⁷Those from the farthest reaches of the earth will remember

    and turn back to *look for* the Eternal One;

All the families of the nations

    will worship You.

²⁸The Eternal One owns the world;

    He exercises His *gentle* rule over all the nations.

²⁹All the wealthy of the world will eat and worship;

    all those who fall in the dust will bow before Him,

    even the life that is headed to the grave.

³⁰Our children will serve Him;

    future generations will hear the story of *how* the Lord *rescued us*.

³¹They will tell the generations to come of the righteousness of the Lord,

    of what He has done.

Psalm 23

A song of David.

¹The Eternal One is my shepherd, He cares for me always.

²He provides me rest in rich, green fields

    beside streams of refreshing water.

    He soothes my fears;

³He makes me whole again,

    steering me *off worn, hard paths* to roads where *truth and*

    righteousness echo His name.

⁴Even in the *unending* shadows of death's darkness,

    I am not overcome by fear.

Because You are with me *in those dark moments,*
>   near with Your protection and guidance,
>   I am comforted.

5You spread out a table before me,
>   *provisions* in the midst of *attack from* my enemies;
You *care for all my needs,* anointing my head with *soothing, fragrant* oil,
>   filling my cup again and again *with Your grace.*
6Certainly Your faithful protection and loving provision will pursue me
>   where I go, always, everywhere.
I will always be with the Eternal One,
>   in Your house forever.

PSALM 23 | **Refreshed by the Eternal One.** There is a deep darkness that causes us to feel painfully alone and uncertain of the future. We experience it when young people go off to war, when facing an enormous challenge that we feel unprepared for, when taking final exams, when facing a judge, when our employment is forcibly terminated, when we are confronted with a terminal illness, and the list continues. Psalm 23 reminds us that God walks beside us, guiding us even in our final moments. He calms our spirits, gives us rest, and when we feel we can't go on, He gently pushes us out of our secure place.

The Eternal One refreshes our spirits in the midst of our dark times; He relieves our suffocating fears. No matter where we are in life—God has promised He will be with us and we will be with Him. He can make His presence known to us by reviving us physically, encouraging our damaged emotions, and connecting us to His Spirit.

Sometimes we actually choose to wallow in our fears rather than trust God. You see, when we are moaning and fearful, we may find ourselves at the center of our loved ones' attention. We may enjoy their hovering concern and care. On the other hand, when we are confident in our place in God's program, we experience the complete exhilaration that comes with overcoming and being at the very center of His attention.

So let the Eternal God do His thing by "filling [you up] again and again with [His] grace."

PSALM 24

A SONG OF DAVID.

¹The earth and all that's upon it belong to the Eternal One.
   The world is His, with every living creature on it.
²With seas as foundations and rivers as boundaries,
   He shaped the continents, fashioned the earth.

³Who can *possibly* ascend the mountain of the Eternal One?
   Who can stand before Him in sacred spaces?
⁴Only those whose hands have been washed and hearts made pure,
   men and women who are not given to lies or deception.
⁵The Eternal One will stand close to them with blessing *and mercy at hand*,
   and the God who redeems will right what has been wrong.
⁶These are the people who chase after Him;
   [like Jacob, they look for the face of God].*

[pause]*

⁷City gates—open wide!
   Ancient doors—stand back!
   For the glorious King shall soon pass your way.
⁸Who is the glorious King?
   The Eternal One who is powerful
   and mightily equipped for battle.
⁹City gates—open wide!
   Ancient doors—stand back!
   For the glorious King shall soon pass your way.
¹⁰Who is the glorious King?
   The Eternal One, Commander of *heaven's* army,
   He is the glorious King.

[pause]

24:6 Most Hebrew manuscripts read "they look for your face, Jacob."
24:6 Literally, selah, likely a musical direction from a Hebrew root meaning "to lift up"

Psalm 25

A SONG OF DAVID.

¹*ALWAYS* I will lift up my soul to You, Eternal One,
²*BECAUSE You are* my God and I put my trust in You.

    Do not let me be humiliated.

    Do not let my enemies celebrate at my expense.
³CERTAINLY none of the people who rely on You will be shamed,

    but those who are unfaithful, who intentionally deceive,

    they are the ones who will be disgraced.

⁴DEMONSTRATE Your ways, O Eternal One.

    Teach me *to understand* so I can follow.
⁵EASE me down *the path of* Your truth.

    FEED me Your word

    because You are the True God who has saved me.

    I wait all day long, *hoping, trusting* in *You.*

⁶GRACIOUS Eternal One, remember Your compassion; *rekindle Your*

    concern and love,

    which have always been *part of Your actions toward those who*

    are Yours.
⁷Do not HOLD against me the sins I committed when I was young;

    instead, deal with me according to Your mercy and love.

    Then Your goodness may be *demonstrated in all the world,*

    Eternal One.

⁸*IMMENSELY* good and honorable is the Eternal One;

    that's why He teaches sinners the way.
⁹With JUSTICE, He directs the humble *in all that is right,*

    and He shows them His way.

¹⁰KIND and true are all the ways of the Eternal One
    to the people who keep His covenant and His words.

¹¹O LORD, *the Eternal One,* bring glory to Your name,
    and forgive my sins because they are beyond number.
¹²MAY anyone who fears the Eternal One
    be shown the path he should choose.

¹³His soul will *NOT only* live in goodness,
    but his children will inherit the land.
¹⁴ONLY those who stand in awe of the Eternal One will have intimacy
      with Him,
    and He will reveal His covenant to them.
¹⁵PERPETUALLY my focus takes me to the Eternal One
    because He will set me free from the traps *laid for me.*

¹⁶*QUIETLY* turn *Your eyes* to me and be compassionate toward me
    because I am lonely and persecuted.
¹⁷*RAPIDLY* my heart beats as troubles build *on the horizon.*
    Come relieve me from these threats.
¹⁸SEE my troubles and my misery,
    and forgive all my sins.
¹⁹TAKE notice of my enemies.
    See how there are so many of them
    who hate me and would seek my violent destruction.
²⁰Watch over my soul,
    and let me face shame and defeat UNASHAMED because You are
      my refuge.
²¹May honor and strong character keep me safe.
    VIGILANTLY I wait for You, *hoping, trusting.*

²²Save Israel from all its troubles,
    O True God.

PSALM 26

A SONG OF DAVID.

¹Declare my innocence, O Eternal One!
>   I have walked blamelessly *down this path*.
>   I placed my trust in the Eternal and have yet to stumble.
²Put me on trial and examine me, O Eternal One!
>   Search me *through and through*—from my deepest longings to every
>   thought that crosses my mind.
³Your unfailing love is always before me;
>   I have journeyed down Your *path of* truth.

⁴My life is not wasted among liars;
>   my days are not spent among cheaters.
⁵I despise every crowd intent on evil;
>   I do not commune with the wicked.

⁶I wash my hands in *the fountain of* innocence
>   so that I might join *the gathering that surrounds* Your altar, O Eternal
>   One.
⁷*From my soul,* I will join the songs of thanksgiving;
>   I will *sing and* proclaim Your wonder *and mystery*.

⁸Your house, home to Your glory, O Eternal One, *radiates its light.*
>   I am fixed on this place *and long to be nowhere else.*
⁹When *Your wrath* pursues those who oppose You,
>   those swift to sin and thirsty for blood,
>   spare my soul and grant me life.
¹⁰These men hold deceit in their *left* hands,
>   and in their right hands, bribery *and lies*.

¹¹But *God,* I have walked blamelessly *down this path,*
>   and this is my plea for redemption.
>   This is my cry for Your mercy.
¹²Here I stand secure and confident
>   before all the people; I will praise the Eternal One.

Psalm 27

A song of David.

¹The Eternal One is my light *amidst my darkness* and my rescue *in times
of trouble.*
So whom shall I fear?
The Eternal One surrounds me with a fortress of protection.
So nothing should cause me alarm.

²When my enemies advanced
to devour me alive,
They tripped and fell *flat on their faces into the soil.*

³When the armies *of the enemy* surround me,
I will not be afraid.
When death calls for me in the midst of war,
my soul is confident *and unmoved.*

⁴I am pleading with the Eternal for this one thing,
my *soul's* desire:
To live with Him all of my days—
in *the shadow of* His temple,
To behold His beauty and ponder His ways
in the company of His people.

⁵His house is my shelter and secret retreat.
It is there I find peace in the midst of storm and turmoil.
Safety sits with me in the hiding place of God.
He will set me on a rock, high *above the fray.*

⁶*God* lifts me high above those with thoughts
of death and deceit that call for my life.
I will enter *His presence,* offering sacrifices *and praise.*
In His house, I am overcome with joy
As I sing, yes, *and play music* for the Eternal One *alone.*

⁷*I cannot shout any louder.* Eternal One—hear my cry
    and respond with Your grace.
⁸The prodding of my heart leads me to chase after You.
    I am seeking You, Eternal One—*don't retreat from me.*
⁹*You have always answered my call.*
    Don't hide from me now.

Don't give up on me in anger at Your servant.
    You have always been there for me.
Don't throw me to the side and forget me,
    my God and only salvation.
¹⁰My father and mother have deserted me,
    yet the Eternal One will take me in.

¹¹O Eternal One, show me Your way,
    shine Your light brightly on this path, and make it level for me,
    for my enemies are lurking *in the recesses and ravines along the way.*
¹²*They are watching*—hoping to seize me.
Do not release me to their desires *or surrender me to their will!*
    Liars are standing against me,
    breathing out cruel lies *hoping that I will die.*

PSALM 27 | **God Didn't Wander Off.** If you are like most folks, you had a best friend while growing up or maybe a special college roommate who was your constant companion. To others it seemed that you were exclusive friends, sheltering one another from the struggles of youth. You shared everything; you almost had the same dreams. When you finally get back together with such a special person after a few years apart, you note that the friendship is still there, but that it is somehow different. You have gone in different directions, and your memories, not the future, are what bind you together. It can be the same way between you and God.

When life slams us with changes we don't expect or we focus too hard on handling the business at hand on our own, we may find ourselves totally out of touch with the Eternal One. It may seem God has gone away and is hiding from us. The truth is, though, that it isn't God who has wandered off; *we* have. At such

¹³*I will move past my enemies with this one, sure hope:*
> that with my own eyes, I will see the goodness of the Eternal One
> in the land of the living.

¹⁴*Please answer me:* Don't give up.
> Wait for the Eternal One in expectation, and be strong.
> Again, wait for the Eternal One.

PSALM 28

A SONG OF DAVID.

¹Eternal One, I am calling out to You;
> You are the foundation of my life. *Please,* don't turn Your ear from
> > me.
> If You respond to my pleas with silence,
> > I will lose all hope like those silenced by death's grave.

²Listen to my voice.
> You will hear me begging for Your help
> With my hands lifted up *in prayer,*
> > my body turned toward Your holy home.

times, we pray long and hard, but immediate, clear-cut answers don't always come. Without a continuing connection, our friendship with God is strained and distant. Just remember that God is constant; He didn't move away, you did.

David says in verse 9, "Don't give up on me . . . You have always been there for me. Don't throw me to the side and forget me." God never gave up on David. Even today the promise God made to David about his throne continuing forever is still true. David moved away from God, but fortunately he recognized the need to get connected again. He says, "Show me Your way, shine Your light brightly on this path."

To stay connected with the Eternal One, it is important that we remain close to Him or that we come close again, if we have moved away. Walking with God every day means sharing with Him the most intimate areas of our lives: our fears, our sins, our loves, our dreams.

³*I beg You;* don't punish me with the most heinous men.
    They spend their days doing evil.
Even when they engage their neighbors in pleasantness,
    they are scheming against them.
⁴Pay them back for their deeds;
    hold them accountable for their malice.
Give them what they deserve.
⁵Because these are people who have no respect for You, O Eternal One,
    they ignore everything You have done.
So He will tear them down *with His powerful hands;*
    never will they be built again.

⁶The Eternal One should be honored and revered;
    He has heard my cries for help.
⁷The Eternal One is the source of my strength and the shield that guards
        me.
    When I *learn to rest and* truly trust Him,
He sends His help. This is why my heart is singing!
    I open my mouth to praise Him, and thankfulness rises as song.

PSALM 28 | **Our Rush to Rest.** Once again David senses a key ingredient to success in this life. In verse 7 he tells us, "I learn to rest and truly trust Him." Life is always a mess when we are constantly struggling to find time and peace amid chaos. Most of us are not good at resting. We're so locked into our routines—even the parts that are good for us, like exercising and Bible reading—that we don't give ourselves a break. Oh, we may take a vacation every year or a long weekend now and then, but even when we do, we often pack those days so full that we need a rest from our vacation! Our rush to rest wears us out.

What are we to do? David takes the time to cry out in confession and then to praise God. He went to the trouble to write out his praise, which now serves as our model. Just take the first small step: stop for five minutes in the middle of your rush. Stop completely. Breathe deeply and talk quietly with God. Tell Him what you are experiencing, confess your shortcomings, and thank Him for being there with you. When we take a moment to truly rest, in the quiet we can hear God speaking to us. He may even cause our hearts to sing! God's power gets us through every possible situation we could face, and we are nothing without Him. Isn't it time to stop, breathe, and rest? Isn't it time to be carried in the arms of the Shepherd?

⁸The Eternal One gives *life and* power to all His chosen ones;
    to His anointed He is a sturdy fortress.
⁹Rescue Your people, and bring prosperity to Your legacy;
    may they know You as a shepherd, carrying them at all times.

PSALM 29

A SONG OF DAVID.

¹Give *all credit* to the Eternal One, O heavenly creatures;
    give *praise* to the Eternal One for His glory and power.
²Give to the Eternal the glory due His name;
    worship Him with *lavish displays of* sacred splendor.

³The voice of the Eternal One echoes over the great waters;
    God's magnificence roars like thunder.
    The Eternal's presence hovers over all the waters.
⁴The Eternal One's voice explodes in great power *over the earth*.
    The Eternal's voice is both regal and grand.

⁵The Eternal One's voice shatters the cedars;
    the Eternal One's power splinters the great cedars of Lebanon.
⁶He speaks, and Lebanon leaps like a young calf;
    Sirion jumps like a wild, youthful ox.

⁷The voice of the Eternal One cuts through with flames of fire.
⁸The voice of the Eternal One rumbles through the wilderness
    with great quakes; the Eternal causes Kadesh to tremble.

⁹The Eternal One's voice brings life from the doe's womb;
    His voice strips the forest bare,
        and all the people in the temple declare, "Glory!"

¹⁰The Eternal One is enthroned over the great flood;
    His reign is unending.
¹¹We ask You, Eternal One, to give strength to Your people;
    Eternal One, bless them with *the gift of* peace.

Psalm 30

A SONG OF DAVID. FOR THE DEDICATION OF THE TEMPLE.

¹I praise You, Eternal One. You lifted me *out of that deep, dark pit*
    and denied my opponents the pleasure of rubbing in their success.
²Eternal One, my True God, I cried out to You for help;
    You mended the shattered pieces of my life.
³You lifted me from the grave *with a mighty hand,*
    gave me another chance, and saved me from joining those in that
        dreadful pit.

⁴Sing, all you who remain faithful! *Pour out your hearts* to the Eternal with
        praise and melodies;
    let grateful music *fill the air and* bless His name.
⁵His wrath, you see, is fleeting,
    but His grace lasts a lifetime.

PSALM 30 | **That Dreadful Pit.** David finds himself in a "deep, dark pit." He has been chased and harassed and made to feel small by his brothers. But he says that at least he is saved from "that dreadful pit," death and separation from God. David sings, "His wrath, you see, is fleeting, but His grace lasts a lifetime."

If we will look deep into our souls even in those dark moments, we can see the hand of God. In our quiet introspection, we should be able to burst out into praise. David woke from his painful night to be greeted by "joy [that] greets the soul with the smile of morning."

Having experienced such moments, we can easily relate to the idea that God's grace pours through our souls and comes out in grateful melody. His grace is what makes us sing and what helps us get past the pains of life. His grace reminds us that there is nothing we achieve on our own; nothing that is ours if He does not come along beside us. Even out of the "deep, dark pit" God brings light and joy. A heart of gratitude pleases God, so when you praise Him in song—no matter the quality of your voice—it is sweet music to His ears! It is a troubled soul that has found rest in Him.

The deepest pains may linger through the night,
    but joy greets the soul with the *smile of* morning.

⁶When *things were quiet and* life was easy, I said *in arrogance,*
    "Nothing can shake me."
⁷By Your grace, Eternal One,
    I thought I was as strong as a mountain;
But when You *left my side and* hid away,
    I crumbled in fear.

⁸O Eternal One, I called out to You;
    I pleaded for Your compassion *and forgiveness*:
⁹"*I'm no good to You dead!* What benefits come from my rotting corpse?
    My body in the grave *will not praise You.*
No songs will rise up from the dust *of my bones.*
    From dust comes no proclamation of Your faithfulness.
¹⁰Hear me, Eternal Lord—please help me,
    Eternal One—be merciful!"

¹¹*You did it:* You turned my deepest pains into joyful dancing;
    You stripped off my dark clothing
    and covered me with joyful light.
¹²*You have restored my honor.* My heart is ready to explode, erupt in new
        songs!
    It's impossible to keep quiet!
    Eternal One, my God, *my Life-Giver,* I will thank You forever.

PSALM 31

FOR THE WORSHIP LEADER. A SONG OF DAVID.

¹You are my shelter, O Eternal One—*my soul's sanctuary!*
    Shield me from shame;
    rescue me by Your righteousness.
²*Hear me, Lord!* Turn Your ear in my direction.
    Come quick! Save me!

Be my rock, my shelter,
>> my fortress of salvation!

³You are my rock and my fortress—*my soul's sanctuary!*
>> Therefore, for the sake of Your reputation, be my leader, my guide,
>>> *my navigator, my commander.*
⁴Save me from the snare that has been secretly set out for me,
>> for You are my protection.
⁵I entrust my spirit into Your hands.*
>> You have redeemed me, O Eternal One, God of *faithfulness and* truth.

⁶I despise the people who pay respect to breathless idols,
>> and I trust *only* in You, Eternal One.
⁷I will gladly rejoice because of Your gracious love
>> because You recognized *the sadness of* my affliction.
>> *You felt deep compassion when* You saw the pains of my soul.
⁸You did not hand me over to the enemy,
>> but instead, You liberated me and made me secure in a *good and*
>>> spacious land.

⁹Show me Your grace, Eternal One, for I am in a tight spot.
>> My eyes are aching with grief;
>> my body and soul *are withering with miseries.*
¹⁰My life is devoured by sorrow,
>> and my years *are haunted* with mourning.
>> My sin has sapped me of all my strength;
>> my body withers *under the weight of this suffering.*

¹¹To all my enemies I am *an object of* scorn.
>> My neighbors especially are ashamed *of me.*
>> My friends are afraid to be seen with me.
>> When I walk down the street, people go out of their way to avoid me.
¹²I am as good as dead to them. Forgotten!
>> Like a shattered clay pot, *I am easily discarded and gladly replaced.*
¹³For I hear their whispered plans;
>> terror is everywhere!

31:5 Luke 23:46

They conspire together,
    planning, plotting, scheming to take my life.

14But I pour my trust into You, Eternal One.
    I'm *glad to* say, "You are my God!"
15I give the moments of my life over to You, *Eternal One.*
    Rescue me from those who hate me and who hound me *with their*
        threats.
16*Look toward me, and* let Your face shine down upon Your servant.
    Because of Your gracious love, save me!
17Spare me shame, O Eternal One,
    for I *turn and* call to You.
  Instead, let those who hate me be shamed;
    let death's silence claim them.
18Seal their lying lips *forever,*
    for with pride and contempt *boiling in their hearts,*
        they speak boldly against the righteous *and persecute those who poured*
            their trust into You.

19Your overflowing goodness
    You have kept for those who live in awe of You,
  And You share Your goodness with those who make You their sanctuary.
20You hide them, You shelter them in Your presence,
    safe from the conspiracies of sinful men.
  You keep them in Your tent,
    safe from the slander of accusing tongues.

21Bless the Eternal One!
    for He has revealed His gracious love to me
    when I was trapped like a city under siege.
22I began to panic so I yelled out,
    "I'm cut off. You no longer see me!"
  But You heard my cry for help *that day*
    when I called out to You.

23Love the Eternal One, all of you, His faithful people!
    The Eternal One protects those who are true to Him,
    but He pays back the proud in kind.

²⁴Be strong, and live courageously,
all of you who set your hope in the Eternal One!

PSALM 32

A CONTEMPLATIVE SONG* OF DAVID.

¹How happy is the one whose wrongs are forgiven,
whose sin is hidden *from sight*.
²How happy is the person whose sin the Eternal will not take into
account.*
How happy are those who no longer lie, *to themselves or others*.

³When I refused to admit my wrongs, *I was miserable*,
moaning and complaining all day long
so that even my bones felt brittle.
⁴Day and night, Your hand kept pressing on me; *You wouldn't let me live
this way; You had to get my attention*.
My strength dried up *like water* in the summer heat; *You wore me
down*.

[pause]*

⁵*When I finally saw my own lies,* I owned up to my sins before You,
and I did not try to hide my evil deeds *from You*.
I said *to myself,* "I'll admit *all* my sins to the Eternal One,"
and You *lifted and* carried away the guilt of my sin.

[pause]

⁶So let all who are devoted to You
speak honestly to You now, *while You are still listening*.
For then when the floods come, surely the rushing water
will not even reach them.

32:title Hebrew, *maskil*
32:1-2 Romans 4:7-8
32:4 Literally, selah, likely a musical direction from a Hebrew root meaning "to lift up"

⁷You are my hiding place.
    You will keep me out of trouble
    and envelop me with songs that remind me I am free.

[pause]

⁸I will teach you and tell you the way to go *and how to get there*;
    I will give you good counsel, and I will watch over you.
⁹But don't be *stubborn and* stupid like horses and mules
    who, if not reigned by leather and metal,
    will run wild, ignoring their masters.

¹⁰Tormented *and empty* are wicked *and destructive* people,
    but the one who trusts in the Eternal One is wrapped tightly in His
        gracious love.
¹¹Express your joy; be happy in the Eternal, you who are good and true.
    Go ahead, shout *and* rejoice aloud, you whose hearts are *honest and*
        straightforward.

PSALM 33

¹Release your heart's joy *in sweet music* to the Eternal One.
    When the upright passionately sing glory-filled songs *to Him,*
        everything is in its right place.
²Worship the Eternal One with your instruments, strings *offering their*
        praise;
    write *awe-filled* songs to Him on the 10-stringed harp.
³Sing to the Eternal a new song;
    play each the best way you can, *and don't be afraid to* be bold with
        your joyful feelings.

⁴For the word of the Eternal One is perfect and true;
    His actions are always faithful *and right.*
⁵He loves virtue and equity;
    the Eternal One's love fills the whole earth.

⁶The *unfathomable* cosmos came into being at the word of the Eternal
  One's *imagination, a solitary voice in endless darkness.*
    The breath of His mouth whispered the sea of stars into existence.
    His word is the womb of all creation.
⁷He gathers every drop of every ocean as in a jar,
    securing the ocean depths as *His watery* treasure.

⁸Let all people stand in awe of the Eternal One;
    let every man, woman, and child live in wonder of Him.
⁹For He spoke, and all things came into being.
    A *single* command *from His lips,* and all creation *obeyed and* stood its
      ground.

¹⁰The Eternal One cripples the schemes of the other nations;
    He impedes the plans of *rival* peoples.
¹¹The Eternal One's purposes will last to the end of time;
    the thoughts of His heart *will awaken and stir* all generations.
¹²The nation whose True God is the Eternal One is *truly* blessed;
    fortunate are all whom He chooses to inherit His legacy.

¹³The Eternal One peers down from heaven
    and watches all of humanity;
¹⁴He observes every soul
    from His divine residence.
¹⁵He has formed every human heart, *breathing life into every human spirit;*
    He knows the deeds of each person, *inside and out.*
¹⁶A king is not delivered by the might of his army.
    Even the *strongest* warrior is not saved by his own strength.
¹⁷A horse is not the way to victory;
    its great strength cannot rescue.

¹⁸Listen, the eye of the Eternal One is upon those who live in awe of Him,
    those who hope in His steadfast love,
¹⁹That He may save them from the darkness of the grave
    and be kept alive during the lean seasons.

²⁰*We live with hope in* the Eternal One. We wait for Him,
    for He is our *Divine* Help and *Impenetrable* Shield.

²¹Our hearts erupt with joy in Him
>
> because we trust His holy name.

²²O Eternal One, drench us with Your endless love,
>
> even now as we wait for You.

PSALM 34

A SONG OF DAVID AS HE PRETENDED TO BE INSANE TO ESCAPE FROM ABIMELECH.

¹I will praise the Eternal One in every moment *through every situation.*
>
> Whenever I speak, my words will always praise Him.

²Everything within me wants to pay tribute to the Eternal One.
>
> Whenever the *poor and* humble hear of His greatness, they will celebrate too!

³*Come and* lift up the Eternal One with me;
>
> let's praise His name together!

⁴*When I needed the Eternal One,* I looked for Him;
>
> *I called out to Him, and* He *heard me and* responded.

He *came and* rescued me from everything that made me so afraid.

⁵Look to Him and shine,
>
> so shame will never contort your faces.

⁶This poor soul cried, and the Eternal One heard me.
>
> He rescued me from my troubles.

⁷The messenger of the Eternal God surrounds
>
> everyone who walks with Him and is always there to *protect and* rescue us.

⁸Taste of His goodness; see how wonderful the Eternal One truly is.
>
> Anyone who puts trust in Him will be blessed *and comforted.*

⁹Revere the Eternal One, you His saints,
>
> for those who worship Him will possess everything important in life.

¹⁰Young lions may grow tired and hungry,
>
> but those intent on knowing the Eternal God will have everything they need.

¹¹Gather around, children, listen to what I'm saying;
>
> I will teach you how to revere the Eternal One.

¹²If you love life
>
> and want to live a good, long time,

¹³Take care with the things you say.
>
> Don't lie or spread gossip or talk about improper things.

¹⁴Walk away from the evil *things of the world,*
>
> and always seek peace and pursue it.

¹⁵For the Eternal One watches over the righteous,
>
> and His ears are attuned to their prayers. *He is always listening.*

¹⁶But the Eternal One will punish evildoers,
>
> *and nothing they do will last.* They will soon be forgotten.

¹⁷When the upright *need help and* cry to the Eternal One, He hears
>
> their cries
>
> and rescues them from all of their troubles.

¹⁸When someone is hurting or brokenhearted, the Eternal One moves in
>
> close
>
> and revives him in his pain.

PSALM 34 | **What We Say *Does* Matter.** Who doesn't want "to live a good, long time"? David has found the secret to a long life: "don't lie . . . walk away from the evil . . . seek peace." This sounds like something your grandmother might have told you. David's advice, though, is not spoken as coming from just another soul living in an evil world. It comes from one who knows he belongs to the Eternal God of heaven.

God is the difference. He hears the cry of the upright: He rescues His own from trouble. He moves in close and comforts. We don't lie because God is truth. We walk away from evil because we are following God's path. We seek peace because we serve the King of Peace.

Probably the most common sin today and maybe one of the most destructive is gossip. What we say about others *does* matter. Words create good or evil, so we must take care with the things we say. We walk with evil when we share in gossip, when we fudge on the truth, when we take advantage of others. We stand against peace when we do any of these things. God would have us stand with Him instead. It all comes down to whom you are serving.

¹⁹Hard times may well be the plight of the righteous—
  they may often seem overwhelmed—
    but the Eternal One rescues the righteous from what oppresses them.
²⁰He will protect all of their bones;
    not even one bone will be broken.
²¹Evil *moves in and ultimately* murders the wicked;
    the enemies of the righteous will be condemned.
²²The Eternal One will liberate His servants;
    those who seek refuge in Him will never be condemned.

PSALM 35

A SONG OF DAVID.

¹Make a case against those who struggle with me, Eternal One.
    Battle against those who battle against me.
²Be my shield and protection;
    stand with me and rescue me!
³Draw the spear and javelin
    to meet my pursuers.
  Reassure my soul and say,
    "I will deliver you."

⁴Shame and dishonor those *ruthless* enemies
    who wish to end my life.
  Turn back those who conspire against me,
    defeated and humiliated!
⁵Let them be separated *from the righteous* as chaff *is separated from the
      grain,*
    blown by the wind,
      driven *far, far* away by the Eternal One's messenger.
⁶Make their way unsure and *dangerously* dark,
    a gauntlet of gloom
      chased through the darkness by the Eternal One's messenger.

⁷For no reason at all, they set a trap for me—*a net, a snare*—
    then, without cause, they disguised a pit to capture my soul—*another*
        cowardly snare.
⁸May they be surprised by their own destruction.
  May they become tangled in their own net
    and fall into the pit *which they, themselves, dug.*

⁹*When that day comes,* my soul will celebrate the Eternal One
    and be glad in His salvation.
¹⁰Every fiber of my being* will shout,
    "Eternal One, there is none like You!
  You save the poor
    from those who try to overpower them
    and rescue the weak and the needy from those who steal from them."

¹¹False witnesses step forward;
    they ask me *strange* questions for which I have no answers.
¹²When I do good *to them,* they do evil to me,
    bringing misery to my soul.
¹³When they were sick,
    I *mourned for them and* wore sackcloth;
    I chose to humble myself by fasting.
  But my prayers came back unanswered.
    ¹⁴So I mourned *more deeply* as if I grieved for my brother or friend;
  I went around bowed down by sorrow, *dressed in black,*
    as if I were weeping for my mother.
¹⁵But when I stumbled, they gathered together
    and celebrated *my fall* with joy;
  People attacked me when I wasn't expecting it;
    they slandered me with no end.
¹⁶Like godless mockers at a festival,*
    their words tore at me.

35:10 Literally, all my bones
35:16 Greek manuscripts read "Like the godless they cruelly mocked."

¹⁷Lord, how long will You *do nothing but* watch?
>   Save me from their evil assaults, *plots, and plunder;*
>   rescue my life from these *hungry beasts, these ruthless* lions!
¹⁸Then I will praise You and thank You at the great gathering
>   in the company of the entire congregation.

¹⁹Do not allow my enemies to boast at my expense,
>   for they despise me without any cause—*
>   yet they wink at me—malicious, taunting winks.
²⁰ Their words have no ring of peace.
>   They plan evil rumors *and incriminations*
>   against those who live peacefully in the land.
²¹They speak *lying* accusations against me;
>   they say, "Aha! Aha! *We know what you've been up to.*
>   We've seen it with our own eyes!"

²²You have seen *what's happening,* Eternal One; don't remain silent!
>   Lord, do not stay far away from me!
²³Wake up; come to my defense!
>   Fight for me, my Lord and my God!
²⁴Pass Your judgment, Eternal One, my True God;
>   do it by the standards of Your righteousness.
>   Do not allow my enemies to boast over me.
²⁵Do not allow them to gloat *over me,*
>   "Aha, we have won! We got what we wanted!"
>   Do not allow them to brag,
>   "We chewed him up and spit him out."

²⁶Shame and confuse those who celebrate my suffering;
>   may those who exalt themselves above me be covered with shame—
>   wrapped in a cloak of dishonor!

²⁷As for those who desire my vindication,
>   may they be joyful and glad.
>   May they forever say,

35:19 John 15:25

"The Eternal One is indeed great!
    He takes pleasure when good things happen to His servant!"
²⁸ *That's why* I will speak of Your righteousness
    and *sing* praises to You all day long.

PSALM 36

FOR THE WORSHIP LEADER. *A SONG* OF DAVID, THE ETERNAL ONE'S
SERVANT.

¹Sin speaks in the depths of the soul
    of those who oppose God; *they listen closely to its urgings.*
You'll never see the fear of God
    in their eyes,
²For they flatter themselves—
    convinced their sin will remain *secret,* undiscovered, and so unhated.
³They speak words of evil and deceit.
    Wisdom and goodness, they deserted *long ago.*
⁴Even as they sleep, they are plotting mischief.
    They journey along a path far from anything good,
    gravitating to trouble, welcoming evil.

⁵Your love, O Eternal One, towers high into the heavens.
    Even the skies are lower than Your faithfulness.
⁶Your justice is like the majestic mountains.
    Your judgments are as deep as the oceans, *and yet in Your greatness,*
        You remember us all.
    You, O Eternal One, offer life for every person and animal.

⁷Your strong love, O True God, is precious.
    All people run for shelter under the shadow of Your wings.
⁸In Your house, they eat and are full at Your table.
    they drink from the river of Your *overflowing* kindness.
⁹You have the fountain of life *that quenches our thirst.*
    Your light has opened our eyes *and awakened our souls.*

¹⁰May Your love continue to grow deeply in the lives of all who know You.
   May Your salvation reach every heart committed to do right.
¹¹Give me shelter from prideful feet that hunt me down
   and wicked hands that push me from Your path.
¹²It is there, *far away from You,* that the wicked will be forced down,
   face to the earth, never again returning to their feet.

PSALM 37*

A SONG OF DAVID.

¹Don't be worried with evil workers
   or envy the gains of people with all-wrong-upside-down ways.
²Soon enough they will wither like grass,
   like green herbs fading *in summer's heat.*

³Believe in the Eternal One, and do what is good—
   live in the land *He provides, roam,* and rest in God's faithfulness.
⁴Take great joy in the Eternal One!
   His gifts are coming, and they are all your heart desires!

⁵Commit your path to the Eternal One; *let Him direct you.*
   Put your confidence in Him, and He will follow through *with you.*
⁶He will spread out righteousness for you as a sunrise *spreads radiance over the land*;
   He will deliver justice for you into the light of the high sun.

⁷Be still. Be patient. Expect the Eternal to arrive *and set things right.*
   Don't get upset when you see the worldly ones rising up the ladder.
   (They will hit the ceiling and fall back down.)
   Don't be bothered by those who are anchored in wicked ways.

⁸So turn from anger. Don't rage,
   and don't worry—these ways frame the doorway to evil.

Psalm 37 Psalm 37 is a Hebrew acrostic poem.

⁹Besides, those who act from evil motives will be cut off from the land;
　　but those who wait, hoping in the Eternal One, will enjoy its riches.

¹⁰You'll see . . . the wicked *won't know what hit them*; you'll blink, and they'll
　　be gone;
　　you'll go out looking for them, but you won't find them.
¹¹But the humble-hearted will inherit the land;
　　they will take pleasure in its peace and enjoy its abundance.

¹²How that wicked man devises evil against God's righteous ones!
　　He grits his teeth, *consumed by hate for the upright*.
¹³But oh, how the Lord laughs at him!
　　He knows the wicked man will get his; the day is coming.

¹⁴The wicked unsheathe their swords, pull taut their bows;
　　the poor and needy are their victims,
　　and evil is on the prowl to kill those with integrity, *God's beloved*.
¹⁵But their swords will bend back to pierce their own hearts—
　　yes, their bows will snap in two.

¹⁶The righteous are better off with the little *God blessed them with*
　　than *living under the curse of* the wealth of the wicked.
¹⁷*Their time is short,* their arms will be broken,
　　but the Eternal One will hold His righteous children high.

¹⁸All their days are *measured and* known by the Eternal;
　　their inheritance is kept safe forever.
¹⁹When calamity comes, they will escape with their dignity.
　　When famine invades the nations, they will be fed to their fill.

PSALM 37 **Setting expectations** is a curious thing. If we expect something of someone else and that person doesn't deliver, we may assume we set our expectations too high, even if we have never actually verbalized our expectations to the one who disappointed us. If we set expectations for ourselves and fail, we may look at lowering our own standards. Psalm 37, however, advises us to "expect" God to act and set things right. After all, what can it mean to believe in God if we don't expect Him to act like God? Many say they have belief without manifesting any real expectation. This is like believing your favorite team will win the championship while you bet that they will lose.

²⁰But immoral ones will find their lives cut short;
>they'll vanish as quickly as wildflowers in the fields.
Yes, enemies of the Eternal One will vanish
>like smoke *into the cool night air.*

²¹Evil people borrow and never repay their debts,
>while the good give generously *from their hearts.*
²²For God's blessed *children* will inherit the land,
>but those cursed by Him stand to gain nothing.

²³*If you are right with God,* He strengthens you for the journey;
>the Eternal One will be pleased with your life.
²⁴And even though you trip up, you will not fall on your face
>because the Eternal holds you by the hand.

²⁵Through my whole life (young and old),
>I have never witnessed God forsaking those who do right,
>nor have I seen their children begging for crumbs,
²⁶Because they are always giving and sharing;
>truly, their children are a joyful blessing.

²⁷Walk away from evil. Do good
>so you, too, will enjoy never-ending life
²⁸Because the Eternal One cherishes justice
>and will not abandon those loyal to Him.

David tells us in verse 28 that "the Eternal One cherishes justice and will not abandon those loyal to Him." There are two major truths here. First, we can expect God to act because He truly loves justice; evil can't prevail with a God who loves justice. Second, He doesn't abandon those who are loyal. Those who are loyal are those who believe, expecting results. He doesn't abandon them, and they don't abandon Him in unbelief. We are to expect and heed the reminder to "be still . . . be patient." God's timing may not be our timing, but He is loyal to those who are loyal.

Are we unrealistic in our expectations concerning God? If we don't have high expectations, then we really don't believe and in turn we are not loyal.

He will guard *and care for* them forever,
 but any child born of evil will be *rooted out, cut down, and* destroyed.
²⁹Those leading God-pleasing lives will inherit His land
 and settle there forever.

³⁰Wisdom fills the mouth of the right-living;
 justice *and truth* roll from their tongues.
³¹The True God's law is imprinted upon their hearts,
 and they do not stumble.

³²The wicked stalk God's good ones,
 looking to kill them,
³³But the Eternal One will never leave them to *the dogs of* evil,
 nor will they be found guilty when the verdict is read.

³⁴Wait for the Eternal One. Keep to His path. *Mind His will.*
 He will *come for you,* exalt you; you will inherit the land.
 Before your very eyes you will see the end of the wicked.

³⁵*I passed by* a wicked man with a cold-blooded nature;
 I looked, and he seemed as large as a cedar of Lebanon.
³⁶But then again, I passed that same way and there was nothing left of him.
 I went out looking for him, but he was nowhere to be found.

³⁷Keep your eye on the innocent. Model your life after the blameless.
 Everyone who loves peace has a future.
³⁸But sinners will be doomed.
 The forecast for the wicked: *utter destruction.*
 There will be none left, *not one child of darkness.*

³⁹The Eternal One saves His faithful;
 He lends His strength in hard times;
⁴⁰The Eternal One comes and frees them—
 frees them from evildoers and saves them *for eternity*—
 simply because they seek shelter in Him.

Psalm 38

A song of David for remembering.

¹O Eternal One, please do not scold me in Your anger;
  though Your wrath is just, do not correct me in Your fury.
²The arrows *from Your bow* have penetrated my flesh;
  Your hand has come down *hard* on me.

³Because Your anger *has infected the depths of my being and stolen my health,*
  my flesh is ill.
 My bones are no longer sound
  because of all the sins I have committed.
⁴My guilt has covered me; *it's more than I can handle;*
  this burden is too heavy for me to carry.

⁵Now sores cover me, infected and putrid sores,
  because of all the foolish things I have done.
⁶I am bent down, *cowering in fear,* prostrate on the ground;
  I spend the day in mourning, *guilty tears stinging and burning my eyes.*
⁷My back aches. *I'm full of fever;*
  my body is no longer whole, *no longer well.*
⁸I am *completely numb,* totally spent, hopelessly crushed.
  The agitation of my heart makes me groan.

⁹O Lord, You know all my desires;
  nothing escapes You; *You hear* my every moan.
¹⁰My heart pounds against my chest; my vigor is completely drained;
  my eyes were once bright, but now the brightness is all gone.
¹¹Even my friends and loved ones turn away when they see this marked man;
  those closest to me are no longer close at all.

¹²Those who want me dead lay traps upon my path;
  those who desire my downfall threaten—*my end is near—*
  they spend their days plotting against me.

¹³Like one who is deaf, my ears do not hear.

Like one who is mute, my tongue cannot speak.
¹⁴The truth is this: I am like one who cannot hear;

I cannot even protest *against them.*

¹⁵Still I wait *expectantly* for You, O Eternal One—

knowing You will answer me *in some way,* O Lord, my True God.
¹⁶I only asked, "When I stumble *on the narrow path,*

don't let them boast or celebrate *my failure.*"

¹⁷I am prepared for what may come; *my time must be short;*

my pain and suffering a constant *companion.*
¹⁸I confess, "I have sinned,"

and I regret the wrong I have done.
¹⁹My enemies are alive *and well,*

they are powerful and on the increase,

and for no reason, they hate me.
²⁰When I do good, my opponents reward me with evil;

though I pursue what is right, they stand against me.

²¹Eternal One, do not leave me *to their mercy;*

my True God, don't be far from me *when they are near.*
²²I need Your help now—*not later.*

O Lord, be my Rescuer.

PSALM 39

FOR THE WORSHIP LEADER, JEDUTHUN.* A SONG OF DAVID.

¹I promised, "I'll be careful on life's journey

not to sin with my words;

I'll seal my lips

when wicked people are around."

39:title 1 Chronicles 9:16

²I kept my mouth shut;
  I had nothing to say—not even anything good—
  which came to grieve me more and more.
³*I felt* my heart become hot inside me
  as I thought on these things; a fire *ignited and* burned.
  Then I said,

⁴"Eternal One, let me understand my end
  and how brief my earthly existence is;
  help me realize my life is fleeting.
⁵You have determined the length of my days,
  and my life is nothing *compared* to You.
Even the longest life is only a breath."

[pause]*

39:5 Literally, selah, likely a musical direction from a Hebrew root meaning "to lift up"

PSALM 39 | **What Is the Goal of Life?** Of course, the goal varies from person to person, but most of us hope others will someday cherish the things we enjoyed as we journeyed through life. We want our important things to serve as a legacy of all we achieved. Why? Because we want to be remembered. We want to know our lives have made a difference.

David is afraid he will be known for being shallow and godless. He confesses, "I am estranged from You, a wanderer like my fathers before me." His desire is to be close to God while pleasing Him. What is keeping him away from God? Sin; specifically the words of his mouth are the source of his separation. He pleads with God, "I'll be careful on life's journey not to sin with my words."

Our words reveal our deep thoughts. A slip of the tongue, a statement in the heat of argument, whispered slander behind someone's back all show the evil inside of us. David tells us that he knows his weakness because "You discipline us for our sins." He is under conviction: "I'll seal my lips . . . kept my mouth shut . . . I am quiet; . . . I keep my mouth closed because this has come from You."

We can't establish a lasting legacy or be truly close to God if we harm others with our words. Words count.

⁶In truth, each of us journeys through life like a shadow.

    We busy ourselves accomplishing nothing, piling up assets we can
        never keep;

We can't even know who will end up with those things.

⁷In light of all this, Lord, what am I really waiting for?
    You are my hope.
⁸Keep me from all the wrong I would do;
    don't let the foolish laugh at me.
⁹I am quiet; I keep my mouth closed
    because this has come from You.
¹⁰Take Your curse from me;
    I can't endure Your punishment.

¹¹You discipline us for our sins.
    Like a moth, You consume everything we treasure;
    it's evident we are merely a breath.

[pause]

¹²Hear me, O Eternal One;
    listen to my pleading,
    and don't ignore my tears
  Because I am estranged from You—
    a wanderer like my fathers before me.
¹³Look away from me so I might have a chance to *recover my joy and* smile
    again
    before I lay this life down and am no more.

PSALM 40

FOR THE WORSHIP LEADER. A SONG OF DAVID.

¹I waited a long time for the Eternal One;
    He *finally* knelt down to hear me. He listened to my *weak and*
    whispered cry.

²He reached down and drew me from the deep, dark hole where I was
        stranded, mired in the muck and clay.
  With a gentle hand, He pulled me out
To set me down safely on a *warm* rock;
        He held me until I was steady enough to continue the journey again.
³*As if that were not enough,*
      because of Him my mind is clearing up.
Now I have a new song to sing—
    a song of praise to the One *who saved me.*

PSALM 40   **A Warm Rock.** David finds himself stranded in a deep, dark hole—mired in muck and clay. Then God reaches down and pulls him out and sets him on a warm rock. Imagine the change from struggling in the cold, dark mire to sunning on a warm rock. What a great God we have!

As followers of the Eternal One, we seek His direction and His will for our lives, and we tell others about His faithfulness to save us from harm. Even so, we have moments when our own sins wash over us in such torrents that we become blind to His presence, even wondering if He is still near . . . still willing to help us. Swimming in the seas of our own troubles, we lose sight of Him and need to search again for His light. David reaches back in his memory to say, "You have done so many wonderful things." Likewise, when we are stuck in the "clay" of living, God gives us the memories of His work to help us get our minds in the right place.

David speaks out, "I have not kept Your righteousness to myself. . . . I haven't been shy to talk about Your love." Remember the words David said in the pit. Those moments of wrestling with our true nature would cause any of us to come up short. We see clearly the chasm between who we are and who God is. We understand that in spite of our best efforts, we fall short of the mark. We want to be rescued because the will of God is etched deeply into our hearts and souls. We cannot swim to the shores of peace and safety without Him. David says, "Right now I can't see because I am surrounded by troubles." In the end, David comes around to the beginning, "You are my help; only You can save me, my True God. Please hurry."

So what do we do when we are in the pit? Remember the work of God previously in our lives, confess our doubts and shortcomings, and call out, knowing He is coming.

Because of what He's done, many people will see
    for the first time, hear for the first time,
And come to trust in the Eternal One.

⁴Surely those who trust the Eternal One—
    who don't trust in proud, *powerful* people
Or in people who care little *for reality,* chasing false gods—
    surely they are happy, as I have become.
⁵You have done so many wonderful things,
    had so many *tender* thoughts toward us, Eternal One, my God,
    that go on and on, ever increasing.
Who can compare with You?

⁶Sacrifices and offerings are not what You want,
    but You've opened my ears,* *and now I understand.*
Burnt offerings and sin offerings
    are not what please You.
⁷So I said, "See, I have come *to do Your will,*
    as it is inscribed of me in the scroll.
⁸I am pleased to live how You want, my God.
    Your law is etched into my heart *and my soul.*"

⁹I have encouraged *Your people* with the message of righteousness,
    in Your great assembly (look and see),
I haven't kept quiet about these things;
    You know this, Eternal One.
¹⁰I have not kept Your righteousness to myself, sealed up in the secret places
    of my heart;
    instead, I *boldly* tell others how You save and how loyal You are.
I haven't been shy to talk about Your love, *nor have I been afraid* to tell
    Your truth
    before the great assembly *of Your people.*

¹¹Please, Eternal One, don't hold back
    Your kind ways from me.

40:6 Greek manuscripts read "but You have prepared a body for me."

I need Your strong love and truth
    to *stand watch over me and* keep me from harm.
[12]Right now *I can't see because* I am surrounded by troubles;
    my sins *and shortcomings* have caught up to me,
    so I am swimming in darkness.
Like the hairs on my head, there are too many to count,
    so my heart deserts me.

[13]O Eternal One, please rescue me.
    O Eternal One, hurry; I need Your help.
[14]May those who are trying to destroy me
    be humiliated and ashamed instead;
May those who want to ruin my reputation
    be cut off and embarrassed.
[15]May those *who try to catch me off guard,*
    those who look at me and say, "Aha, *we've trapped you,*"
    be caught in their own shame instead.

[16]But may all who look for You
    discover true joy and happiness in You;
May those who cherish how You save them
    always say, "O Eternal One, You are great *and are first in our hearts.*"
[17]Meanwhile, I am empty and need so much,
    but *I know* the Lord is thinking of me.
You are my help; only You can save me, my True God.
    Please hurry.

PSALM 41

FOR THE WORSHIP LEADER. A SONG OF DAVID.

[1]Blessed are those who consider the helpless.
    The Eternal One will *stay near them,* leading them to safety in times
        of bitter struggle.

²The Eternal One defends them and preserves them,
>   and His blessing will find them in the land *He gave them*.
>   He moves ahead to frustrate their enemies' plans.
³When sickness comes, the Eternal One is beside them—
>   to comfort them on their sickbeds and restore them to health.

⁴And me? I cry out to Him,
>   "Heal my soul, O Eternal One, and show mercy
>   because I have sinned against You!"
⁵My enemies are talking about me *even now*:
>   "When will death come for him and his name be forgotten?"
⁶As they sit with me *under my roof, their well wishes are* empty lies.
>   They listen to my story
>   and then turn it around to tell their own version on the street.
⁷*Across the city,* crowds whisper lies about me.
>   *Their hate is strong, and* they search for ways to harm me.

⁸*Some are saying:* "Some vile disease has gotten hold of him.
>   The bed he lies in will be his deathbed."
⁹Even my best friend, my confidant
>   who has eaten my bread will stab me in the back.*
¹⁰But You, Eternal One, show mercy to me.
>   *Extend Your gracious hand, and* help me up. I need to pay them back
>   *for what they've done to me.*

¹¹I realize now that Your favor has come to me,
>   for my enemies have yet to declare victory over me.
¹²You know and uphold me—a man of honor.
>   You grant me *strength and* life forever in Your presence.

¹³Blessed is the Eternal One, the True God of Israel.
>   Always and Eternal. Amen and Amen.

41: 9 John 13:18

PSALM 42*

═══════════════════════════════════

FOR THE WORSHIP LEADER. A CONTEMPLATIVE SONG*
OF THE SONS OF KORAH.

¹My soul *is dry and* thirsts for You, True God,
  as a deer thirsts for water.
²I long for the True God who lives.
  When can I stand before Him *and feel His comfort*?
³*Right now I'm overwhelmed by my sorrow and pain;*
  I can't stop feasting on my tears.
People crowd around me and say,
  "Where is your True God *whom you claim will save*?"

⁴With a broken heart,
  I remember times before
When I was with Your people. *They were better days.*
  I used to lead them *happil*y into the True God's house,
Singing with joy, shouting thanksgivings with *abandon,*
  joining the congregation in the celebration.
⁵Why am I so overwrought?
  Why am I so disturbed?
Why can't I just hope in God?
  Despite all my emotions, I will *believe and* praise the One
  who saves me *and is my life.*
⁶My God, my soul is so traumatized;
  the only help is remembering You *wherever I may be*;
From the land of the Jordan to Hermon's high place
  to Mount Mizar.
⁷In the roar of Your waterfalls,
  ancient depths *surge,* calling out to the deep.
All Your waves break over me; *am I drowning?*

Psalm 42 Psalms 42–43 are a single poem in many Hebrew manuscripts.
42:title Hebrew, *maskil*

⁸Yet in the light of day, the Eternal One shows me His love.

When night settles in *and all is dark,* He keeps me company—

His *soothing* song, a prayerful melody to the True God of my life.

⁹*Even still,* I will say to the True God, my rock *and strength*:

"Why have You forgotten me?

Why must I live my life so depressed, crying endlessly

while my enemies have the upper hand?"

¹⁰My enemies taunt me.

They shatter my soul the way a sword shatters a man's bones.

They keep taunting all the day long,

"Where is He, your True God?"

¹¹Why am I so overwrought,

Why am I so disturbed?

| PSALM 42 | **Emotions Are Tricky.** They can lift us up, singing and shouting for joy with a kind of reckless abandon; or they can plunge us back to the very core of our being, leaving us in a drought of misery, thirsting for relief. "My soul is dry and thirsts for You, True God, as a deer thirsts for water." This psalm expresses the highs of living so close to God that it is cause for celebration and also the lows of brokenness, pining for better days.

The refrain brings the dilemma to light here, "Why am I so overwrought? Why am I so disturbed? Why can't I just hope in God?" We are no different. When the good days seem to have left us, we remember them with longing and we cry out for hope again. In that moment, in that cry for hope, we recognize the challenge. We know we must step aside from our emotions, and we must believe again in the One True God, praising Him for all He does to keep us satisfied. Only in Him will we thirst no more!

Even in the face of our detractors taunting us ("Where is He, your True God?"), we must be faithful. The psalm closes with the repeated refrain, "Why am I so overwrought?" But this time instead of stopping with "Why can't I just hope in God?" the psalmist takes a stand. "Despite all my emotions, I will believe and praise the One who saves me, my God." After all, the purpose of a trial is to pass the test. God stretches us so that we may savor the sweetness of His fellowship when we come back to Him.

Why can't I just hope in God?
Despite all my emotions, I will *believe and* praise the One
who saves me, my God.

PSALM 43*

¹Plead for me; *clear my name,* O God. Prove me innocent
before immoral people;
Save me from their lies,
their unjust *thoughts and deeds.*
²You are the True God—my shelter, my protector, *the one whom I lean on.*
Why have You turned away from me? *Rejected me?*
Why must I go around, overwrought, mourning,
suffering under the weight of my enemies?

³*O my God,* shine Your light and truth
to help me see clearly,
To lead me to Your holy mountain,
to Your home.
⁴Then I will go to God's altar *with nothing to hide.*
I will go to God, my rapture;
I will sing praises to You and play my strings,
Unloading my cares, unleashing my joys, to You, God, my God.

⁵O my soul, why are you so overwrought?
Why are you so disturbed?
Why can't I just hope in God? *Despite all my emotions,* I will hope in God
again.
I will *believe and* praise the One
who saves me and is my life,
My Savior and my God.

Psalm 43 Psalms 42–43 are a single poem in many Hebrew manuscripts.

PSALM 44

FOR THE WORSHIP LEADER. A CONTEMPLATIVE SONG* OF THE SONS OF KORAH.

¹With our own ears, O God, we have heard the stories
　　our ancestors recited of Your deeds in their days, days long past.
　　How You saved the day.
²With a powerful hand, You drove the nations *from this land,*
　　but then You planted our parents here.
You fought for us against people of this land;
　　You set our parents free *to enjoy its goodness.*
³They did not win the land with their swords.
　　It wasn't their strength that won them victory.
It was *Your strength*—Your right hand, Your arm,
　　and the light of Your presence *that gave them success,*
　　for You loved them.

⁴You are my King, my God!
　　You ordained victories for Jacob *and his people*!
⁵You are *our victory,* pushing back the enemy;
　　at the sound of Your name, we crush the opposition.

44:title Hebrew, *maskil*

PSALM 44 **Believe Without Reservation.** At one time or another, each of us has been in a situation where someone is droning on about how great life is. It may be that God has given wealth or easy living; or maybe God has stepped in and delivered that person from a terrible situation; or maybe He has brought the perfect mate into this person's life. All the while you feel worse and worse, because you have financial problems or don't feel accepted or have an abusive spouse.

　　Well, this is the way the psalmist felt. After all those stories of the blessings and deliverance of God that the old folks would share, the Jews were stuck without a land and without friends. They were possibly in exile or under attack from their neighbors. Everyone was against them; and when they cried out to God, there was no answer. What was wrong? Where was God? Doubt naturally comes and self-pity

⁶I don't trust in my weapons
    or in my strength to win me victory.
⁷But You rescue us from our foes;
    You shame our enemies.
⁸We shout Your name all day long;
    we will praise Your name forever!

[pause][*]

⁹*But wait, God, where have You gone?* Why have You shamed us?
    Why do our armies stand alone?
¹⁰Without Your help we must retreat from our enemy,
    and the very ones who despise us pillage us.
¹¹You have offered us up *to our enemies,*
    like sheep to the slaughter, *meat for their feast,*
    and You have dispersed us among the nations.
¹²You sold Your people for mere pennies,
    and You gained nothing from the deal.

44:8 Literally, selah, likely a musical direction from a Hebrew root meaning "to lift up"

grows. Is that all of the story? During several different periods, entire generations needed to be purged from Israel, because of their hard hearts. They had lost their way, and God was preparing to bring His remnant back into favor.

So what is the lesson for us? God responds to faith; we must believe without reservation. We must look for the work of God in all situations. We must be like the psalmist and call out in faith, "Rise up and help us; restore us for the sake of Your boundless love." History tells us that God did just that. He brought the people back into the land, raised up a new temple, restored fellowship with them, and a few generations later brought the Messiah.

God is still there, and He is still concerned about people of faith. Ask with a believing heart and expect Him to respond.

¹³You have made us a joke to our *friends and* neighbors,
    mocked and ridiculed by all those around us.
¹⁴You have brought us infamy among the nations
    and made us an object of scorn and laughter to our neighbors.
¹⁵Disgrace follows me everywhere I go; *I am constantly embarrassed.*
    Shame is written across my face
¹⁶Because of the taunting and berating of those who are against me,
    because the enemy seeks revenge against me.

¹⁷All this has happened to us,
    yet we have never forgotten You;
    we have not broken Your covenant with us.
    We remembered You and our promises.
¹⁸Our hearts stayed true to You;
    we have never left Your path; *we follow on.*
¹⁹Yet You have *tested us,* left us defeated in a land of jackals,
    and shrouded us with the veil of death.

²⁰Even if we had forgotten the name of our God
    or offered praise to another god,
²¹Would not the True God have known it?
    For He can see the hidden places of our hearts.
²²On Your behalf, our lives are endangered constantly;
    we are like sheep awaiting slaughter.*

²³Wake up, Lord! Why do You slumber?
    Get up! Do not reject us any longer!
²⁴Why are You still hiding from us?
    Why are You still ignoring our suffering and trouble?
²⁵*Look and You will see* our souls now dwell in the dust;
    our bodies hug the earth.
²⁶Rise up and help us;
    restore us for the sake of Your boundless love.

44:22 Romans 8:36

PSALM 45

For the worship leader. A contemplative song* of the sons of Korah to *the tune* "The Lilies."* A love song.

¹My heart is bursting with a new song;
lyrics to my king *erupt like a spring*
for my king, to my king;
my tongue is the pen of a poet, ready *and willing*.

²Better by far are you than all others, *my king;*
gracious words flow from your lips;
indeed, God has blessed you forever.
³With your sword at your side, you are glorious, majestic,
a mighty warrior.

⁴Ride on in splendor; ride into battle victorious,
for the sake of truth, humility, and justice.
Perform awesome acts, trained by your *powerful* right hand.
⁵Razor-sharp arrows *leap from your bow*
to pierce the heart of the king's foes;
they lie, defeated, before you.

⁶O God, Your throne is eternal;
You will rule your kingdom with a scepter of justice.
⁷You have loved what is right and hated what is evil.

That is why God, your God, has anointed you
with the oil of gladness *and lifted you* above your companions.*
⁸All of your clothing *is drenched* in *the rich scent of* myrrh, aloes, and
cassia;

45:title Hebrew, *maskil*
45: title Hebrew, *shoshannim,* white lily-like flowers, perhaps the melody to which the song is sung
45:6-7 Hebrews 1:8-9

In palaces decked out with ivory, *beautiful* stringed instruments play for
    your pleasure.
    ⁹*At a royal wedding* with the daughters of kings among the guests of
    honor,
    your bride-queen stands at your right, adorned in gold from Ophir.

¹⁰Hear this, daughter; pay close attention to what I am about to say:
    You must forget your people and *even* your father's house
    ¹¹because the king yearns for your beauty.
Humble yourself before him, for he is *now* your lord.
    ¹²The daughter of Tyre arrives with a gift;
    the wealthy will *bow and* plead for your favor.
¹³A stunning bride, the king's daughter waits within;
    her clothing is *skillfully* woven with gold.
    ¹⁴She, in her richly embroidered gown, is carried to the king,
    her virgin companions following *close behind.*

¹⁵They walk in a spirit of celebration *and gratefulness.*
    In delight, they enter the palace of the king.

¹⁶O king, in this place where your ancestors *reigned,* you will have sons;
    you will make them princes throughout all the land.
¹⁷I will make sure your name is remembered by all *future* generations
    so that the people will offer you thanks and praise *now and* forever.

PSALM 46

FOR THE WORSHIP LEADER. A SONG OF THE SONS OF KORAH, A SONG
FOR SOPRANOS.*

¹God is our shelter and our strength.
    When troubles seem near, God is nearer, and He's ready to help.
So why run and hide?
²No fear, *no pacing, no biting fingernails.*
    When the earth spins out of control, *we are sure and fearless.*

46:title Hebrew, *alamoth,* meaning is uncertain, perhaps "young women."

When mountains crumble and the waters run wild, *we are sure and*
   fearless.
³Even in heavy winds and huge waves,
   or as mountains shake, *we are sure and fearless.*

[pause]*

⁴A *pure* stream flows—*never to be cut off*—
   bringing joy to the city where God makes His home,
   the sacred site where the Most High *chooses to* live.
⁵The True God *never sleeps and* always resides in the city *of joy*;
   He makes it unstoppable, unshakable.
   When it awakes at dawn, the True God has already been at work.

46:3 Literally, selah, likely a musical direction from a Hebrew root meaning "to lift up"

PSALM 46 **God Never Sleeps.** Consider what it means to feel protected, safe, and secure in a world threatened by weapons of mass destruction. In a world where it seems that "the earth spins out of control" and "mountains crumble and the waters run wild," we have a sure God. Consider, too, what it means to know that the Eternal One never sleeps, is always ready to defend and protect, and has the ability to turn any weapon into scrap. He is "unstoppable, unshakable" and is busy working on our behalf while we sleep.

We recognize that earth is a battlefield and we are not always sure about our safety. But we *can* be sure that God watches out for our good. The psalm says He is our shelter. Not just that He protects us, but that He Himself is the very shelter. He is the fortress we take cover in or the citadel itself. It is as though He tucks us under His wing. The text actually says He surrounds us with Himself so that nothing can harm us.

With all this what is our responsibility? We are to "be still, be calm, see, and understand [He is] the True God." We don't have an imposter Savior, and our faith should not be fake either. It always comes back to faith or trust. And look who we are to have faith in: God who brings to bear all the resources of the angelic realm! He is "the Commander of heavenly armies," and we can call on Him. So then, why are we so anxious?

Remember: "Be calm and see."

⁶Trouble is *on the horizon* for the outside nations, *not long until* kingdoms
  will fall;
  God's voice thunders and the earth shakes.
⁷*You know* the Eternal One, the Commander of *heavenly* armies, surrounds
  us *and protects us*;
  the True God of Jacob is our shelter, *close to His heart.*

[pause]

⁸Come, gaze, *fix your eyes* on what the Eternal One can do.
  Amazing, He has worked desolation here on *this battlefield,* earth.
⁹God can stop wars anywhere in the world.
  He can *make scrap of all weapons*: snap bows, shatter spears,
  and burn shields.
¹⁰"Be still, *be calm, see,* and understand I am the True God.
  I am honored among all the nations.
  I am honored over all the earth."
¹¹*You know* the Eternal One, the Commander of *heavenly* armies, surrounds
  us *and protects us*;
  the True God of Jacob is our shelter, *close to His heart.*

[pause]

PSALM 47

FOR THE WORSHIP LEADER. A SONG OF THE SONS OF KORAH.

¹Clap your hands, all of you;
  raise your voices joyfully and loudly.
  Give honor for the True God *of the Universe*;
²Here's why: The Eternal One, the Most High, is awesome *and deserves our
  great respect*.
  He is the great King over everything in this world.
³He's helped us win wars, suppressed our enemies,
  and made nations *bow* at our feet.

⁴He decides *the extent of* our inheritance *and selects the land where we and*
    our children will live,
        for we are the pride of Jacob, the ones He loves.

[pause]*

⁵The True God ascends *the throne acclaimed* by shouts of the people.
    The Eternal One *is announced* by the blast of a trumpet.
⁶Sing! Shout! *Play instruments!*
    Praise our God and King; sing praises *to Him who is worthy.*
⁷For He is the King of all the earth. *Sing praise, all who can.*
    Put words to music, and then sing praises
⁸*At the feet of the* God who sits on His holy throne,
    ruling over all the nations.
⁹All those with influence in this world—princes, *kings, and satraps*—
    gather with those who follow Abraham's God.
For these defenders belong to God
    who reigns over the nations!

Psalm 48

A SONG OF THE SONS OF KORAH.

¹The Eternal One is great *and mighty,* worthy of great praise
    in the city of our True God, upon His holy mountain.
²Situated high above, Mount Zion is beautiful to see,
    the pleasure of the entire earth.
Mount Zion, in the north,*
    is the city of the great King.
³In her palaces, the True God
    has revealed Himself as a mighty fortress.

47:4 Literally, selah, likely a musical direction from a Hebrew root meaning "to lift up"
48:2 Hebrew, *zaphon*

⁴*Not long ago, enemy* kings gathered together
   and moved forward as one *to attack the city.*
⁵When they saw Mount Zion, they were amazed;
   amazement became fear, *then panic.* They fled *for their lives.*
⁶They were overtaken by terror, trembling in anguish
   like a woman in childbirth.
⁷*God,* You shattered the ships of Tarshish
   with the *mighty* east wind.
⁸As we have heard *stories of Your greatness,*
   now we have also seen it *with our own eyes*
   right here, in the city of the Eternal One, the Commander of *heavenly*
      armies.
   Right here, in our God's city,
      the True God will preserve her forever.

   [pause]*

⁹We have meditated upon Your loyal love, O God,
   within Your *holy* temple.
¹⁰Just as Your name reaches to the ends of the earth, O God,
   so Your praise flows there too;
   Your right hand holds justice.
¹¹So because of Your judgments,
   may Mount Zion be delighted!
   May the villages of Judah celebrate!

¹²Explore Zion; make an accounting,
   note all her towers;
¹³Reflect upon her defenses;
   stroll through her palaces
   So that you can tell the coming generation all about her.
¹⁴For so is God,
   our True God, forever and ever;
   grand and strong and beautiful,
   He will be our guide till the end.

48:8 Literally, selah, likely a musical direction from a Hebrew root meaning "to lift up"

Psalm 49

FOR THE WORSHIP LEADER. A SONG OF THE SONS OF KORAH.

¹Listen up, everyone!

All you who reside in this world, give an ear!
²*Everyone*—rich and poor,

young and old, wise and foolish, humble and mighty—
³My mouth will overflow with wisdom;

the reflections of my heart will guide you to understand *the nature of
life.*
⁴I will tune my ear to *the words of* a proverb;

to the sounds of a harp, I will reveal my riddle.

PSALM 49 **What Matters?** "Do not be afraid of the rich and powerful as their prestige and honor grow, for they cannot take anything with them when they die. Their fame and glory will not follow them into the grave." Doesn't this sound familiar? It's the truth! It's a reminder that no matter what wealth we manage to accumulate or what power we give to others because of their wealth, there's still only one result. Its importance expires with us. This psalm promises to reveal a riddle.

So what difference does it make what we do in life then? The difference is in *what* we treasure. *That* really does matter. The verse directly preceding the opening quote says, "But God will reach into the grave and save my life from its power. He will fetch me and take me into His eternal house."

God has much to say about our real life that stretches into eternity. What we value won't decay and wash away into the darkness? What we have will last beyond the riches of this world? Of course, we know the psalm is talking about our connection to the Eternal One who restores us to Himself.

We read, "One person can't grant salvation to another or make a payment to the True God for another." But God *can.* True riches are in the work of Jesus, the Son of God, in making payment for us.

What the psalmist couldn't see is how God completed the riddle. If you can't take your riches with you, how can you be truly wealthy forever? Jesus paid the price we could never pay, and we share in the inheritance for all eternity.

⁵Why should I be afraid when dark evils swirl about me,
　　when I am walking among the sin of evildoers—
⁶Those who depend on their own fortunes,
　　who boast about their earthly riches?
⁷One person can't grant salvation to another
　　or make a payment to the True God for another.
⁸Redeeming a life is costly;
　　no premium is enough, ever enough,
⁹That one's body might live on forever
　　and never fear the grave's decay.

¹⁰Everyone knows that even the wisest ones die,
　　perishing together with the foolish and the stupid.
　For all die—beggars and kings, fools and wise men.
　　Their wealth remains behind for others.
¹¹*Although they wish to dwell in fine houses* forever, their graves are their real
　　　resting places.
　　Their homes are for all future generations,
　　yet *for a while* they have named lands after themselves.
¹²[No one, regardless of how *rich or* important, can live forever;
　　he is]* just like the animals that perish *and decay.*

¹³This is the destiny of those foolish souls *who have faith only in themselves*;
　　this will be the end of those happy to follow in their ways.

　[pause]*

¹⁴The fate of fools is the grave, and just like sheep,
　　death will feast on them.
　The righteous will rule over them at dawn,
　　their bodies, their outward forms, rotting in the grave
　　far away from their great mansions.
¹⁵But God will reach into the grave and save my life from its power.
　　He will fetch me *and take me into His eternal house.*

　[pause]

49:12 Greek manuscripts read "Anyone who is rich without understanding."
49:13 Literally, selah, likely a musical direction from a Hebrew root meaning "to lift up"

¹⁶Do not be afraid of the rich *and powerful*
     as their prestige and honor grow,
¹⁷For they cannot take anything with them when they die.
     Their fame and glory will not follow them into the grave.
¹⁸During their lives, they seek every blessing *and advantage*
     because others praise you when you've done well.
¹⁹But they will soon join their ancestors, for all of time,
     among the tombs of the faithless—a place of no light.
²⁰Anyone who is *rich or* important without understanding
     is just like the animals that perish *and decay.*

PSALM 50

A SONG OF ASAPH.

¹The Mighty God, the Eternal One—*God of past, present, and future*—
     has spoken over the world,
         calling together all things from sunrise to sunset.
²From Zion, that perfectly beautiful *holy* place,
     shines *the radiance of* God.

³Our God will come, and He will not enter on a whisper.
     A fire will devour *the earth* before Him;
         the *wind will* storm wildly about Him.
⁴He calls heaven above and earth *below*
     to assist in bringing judgment on His people.
⁵"Gather up those who are aligned with Me; bring them to Me;
     bring everyone who belongs to Me who have made covenant
         sacrifice."
⁶And the heavens shout of His justice,
     for He is the True God, an *honest* judge.

[pause]*

50:6 Literally, selah, likely a musical direction from a Hebrew root meaning "to lift up"

⁷"Listen, My people, I have something to say:
>   O Israel, My testimony comes against you;
>   I am God, your God.
⁸I am not going to scold you because of your sacrifices;
>   your burnt offerings are always before Me.
⁹I will not accept the *best* bull from your fields
>   or goats from your meadow,
¹⁰For they are already Mine, just as the forest beast
>   and the cattle grazing over a thousand hills *are Mine*.
¹¹Every bird flying over the mountains I know;
>   every animal roaming over the fields belongs to Me.

¹²"I would not come to you if I were hungry,
>   for the world and all it contains are Mine.
¹³Do *you really think* I eat bull meat?
>   Or drink goat's blood?
¹⁴Set out a sacrifice I can accept: your thankfulness.
>   Be true to your word to the Most High.
¹⁵When you are in trouble, call for Me.
>   I will *come and* rescue you, and you will honor Me."

¹⁶But to those acting against Him, God says,
>   "Who do you think you are? Listing off My laws,
>   acting as if your life is in alignment with My ways?
¹⁷For *it's clear that* you despise My guidance;
>   you throw My *wise* words over your shoulder.
¹⁸You play with thieves,
>   spend your time with adulterers.

¹⁹Evil runs out of your mouth;
>   your tongue is wrapped in deceit.
²⁰You sit back and gossip about your brother;
>   you slander your mother's son.
²¹While you did these things, I kept silent;
>   *somehow* you got the idea that I was like you.
> But now *My silence ends, and* I am going to indict you.
>   I'll state the charge against you *clearly,* face-to-face.

²²"All you who have forgotten *Me, your* God, should think about what I have
said,
or I will tear you apart and leave no one to save you.
²³Set out a sacrifice *I can accept*: your thankfulness. Do this, and you will
honor Me.
Those who straighten up their lives
will know the saving grace of God."

PSALM 51

FOR THE WORSHIP LEADER. A SONG OF DAVID AFTER NATHAN THE
PROPHET ACCUSED HIM OF INFIDELITY WITH BATHSHEBA.

¹Look on me with a heart of mercy, O God,
according to Your generous love.
According to Your great compassion,
wipe out *every consequence of* my *shameful* crimes.
²Thoroughly wash me, *inside and out,* of all my crooked deeds.
Cleanse me from my sins.

³For I am *fully* aware of all I have done wrong,
and my guilt is there, staring me in the face.
⁴It was against You, only You, that I sinned,
for I have done what You say is wrong, right before Your eyes.
So when You speak, You are in the right.
When You judge, Your judgments are pure and true.*
⁵For I was guilty from the day I was born,
a sinner from the time my mother became pregnant with me.

⁶But still, You long *to enthrone* truth throughout my being;
in unseen places deep within me, You show me wisdom.
⁷Cleanse me *of my wickedness* with hyssop, and I will be clean.
If You wash me, I will be whiter than snow.

51:4 Romans 3:4

⁸Help me hear joy and happiness *as my accompaniment,*
    so my bones, which You have broken, will *dance in* delight instead.
⁹Cover Your face so You will not see my sins,
    and erase my guilt *from the record.*

¹⁰Create in me a clean heart, O God;
    restore within me a sense of being brand new.
¹¹Do not throw me far away from Your presence,
    and do not remove Your Holy Spirit from me.
¹²Give back to me the *deep* delight of being saved by You;
    let Your willing Spirit sustain me.

¹³If You do, I promise to teach rebels Your ways
    and help sinners find their way back to You.
¹⁴Free me from the guilt *of murder,* of shedding *a man's* blood,
    O God who saves me.
    Now my tongue, *which was used to destroy,* will be used to sing with
        deep delight of how right *and just* You are.

¹⁵O Lord, *pry* open my lips
    that this mouth will sing *joyfully* of Your greatness.
¹⁶I would surrender *my dearest possessions or destroy all that I prize to prove*
        my regret,
    but You don't take pleasure in sacrifices or burnt offerings.
¹⁷What sacrifice I can offer You is my broken spirit
    because a broken spirit, O God,
    a heart that honestly regrets the past,
  You won't detest.

¹⁸Be good to Zion; grant her Your favor.
    Make Jerusalem's walls steady and strong.
¹⁹Then there will be sacrifices made,
    burnt offerings and whole burnt offerings,
  With right motives that will delight You.
    And *costly* young bulls will be offered up to Your altar, *only the best.*

PSALM 52

FOR THE WORSHIP LEADER. A CONTEMPLATIVE SONG* OF DAVID WHEN THE EDOMITE DOEG TOLD SAUL THAT DAVID HAD RECEIVED HELP FROM AHIMELECH.

¹Why do you boast of all the trouble you stir up, O mighty one,
      when the constant, unfailing love of God is what truly lasts?
²*Have you listened to yourself?*
Your tongue is like a sharp razor,
      full of lies *that slash and tear* right to the soul.
³You've fallen in love with evil and have no interest in *what He calls* good.
      You prefer your own lies to speaking what is true.

[pause]*

⁴You love words that destroy people, *don't you,*
      lying tongue?

52:title Hebrew, *maskil*
52:3 Literally, selah, likely a musical direction from a Hebrew root meaning "to lift up"

PSALM 52 | **Serious Consequences.** We often are drawn to the rich worship of the psalms and scurry past some of the darker passages. David can be joyous, but he can also be painfully honest. If you read this psalm carefully and allow its honest emotions to roll over you, you will be downright scared.

David speaks to his enemy, "You have fallen in love with evil." Then comes the warning, "He will come into your home, snatch you away, and pull you from the land of the living." It is time to pay attention. There are serious consequences to standing against God.

We hope God will somehow see past the scars of life, our sins of disobedience, and hearts gone astray. We hope He will issue us a new scorecard, a clean slate, a "paid in full" document so we can start again to follow His ways more carefully. But it is not a given that this will happen for us.

(continued on next page)

⁵*You won't be smiling when* the True God *brings His justice and* destroys you
forever.
He will come into your home, snatch you away,
and pull you from the land of the living.

[pause]

⁶Those who are just will see *what happens to* you and be afraid.
And some of them will laugh and say,
⁷"Hey, look! Over there is the one who didn't take
shelter in the True God;
Instead, he trusted in his great wealth
and got what he wanted by destroying others!"

⁸But my life is *abundant*—like a lush olive tree
cared for at the house of the *one* True God.
I put my trust in His kind love
forever and ever; *it will never fail.*
⁹Because of all You have done,
because You have entered my life story and weaved it into Your own,
I will *humble myself and* thank You forever.
With Your faithful people at my side,
I will put my hope in Your good reputation.

(continued from previous page)

There is one essential step that must happen first. "I put my trust in His kind love forever and ever, it will never fail. Because of all You have done." It isn't enough to be sorry or sad that our dirty little secret has been discovered. We must trust and obey. In truth, we know the longing to be restored and renewed and issued a clean heart is fulfilled through God's gracious gift to us. His Spirit does indeed sustain us and restore us to wholeness. First, we trust; then, we obey.

The psalmist David has given us the answer to what obedience looks like: We show the presence of God in our lives and so follow our urge to point the way back for others who have the same longing to be restored to Him. When we trust God, it is natural to speak with enthusiasm and boldness about the mercy of the Eternal!

PSALM 53

FOR THE WORSHIP LEADER. A CONTEMPLATIVE SONG* OF DAVID.
A SONG FOR THE DANCE.*

¹The foolish are convinced deep down that there is no God.
Their souls are polluted, and they commit gross injustice.
Not one of them does good.

²From heaven the *one* True God examines the earth
to see if any understand *the big picture,*
if any seek to know the True God.

³All have turned back *to their wicked ways*; they've become *totally* perverse.
Not one of them does good,
not even one.

⁴Do the wicked relish their ignorance,
the wicked ones who consume My people as if they were bread
and fail to call upon the True God?

⁵They trembled with great fear,
though they'd never been afraid before,
Because the True God ravaged the bones of those who rose against you.
You humiliated them because the True God spat them out.

⁶Oh, that the liberation of Israel would come out of Zion!
When the True God reclaims His people,
let Jacob celebrate; let Israel rejoice.

53:title Hebrew, *maskil*
53:title Hebrew, *mahalath,* meaning is uncertain.

PSALM 54

FOR THE WORSHIP LEADER. A CONTEMPLATIVE SONG * OF DAVID WHEN *HIS FRIENDS,* THE ZIPHITES, BETRAYED HIM TO SAUL. ACCOMPANIED BY STRINGS.

¹Liberate me, O God, by *the authority of* Your name.
    Vindicate me through Your *legendary* power.
²Hear my prayer, O God;
    let the words of my mouth reach Your *sympathetic* ear.

³*The truth is, these* strangers are rallying against me;
    cold-blooded men seek to slay me;
    they have no respect for You.

[pause]*

⁴But see now! God comes to rescue me;
    the Lord is my *valiant* supporter.
⁵He will repay my enemies for the harm they have done; *they are doomed!*
    According to Your faithful promises, silence them.

54:title Hebrew, *maskil*
54:3 Literally, selah, likely a musical direction from a Hebrew root meaning "to lift up"

PSALM 55 | **Either in Control or Trusting.** Ahithopel had been David's trusted advisor, but when David's son Absalom rebelled against him and gained the affection of Israel, Ahithopel turned against David and helped Absalom. The pain ran deep in David, "But it is you! A man like me, my old friend, my companion." Later, he says, "My friend has become a foe, breaking faith, tearing down peace. He's betrayed our covenant." The times were extremely tough, and there seemed no way out. But David persisted in calling out to God. "Evening, morning, and noon I will plead; I will grumble and moan before Him until He hears my voice."

Whining is not typically seen as an appropriate approach for getting what we want; but in David's case, his moaning and groaning reflect his persistence.

⁶I will sacrifice to You willingly;

> I will lift Your name by shouts of thanksgiving, O Eternal One, for
> > Your name is good.

⁷God has pulled me out from every one of the troubles *that encompass me*,

> and I have seen *what it means to stand over* my enemies in triumph.

Psalm 55

For the worship leader. A contemplative song* of David *accompanied* by strings.

¹*Hear me,* O God.

> Tune Your ear to my plea,
> and do not turn Your face from my prayer.

²Give me Your attention.

> Answer *these sighs of sorrow*;
> my troubles have made me restless—I groan from anxiety.

55:title Hebrew, *maskil*

He's not going to stop until God answers. The lesson for us here is not just about persistence or even whining. The lesson is that we can rely on God to rescue us from our enemies. Over and over in the psalms, we see the same theme, "Trust in God; He will rescue you." We see it often because people naturally turn away from God rather than toward Him. There seems to be a real need in us to be in control. Being in control is the opposite of trusting God and seeking His will over our own.

Recognizing the sovereignty of God and our humble position is the key to experiencing the gracious acts of God. We can confidently believe that our troubles will end in God's timing, knowing that He truly cares enough to act. It is our pride and resistance that keep us from His mercy.

³All because of my enemy! Because his voice speaks against me,
     his wickedness torments me!
He casts down misfortune upon me;
     his anger flares; his grudges grow against me.

⁴My heart seizes within my chest; *I am in anguish!*
     I am terrified my life could end *on any breath.*
⁵I shiver and shudder in fear;
     I can't stop because this horror is just too much.
⁶I said, "If only my arms were wings like the dove's!
     I would fly away *from here* and find rest—
⁷Yes, I would venture far
     and weave a nest in the wilderness.

     [pause]*

⁸"I would rush to take refuge
     away from the violent storm and pounding winds."

⁹Throw them off, O Lord. Confuse their speech, *and frustrate their plans,*
     for violence and contention are *building* within the city.
I can see it *with my own eyes.*
¹⁰They plot day and night, scurrying the city walls *like rats,*
     trouble and evil lurking *everywhere.*
¹¹In the heart of the city, destruction awaits.
     Oppression and lies swarm the streets,
     and they will not take leave; *no, they will not go.*

¹²If it were just an enemy sneering at me,
     I could take it.
If it were just someone who has *always* hated me treating me like dirt,
     I'd simply hide away.
¹³But it is you! A man like me,
     my old friend, my companion.
¹⁴We enjoyed sweet conversation,
     walking together in the house of God among the pressing crowds.

55:7 Literally, selah, likely a musical direction from a Hebrew root meaning "to lift up"

¹⁵Let death sneak up on them,
  swallow them alive into the pit of death.
  Why? Because evil stirs in their homes; *evil is* all around them.
¹⁶But I, I shall call upon God,
  and *by His word,* the Eternal One shall save me.
¹⁷Evening, morning, and noon *I will plead*;
  I will grumble and moan *before Him*
  until He hears my voice.
¹⁸And He will rescue my soul, *untouched,*
  plucked safely from the battle,
  despite the many who are warring against me.
¹⁹God, enthroned from ancient times *through eternity,*
  will hear my prayers and strike them down.

[pause]

For they have refused change;
  they *supply their every need and* have no fear of God.

²⁰My friend has become a foe, *breaking faith,* tearing down peace.
  He's betrayed our covenant.
²¹Oh, how his *pleasant* voice is smoother than butter,
  while his heart is enchanted by war.
Oh, how his words are smoother than oil,
  and yet each is a sword drawn *in his hand.*

²²Cast your troubles upon the Eternal One;
  His care is unceasing!
He will not allow
  His righteous to be shaken.

²³But You, O God, You will drive them
  into the lowest* pit—
Violent, lying people
  won't live beyond their middle years.
But I place my trust in You.

55:23 Greek manuscripts read "pit of destruction." The idea is the grave or place of death.

PSALM 56

FOR THE WORSHIP LEADER. A PRAYER* OF DAVID TO *THE TUNE* "SILENT DOVE *IN THE* DISTANCE,"* WHEN THE PHILISTINE OPPRESSORS SEIZED HIM IN GATH.

¹Show mercy to me, O God, because people are crushing me—
    grinding me down like dirt underfoot—all day long.
    No matter what I do, I can't get myself out from under them.
²My enemies are crushing me, *yes* all day long, *O Highest of High,*
    for many come proud and raise their hands against me.
³When struck by fear,
    I let go, depending *securely* upon You *alone.*
⁴In God—whose word I praise—
    in God I place my trust. I shall not let fear come in,
    for what can measly men do to me?
⁵All day long they warp my words;
    all their thoughts against me are *mangled by* evil.
⁶They conspire, then lurk about.
    They eye my every move,
  Waiting to steal my very life.
⁷Because they are wicked *through and through,* drag them out.
    In Your *just* anger, O God, cast them down!

⁸You have taken note of my journey *through life,*
    caught *each of* my tears in Your bottle.
    But *God,* are they not *also blots* on Your book?
⁹Then my enemies shall turn back *and scatter*
    on the day I call out *to You.*
    This I know *for certain*: God is on my side.
¹⁰In God whose word I praise
    and in the Eternal One whose word I praise—

56:title Hebrew, *miktam,* meaning is uncertain.
56:title Hebrew, *yonath elem rehokim,* meaning is uncertain.

[11]In God I have placed my trust. I shall not let fear come in,
    for what can *measly* men do to me?

[12]I am bound by Your promise, O God.
    My life is my offering of thanksgiving to You,
[13]For You have saved my soul from *the darkness of* death,
    steadied my feet from stumbling
So I might *continue to* walk before God,
    embraced in the light of the living.

PSALM 57

FOR THE WORSHIP LEADER. A PRAYER* OF DAVID TO *THE TUNE* "DO NOT DESTROY,"* WHEN HE HID FROM SAUL IN A CAVE.

[1]Mercy. May Your mercy come to me, O God,
    for my soul is safe within You, *the guardian of my life.*
I will seek protection in the shade of Your wings
    until the destruction has passed.
[2]I cry out to God, the Most High,
    to God who always does what is good for me.
[3]Out of heaven my rescue comes.
    He dispatches His mercy and truth
And goes after whoever tries to run over me.

[pause]*

[4]I am surrounded by lions;
    I lie in a den of ravenous beasts.
Those *around me* have spears and arrows for teeth,
    a sharpened blade for a tongue.

57:title Hebrew, *miktam,* meaning is uncertain.
57:title Hebrew, *al-tashheth,* meaning is uncertain.
57:3 Literally, selah, likely a musical direction from a Hebrew root meaning "to lift up"

⁵O God, be lifted up above the heavens;
    may Your glory cover the earth.

⁶Yet my foes cast a net to catch my feet *and bring me to my knees.*
    I am weary from all of this.
They dug a pit to snare me
    but fell into their own trap.

[pause]

⁷My heart is ready, O God;
    my heart is ready,
And I will sing! Yes, I will sing praise!
    ⁸Wake up, my glory!
Wake up, harp and lyre;
    I will stir the sleepy dawn *with praise*!

PSALM 57 | **Heartfelt Gratitude.** A light seems so much brighter when it shines in complete darkness. The glory and mercy of the Eternal One are so much more magnificent when He reaches into our struggles to bring us good. David has more than his share of struggles and troubles. It is natural that he greatly rejoices when God delivers him. We may not have experienced the same joy because we haven't been open to God's intervention or we haven't recognized His work. Praise and worship songs are great ways to honor the Eternal One. Imagine if we were so filled with thanksgiving that we sang the words to these songs with the kind of enthusiasm exhibited in the words of this psalm. Imagine feeling so ready to praise God that we want to wake up the sleeping earth to declare His greatness! The joy of deliverance is so great that it can't be contained.

Remember the relief and the freedom you experienced when you first experienced God's love. A heart of gratitude focused on the Lord raises its voice to sweep past the clouds and fill the expanse of the universe with praise. As our love and our gratitude mature, we should not forget the payment that was made on our behalf. Look at the overwhelming desire to praise in this psalm. "My heart is ready . . . I will sing . . . wake up, my glory . . . stir the sleepy dawn . . . I will sing of Your greatness." We can sing of His love wherever we are. All we have to do is remember where we came from and where we would be without the grace of the Eternal One.

⁹I will offer You my thanks, O Lord, before the nations *of the world*;
  I will sing of Your greatness no matter where I am.
¹⁰For Your amazing mercy ascends far into the heavens;
  Your truth rises above the clouds.
¹¹O God, be lifted up above the heavens;
  may Your glory cover the earth.

PSALM 58

FOR THE WORSHIP LEADER. A PRAYER* OF DAVID TO *THE TUNE*
"DO NOT DESTROY."*

¹Can you, *panel of* judges, *get anything right?*
  When you judge people, do you tell the truth and pursue justice?
²No, *your real selves have been revealed.* You have wickedness in your heart,
  and many people have suffered by your hands.

³Evildoers are naturally offensive, wayward at birth!
  They were born telling lies *and willfully wandering from the truth.*
⁴*Their bite is painful;* their venom is like the *deadly* poison of a snake;
  they are like a cobra that closes up its ears
⁵To escape the voice of the charmers,
  no matter how enchanting the spells may be.

⁶O God, shatter their teeth in their mouths!
  Render the young lions *harmless;* break out their fangs, O Eternal
    One.
⁷Let them run off like the waters *of a flood,*
  and though they aim their arrows, let them fly without their heads.
⁸Let them melt like a snail that oozes along;
  may they be like a stillborn that *never catches its first breath,* never sees
    the sun.

58:title Hebrew, *miktam,* meaning is uncertain.
58:title Hebrew, *al-tashheth,* meaning is uncertain.

⁹Before your *cook* pots know the *furious flame of a* fire of thorns—
whether green or burning—He will blow the wicked away.

¹⁰Cheers will rise as the right-living watch Him settle the score,
their feet washed in the blood *after the onslaught* of the wicked.
¹¹And it will be heard, "Those who seek justice will be rewarded.
Indeed, there is a God who brings justice to the earth!"

PSALM 59

FOR THE WORSHIP LEADER. A PRAYER* OF DAVID TO *THE TUNE* "DO
NOT DESTROY,"* WHEN SAUL SENT ASSASSINS TO DAVID'S HOUSE.

¹Rescue me! *Save me,* O my God, from my enemies;
set me in a safe place, far above any who come to attack me.
²Rescue me from those malicious people,
and save me from blood-thirsty murderers.

³They have staked out my life; *they are going to ambush me!*
Those brutes are aligned, ready to attack me
For no good cause, my Eternal One. *I have not crossed them.*
⁴I've done nothing wrong, yet they rush ahead to start the assault.
I beg You to help me; come and see for Yourself!
⁵*I plead with* You, Eternal One, Commander of *heavenly* armies, True God
of Israel,
to get up and punish these people;
do not let any betrayer off the hook; show no mercy to malicious
evildoers!

[pause]*

59:title Hebrew, *miktam,* meaning is uncertain.
59:title Hebrew, *al-tashheth,* meaning is uncertain.
59:5 Literally, selah, likely a musical direction from a Hebrew root meaning "to lift up"

⁶Treacherous souls return to the city in the evening;
　　they prowl about,
　　howling like dogs.
⁷Watch them! Snarling, dribbling *their malicious insults.*
　　Their words *cut loose* from their lips like swords,
　　and *in their backstabbing* they say, "Who's listening anyway?"

⁸But You, O Eternal One, laugh at them;
　　You make fun of all the nations.
⁹I will watch for You, for You keep me strong.
　　God, You are my security!
¹⁰My God is *one step* ahead of me with His mercy;
　　He will show me the victory I desire over my enemies.
¹¹Don't wipe them out, or my people may *one day* forget.
　　Instead, use Your power to scatter and bring them to ruin.
　　O Lord, You are our protection.
¹²Sin pours from their mouths, *cruel* words from their lips.
　　May they be caught in their pride.
For their *foul* curses and lies,
　　¹³devour them with *Your* wrath,
　　eat them up, leave no one alive.
Then people will surely know that the *one* True God rules over Jacob,
　　even to the *far* ends of the earth.

[pause]

¹⁴Treacherous souls return to the city in the evening;
　　they prowl about,
　　howling like dogs.
¹⁵They search through the city, scavenging for meat
　　as they growl *and grumble* in dissatisfaction.

¹⁶But me? I will sing of Your strength.
　　I will awake with the sun to sing of Your loving mercy
Because in my most troubled hour,
　　You defended me. You were my shelter.

¹⁷I will *lift my voice to* sing Your praise, O my Strength—
　　for You came to my defense.
　　O God, You have shown me Your loving mercy.

PSALM 60

FOR THE WORSHIP LEADER. A PRAYER* OF DAVID AFTER HIS VICTORY
OVER THE ARAMEANS, JOAB'S RETURN, AND THE STRIKING DOWN OF
12,000 EDOMITES IN THE VALLEY OF SALT. *A SONG* FOR INSTRUCTION TO
THE TUNE "A LILY REMINDS US."*

¹God, You have turned away from us; You have shattered us *into a million*
　　tiny pieces;
　　You have boiled with anger. Now put us back together, *and refresh us*
　　with Your mercy.
²You have made the earth shake; You have cracked it open *effortlessly*.
　　Heal the fissures in the earth, for it is unsteady.
³You have caused Your people to suffer;
　　You have provided us with wine that makes us stagger.

⁴You have unfurled a banner for those who revere You,
　　a signal to gather *in safety* out of the enemy's reach.

　　[pause]*

⁵So that Your treasured ones may be saved,
　　rescue us with Your right hand, and answer our pleas!

⁶God's voice has been heard in His holy sanctuary:
　　"I will celebrate; I will allocate Shechem
　　and the Succoth Valley *to My people*.

60:title Hebrew, *miktam,* meaning is uncertain.
60:title Hebrew, *shushan eduth,* meaning is uncertain.
60:4 Literally, selah, likely a musical direction from a Hebrew root meaning "to lift up"

⁷Gilead belongs to Me, and so does Manasseh;

Ephraim is the helmet that protects My head;

Judah is the scepter through which I rule;

⁸Moab is the washpot in which I rinse *My feet*.

I will throw My shoe over Edom *in conquest*;

prepare for My victory, Philistia. Cry out because of Me!"

⁹But who will take me into the fortified city?

Who will lead me into Edom?

¹⁰Have You not turned Your back on us, O God?

Will You *stay away and* not accompany our armies, O God?

¹¹Help us against our enemy; *we need Your help!*

It's useless to trust in *the hand of* man for liberation.

¹²*Only* through God can we be successful.

It is God *alone* who will defeat our enemies *and bring us victory*!

Psalm 61

For the worship leader. *A song* of David *accompanied* by strings.

¹Hear me, O God, when I cry;

listen to my prayer.

²You are the One I will call when pushed to the edge,

when my heart is faint.

Shoulder me to the rock above me.

³For You are my protection,

an impenetrable fortress from my enemies.

⁴Let me live in Your sanctuary forever;

let me find safety in the shadow of Your wings.

[pause]*

61:4 Literally, selah, likely a musical direction from a Hebrew root meaning "to lift up"

⁵You have heard the promises I made, O God.
>You have laid upon me the legacy due to those who fear Your name.

⁶Extend the king's life, *day after day;*
>increase his years for many generations.
⁷May he be ever present before God,
>*attended and* guarded by Your loyal love and truth.

⁸So I will never stop singing Your praise;
>as long as I live, I will fulfill my promise.

PSALM 62

FOR THE WORSHIP LEADER, JEDUTHUN. A SONG OF DAVID.

¹My soul quietly waits for the True God alone;
>my salvation comes from Him.
²He alone is my rock and my deliverance,
>my citadel *high on the hill*; I will not be shaken.

³How long will you attack a man?
>How long will all of you strive to crush your prey
>when he's like a leaning fence or a wall on the verge of collapse?
⁴Their only purpose *in life* is to knock him down from his prominent
>position;
>they love deceit.
When others are around, they speak a blessing *on someone,*
>but inwardly they are mumbling a curse.

[pause]

⁵My soul quietly waits for the True God alone
>because I hope only in Him.
⁶He alone is my rock and deliverance,
>my citadel *high on a hill*; I will not be shaken.
⁷My salvation and my significance depend *ultimately* on God;
>the core of my strength, my shelter, is in the True God.

[8]Have faith in Him in all circumstances, *dear* people.
>Open up your heart to Him;
>the True God shelters us *in His arms.*

[pause]

[9]*Don't put confidence in what other people do.*
Human beings disappear like a breath;
>*even* people of rank live artificial lives.
Their weight is that of a breath in a balance—*nothing.*
>Added together, they're still lighter than air.
[10]Do not resort to oppression;
>resist the temptation of ill-gotten gain.
>If you achieve wealth, don't let your heart get attached.

[11]The True God spoke this once,
>and twice I've heard:

PSALM 62 | **Finding True Worth.** We all want to be greatly loved by someone and to be held in respect by most. We want to be seen as having value or significance. Searching for significance is a passion for many of us today. We struggle to find value in a world where traditional values are often turned upside down. Falling to the temptation to compare ourselves with others, we try to determine where we have fallen short of what others have achieved or why we have succeeded when they have not. But do such comparisons yield truth? To be viewed as successful or wealthy becomes increasingly more difficult because the goal keeps changing. There never seems to be a point when we can be satisfied.

We are reminded that looking at anyone or anything in this world for validation is a false measure, which leaves us empty with nothing to hold. "Human beings disappear like a breath . . . added together, they're still lighter than air." There is no lasting substance in the world's validation. The Eternal One is the only One who can judge our true significance. "For You pay every person back according to his deeds." David is not speaking of accomplishments; rather, the "deeds" are those acts we perform in response to God's love for us. It is the living out of a relationship with the Eternal. Our confidence, our sense of worth can only come from one place, the One who holds our hearts . . . the God who chose us to be His own.

That *You,* the True God, hold all power;
    ¹²and Your love never fails, O Lord,
For You pay every person back
    according to his deeds.

PSALM 63

A SONG OF DAVID WHILE IN THE WILDERNESS OF JUDAH.

¹O True God, You are my God, *the One whom I trust.* I seek You *with every fiber of my being*
    in this dry and weary land with no water in sight,
My soul is dry and longs for You.
    My body aches for You, *for Your presence.*
²I have seen You in Your sanctuary
    and have been awed by Your power and glory.
³Your steadfast love is better than life itself,
    so my lips will give You *all my* praise.
⁴I will bless You with every breath of my life;
    I will lift up my hands in *praise to* Your name.

⁵My soul overflows with satisfaction, as when I feast on *foods rich in marrow and fat;*
    with *excitement in my heart and* joy on my lips, I offer You praise.
⁶Often at night I lie in bed and remember You,
    meditating on Your *greatness* till morning *smiles through my window.*
⁷You have been my *constant* helper;
    therefore, I sing for joy under the protection of Your wings.
⁸My soul clings to You;
    Your right hand *reaches down and* holds me up.

⁹But as for those who try to destroy my life,
    they will descend *into eternal shadows,* deep beneath the earth.
¹⁰They will fall by the sword,
    and wild dogs will feast on their corpses.

[11]But the king will find his joy in the True God;
    all who make pledges and invoke His name will celebrate,
    while the mindless prattle of *cheaters and* deceivers will be silenced.

PSALM 64

FOR THE WORSHIP LEADER. A SONG OF DAVID.

[1]O True God, hear my voice! Listen to my complaint!
    Guard my life; *keep me safe* from my enemy's threats.
[2]Hide me from the sinful circle that conspires against me,
    from the band of rebels out to make trouble,
[3]Who sharpen their tongues into swords,
    who take aim with poisonous words like arrows.
[4]They hide in the shadows and shoot at the innocent;
    they shoot at them without warning and without any fear.
[5]They persist in their evil purpose
    and plan in secret to lay their traps.
 And they say, "Who will see them?"
    [6]They plot their offense *with precision* and say,
"Now we have the perfect crime."
    The human heart and mind are deep *and complex.*

[7]But without hesitation the True God will shoot at them;
    His arrow will *surely* wound them.
[8]He will use their very own words to bring them to destruction;
    all who see will be appalled at *what happens to* them.
[9]Then everyone will fear the True God;
    they will proclaim His deeds
    and will reflect upon all He has done.

[10]The righteous will delight in the Eternal One
    and will take shelter in Him.
 All those with an honest heart will glorify Him!

PSALM 65

FOR THE WORSHIP LEADER. A SONG OF DAVID.

¹*All will stand in awe to* praise You.
    Praise will sweep through Zion, *the Sacred City,* O God.
    Solemn vows uttered to You will now be performed.
²You hear us pray *in words and silence*;
    all humanity comes into Your presence.
³Injustice overwhelms me!
    But You forgive our sins, *restoring as only You can.*
⁴You invite us near, drawing us
    into Your courts—what an honor *and a privilege*!
We feast until we're full on the goodness of Your house,
    Your sacred temple *made manifest.*

⁵*You leave us breathless* when Your awesome works answer us by putting
        everything right.
    God of our liberation—
You are the hope of all *creation,* from the far corners of the earth
    to distant *life-giving* oceans.
⁶With immense power, You erected mountains.
    Wrapped in strength, *You compelled*

PSALM 65 | **Who Can Deny that God Exists?** David points to the oceans, mountains, people, crops, pastures, and livestock. They all work together because there is a Creator and Sustainer who coordinates them! We can observe God's work in all of creation for God designed Earth as a totally sustainable planet—a place where human beings could thrive and deliver His promises to each other. We become breathless when we see His work all through history continually setting things right. He has been more than gracious to give us undeniable signs of His presence in our daily lives.

It is true though that people need understanding of a future to be motivated. God knows we need direction and a sense that we are indeed moving along the

⁷Choppy seas,
>   crashing waves,
>   and crowds of people
> To sit in *astonished* silence.
⁸Those who inhabit the boundaries of the earth are awed by Your signs,
>   *strong and subtle hints of Your indelible presence.*
> Even the dawn and dusk respond to You with joy.

⁹You spend time on the *good* earth,
>   watering and nourishing *the networks of the living.*
> God's river is full of water!
>   By preparing the land,
>   You have provided us grain *for nourishment.*
¹⁰You *are the gentle equalizer*: soaking the furrows,
>   smoothing soil's ridges,
> Softening *sun-baked* earth with *generous* showers,
>   blessing the fruit *of the ground.*
¹¹You crown the year with a fruitful harvest;
>   the paths are *worn down by carts* overflowing with unstoppable
>   growth.
¹²Barren desert pastures yield *fruit*;
>   *craggy* hills are now dressed for celebration.
¹³Meadows are clothed with frolicking flocks *of lambs*;
>   valleys are covered with *a carpet of autumn-harvest* grain,
>   the land shouts and sings in joyous celebration.

---

path He designed for us. He has provided a road map with sufficient signs along the way. As David looks around, he sees with great joy the plan of God unfolding. He says, "The land shouts and sings in joyous celebration." We have a unique role in God's creation; we have responsibility and we alone among the species have a role with God in determining the future. As God's creatures doing His will, we assist in moving forward His plan along the path He has chosen. "You invite us near, drawing us into Your courts." What a joy to be invited to participate in dominion over the earth and to be voluntary members of God's kingdom!

PSALM 66

FOR THE WORSHIP LEADER. A SONG.

¹Shout out to God, all the earth. Erupt with joy *to the one True God*!
²Sing of the glory due His name!
   Offer Him the most magnificent praises!
³Say to God, "All You have done is wondrous and causes fear!
   Your power is mighty, and Your enemies pretend to submit to You.
⁴The entire earth will *bow down to* worship You
   and will sing glory-songs to You;
   they will sing praises to Your name!

[pause]*

⁵Come and witness the True God's *endless* works.
   His *miraculous* deeds done on behalf of humanity inspire fear.
⁶He transformed the sea into dry land;
   our people passed through the river on foot!
Rejoice in Him; *celebrate what He did* there*!*
   ⁷By His great might, He rules forever;
His eyes watch over all the nations,
   so no one should go up against Him.

[pause]

⁸Everyone, bless our True God!
   Let praise-filled voices be heard *near and far—at home and on foreign
      soil*!
⁹*Praise the One* who *gives us life and* keeps us safe,
   who does not allow us to stumble *in the darkness*.
¹⁰For You have put us to the test, O God;
   You have refined us as silver is refined.
¹¹You trapped us with a snare;
   You have laid upon our backs a heavy burden.

66:4 Literally, selah, likely a musical direction from a Hebrew root meaning "to lift up"

¹²You *allowed us to be conquered and* let our enemies run over us.
    We journeyed *through dangers,* through fire and flood,
  But You led us *finally* to a *safe* place, a land rich and abundant.

¹³I will come into Your temple with burnt offerings;
    I will fulfill my promises to You—
¹⁴The oaths that parted my lips
      and *were promises* my mouth *freely* made when I was *suffering and* in
        anguish.
¹⁵I will bring You my sacrifices—plump beasts
      and the sweet smoke of *consecrated* rams—
  I will also offer You bulls and goats.

  [pause]

¹⁶Come and listen, everyone who reveres the True God,
    and I will tell you what He has done for me.
¹⁷I cried out to Him with my mouth,
    and I praised Him with my tongue.
¹⁸If I entertain evil in my heart,
    the Lord will not hear me.
¹⁹But surely God has heard me;
    He has paid attention to *the urgency of* my request.

²⁰May the True God be blessed,
      for He did not turn away from my prayer
      nor did He hold back His loyal love from me.

Psalm 67

For the worship leader. A song *accompanied* by strings.

¹May God pour His grace and blessings into us
    and turn His face to shine *His light* on us.

[pause]*

67:1 Literally, selah, likely a musical direction from a Hebrew root meaning "to lift up"

²So *all* those on earth will learn *to follow* Your way
   and see Your saving power come to *redeem* all nations.
³May all people *live to* praise You, Our True God;
   may all come to praise You.

⁴May *all* nations celebrate *together,* singing joy-filled songs *of praise to You*
   because You judge the people fairly
   and give guidance to *all* the nations of the earth.

[pause]

⁵May the people praise You *with their whole hearts,* O God;
   may every man, woman, and child on the earth praise You.

⁶The land has supplied a *bountiful* harvest,
   and the True God, our God, has poured out His blessings to us *all.*
⁷God is the source of our blessings;
   may every corner of the earth respect and revere Him.

PSALM 68

FOR THE WORSHIP LEADER. A SONG OF DAVID.

¹May the True God rise up *and show Himself;*
   May those *who are united* against Him be dispersed,
      while the people who hate Him run away at the sight of Him.
²As smoke disappears when it is blown *by the wind,*
   may You blow away Your enemies *forever.*
As wax melts in the presence of fire,
   may the wicked heart melt away in God's presence.
³But may those who are righteous rejoice
   in the presence of the True God, so may they be glad and rejoice.
   Yes, let them celebrate with joy!

⁴Sing songs of praise to the name that belongs to the True God!
   Let your voices ring out in songs *of praise* to Him, *the One* who rides
      through the deserted places.

His name is the Eternal One;
    celebrate in His *glorious* presence.

5The True God who inhabits sacred space
    is a father to the fatherless, a defender of widows.
6He makes a home for those who are alone.
    He frees the prisoners and leads them to prosper.
Yet those who rebel *against Him* live in the barren land *without His*
      blessings and prosperity.

7O True God, when You led Your *enslaved* people *from Egypt,*
    when You journeyed *with us* through the wilderness,

[pause]*

8The whole world trembled! The sky poured down rain
    at *the power of* Your presence; even Mount Sinai trembled in *Your*
      presence,
    the presence of the True God, the God of Israel.
9You sent a heavy downpour *to soak the ground,* O True God.
    You refreshed the land—*the land* Your people would inherit—when
      it was *parched* and dry.
10Your *covenant* people made their homes in the land,
    and because You are so good, You provided for those crushed by
      poverty, O True God.

11The Lord gives the word;
    there are very many women ready to tell the good news:
     12"Kings who lead the armies are on the run! They are on the run!
And the woman who stays at home *is ready, too,*
    ready to enjoy the treasures *that they've left behind!*"
13When they lay down among the campfires *and open the saddlebags,*
     imagine what they'll find—
    a *beautiful* dove, its wings covered with silver,
    its feathers a shimmering gold.

68:7 Literally, selah, likely a musical direction from a Hebrew root meaning "to lift up"

¹⁴When the Almighty scattered the kings from that place,
  it was snowing in Zalmon.

¹⁵O Mount Bashan, you *mighty* mountain of the True God;
  mountain of many peaks, O Mount Bashan.
¹⁶Why are you so jealous, O mountain of many peaks,
  when you look at the mountain the True God has chosen as His
    dwelling place?
  The Eternal One will surely abide on *Mount Zion* forever.

¹⁷The chariots of God are innumerable;
  there are thousands upon thousands of them.

PSALM 68 | **Innumerable Chariots.** Where most of David's psalms are personal pleadings or he is writing as a worship leader, this psalm is truly the praise from the king of Israel. He steps the nation through the phases of mercy shown to them by the Eternal God. First of all, Israelites—whether orphans, widows, prisoners, men, women, or rulers—have God protecting them against their enemies. They are instructed, "Let your voices ring out in songs of praise." He then celebrates deliverance from Egyptian slavery and the opening up of the promised land; he rejoices that God chose Mount Zion over all other mountains for His home and how their enemies were subdued; and he finishes with national worship that draws other rulers to Zion, calling all the earth to fall down in praise of the Eternal One.

The entire nation, even the entire world, is called to worship Israel's God. There is something grand and pure about all of God's people coming together and collectively saying, "O True God, You are awesome from the holy place where You dwell."

Those who are ready open their hearts and rejoice with God in the things that bring joy to Him, who keeps them sheltered and filled with truth. They understand the treasures that are overlooked by those who seek earthly gain and are awed by God's goodness and willingness to provide.

The Lord comes into their midst able to carry their heavy loads for them because "the chariots of God are innumerable; there are thousands upon thousands of them." He comes near no matter where we are as well, ready to give us all we need. David is saying more than that God is worthy because He helps us; he is saying that God is worthy, magnificent, mighty, glorious, and gracious.

The Lord is in their midst, just as He was at Mount Sinai.
He has come into the holy place.

¹⁸When You ascended the sacred mountain,
with Your prisoners in tow, Your captives *in chains,*
You *sat in triumph* receiving gifts from men,
Even from those who rebel *against You,* so that *You,* the Eternal God,
might take up residence there.

¹⁹Blessed be the Lord
who carries our heavy loads every day,
the True God who is our salvation.

[pause]

²⁰*We know* our God is the God who delivers us,
and the Eternal One, the Lord, is the One who saves us from *the grip
of* death.

²¹The True God will certainly shatter the skulls of those who oppose Him;
He'll smash the hairy head of the man who continues on his sinful
ways.

²²The Lord said,
"I will bring the enemy back from Bashan.
I will bring them back from the deepest parts of the sea,

²³So that you may plant your feet in their blood
and your dogs may lick up their portion of the foe."

²⁴The *solemn* march in Your honor, O True God, has come into view;
the march that celebrates my God, my King, has come into the
sanctuary.

²⁵The singers went first, and the musicians came last
between *rows of* girls who played tambourines.

²⁶Come, let us gather to bless the True God
and to praise the Eternal One, He who is the fountain of Israel, *the
source of our life!*

²⁷Look! There *are the rulers of* Benjamin, the youngest in the lead.
A great crowd follows
The princes of Judah,
the princes of Zebulun, the princes of Naphtali.

²⁸[Your God *is the One who* has given you strength];*

    show Your power, O True God, as You have done for us.

²⁹Because of Your *magnificent* temple in Jerusalem,

    many kings will *line up to* bring You gifts.

³⁰Reprimand the beasts in the tall grass,

    the herds of bulls that are with the people's calves,

Trampling over the pieces of silver.

    He has driven out the people who love to be at war.

³¹Ambassadors will come from Egypt;

    the people of Ethiopia* will reach out their hands to the *one* True God.

³²Let all the kingdoms of the earth sing to the True God.

    Sing songs of praise to the Lord.

[pause]

³³To Him who rides high up beyond the heavens, which have been since
        ancient times,

    watch *and listen.* His voice speaks, and it is powerful *and strong.*

³⁴Attribute power to the *one* True God;

    His royal splendor is *evident* over Israel,

    and His power courses through the clouds.

³⁵O True God, You are awesome from the holy place where You dwell.

    The True God of Israel Himself

    grants strength and power to His people.

Blessed be *our* God!

PSALM 69

FOR THE WORSHIP LEADER. *A SONG* OF DAVID TO *THE TUNE* "LILIES."*

¹*Reach down for me,* True God; deliver me.

    The waters have risen to my neck; *I am going down!*

68:28 Other manuscripts read "Call on Your strength, O God."
68:31 Literally, Cush
69:title Hebrew, *shoshannim,* white lily-like flowers, perhaps the melody to which the song is sung

²My feet are swallowed in this murky bog;
   I am sinking—there is no sturdy ground.
I am in the deep;
   the floods are crashing in!
³I am weary of howling;
   my throat is scratched dry.
I still look for my God
   even though my eyes fail.

⁴My enemies despise me without any cause;
   they outnumber the hairs on my head.
They torment me with their power;
   they have absolutely no reason to hate me.
Now I am set to pay for crimes
   I have never committed!
⁵O True God, my foolish ways are plain before You;
   my mistakes—no, nothing can be hidden from You.

PSALM 69 **Humiliation of the Savior.** This is an interesting play between the struggles and the woes of David and a picture of the humiliation and insults Jesus would experience. As we reflect on the insults and injuries that Jesus suffered for our sakes, we are given pause to think of Him humiliated and disgraced by His enemies—those who poisoned His Spirit and left Him to die. We read this and imagine that if only we had been there, we would not have participated in such things. We would never have given Him vinegar to drink, and yet we may have to examine our integrity. Through all of the woes of the psalm, we see God standing above, making sure His beloved (both David and Jesus) survives the trial before him. David asks special grace for himself: "Don't let Your hopeful followers face disgrace because of me . . . Don't let Your seekers be shamed on account of me."

(continued on next page)

⁶Don't let Your hopeful followers face disgrace because of me,
    O Lord, Eternal One, Commander of *heaven's* armies;
Don't let Your seekers be shamed on account of me,
    O True God of Israel.
⁷I have been mocked when I stood up for You;
    I cower, shamefaced.
⁸*You know* my brothers and sisters?
    They now reject me—*they act as if I never existed.*
    I'm like a stranger to my own family.

⁹And here's why: I am consumed with You, completely devoted to
        protecting Your house;
    when they insult You, they insult me.
¹⁰When I mourn and discipline my soul by fasting,
    they deride me.
¹¹And when I put on sackcloth,
    they mock me.
¹²Those who sit at the gate gossip about me;
    I am *shamed by* the *slurred* songs of drunkards.

¹³But, Eternal One, I just pray the time is right
    that You would hear me. And, True God,
    because You are enduring love, that You would answer.

(continued from previous page)

When we apply this to ourselves, will we be able to face the sufferings of a Christ-follower as David did as king of Israel and as Jesus did on the cross. Will our conduct further the kingdom of God? Is there anything about the way we live now—the choices we make each day—that may grieve His Spirit, causing Him to suffer anew and be humiliated all over again? Are we even conscious of the things we do to deny Him?

The grace of God keeps peeking out throughout this psalm: "All you seekers-after-God will revive your souls! The Eternal One listens to the prayers of the poor and has regard for His people held in bondage." Throughout this grand song is the picture of the followers of God suffering as some are being called to be models, like David, standing firm against great odds.

In Your faithfulness, please, save me.

^{14}Pluck me from this murky bog;

don't let it pull me down!

Pull me from this rising water;

take me away from my enemies *to dry land*.

^{15}Don't let the flood take me under

or let me, Your servant, be swallowed into the deep

or let the yawning pit seal me in!

^{16}O Eternal One, *hear me*. Answer me. For Your enduring love is good

comfort;

in Your great mercy, turn toward me.

^{17}Yes, shine Your face upon *me,* Your servant;

put an end to my anguish—don't wait another minute.

^{18}Come near; rescue me!

Set me free from my enemies.

^{19}You know all my opponents;

You see them, see the way they treat me—

humiliating me with insults, trying to disgrace me.

^{20}All this ridicule has broken my heart,

killed my spirit.

I searched for sympathy, and I came up empty.

I looked for supporters, but there was no one.

^{21}*Even more,* they gave me poison for my food

and offered me *only sour* vinegar to drink.

^{22}Let them be ambushed at the *dinner* table,

caught in a trap when they least expect it.

^{23}Cloud their vision so they cannot see;

make their bodies shake, *their knees knock in terror*.

^{24}Pour out Your *fiery* wrath upon them!

Make a clean sweep; engulf them with Your flaming fury.

^{25}May their camps be bleak

with not one left in any tent.

^{26}Because they have persecuted the one You have struck,

add insult to those whom You have wounded.

²⁷Compound their sins; *don't let them off the hook!*
  Keep them from entering into Your mercy.
²⁸Blot out their names from Your book of life
  so they will not be recorded alongside those who are upright *before You.*
²⁹I am living in pain; I'm suffering,
  so save me, True God, and keep me safe *in troubled times*!

³⁰The name of the True God will be my song,
  an uplifting tune of *praise and* thanksgiving!
³¹My praise will please the Eternal One more than *if I were to sacrifice* an ox
  or the finest bull. (Horns, hooves, *and all!*)
³²Those who humbly serve will see and rejoice!
  All you seekers-after-God will revive your souls!
³³The Eternal One listens to the *prayers of the* poor
  and has regard for His people held in bondage.

³⁴*All God's creation:* join together in His praise! All heaven, all earth,
  all seas, all creatures of the ocean deep!
³⁵The True God will save Zion
  and rebuild the cities of Judah
  So that His servants may own it and live there *once again.*
³⁶Their children and children's children shall have it as their inheritance,
  and those who love His name will live in it.

PSALM 70

For the worship leader. *A song* of David for remembering.

¹O God, hurry to save me;
  Eternal One, hurry to my side.
²For those who seek to kill me,
  God, may they burn in disgrace and humiliation!
  Repulse the attacks; ridicule the efforts
  of those taking pleasure in my pain.

³I hear their taunts: "Nah, nah, nah . . . ."
>   Let those hecklers fall back *upon their brays*—ashamed *and*
>   *confused*—

⁴But let those who pursue You
>   celebrate and have joy because of You.
> And let the song of those who love Your saving *grace*
>   never cease: "God is great!"
⁵But I am poor and in *serious* need,
>   so hurry to my side, God,
> because You are my helper, my liberator.
>   Eternal One, please don't wait.

PSALM 71

¹I have found shelter in You, Eternal One;
>   *I count on You to* shield me always from humiliation and disgrace.
²Rescue and save me in Your justice.
>   Turn Your ear to me, and *hurry to* deliver me *from my enemies.*
³Be my rock of refuge where I can always hide.
>   You have given the order to keep me safe;
>   You are *my solid ground*—my rock and my fortress.

⁴Save me from the power of sinful people, O my God,
>   from the grip of unjust and cruel men.
⁵For You are my hope, Eternal One;
>   You, Lord, have been *the source of* my confidence since I was young.
⁶I have leaned upon You since I came into this world;
>   *I have relied on You since* You took me *safely* from my mother's body,
> So I will ever praise You.

⁷Many find me a mystery,
>   but You are my rock and my shelter—*my soul's asylum.*
⁸My mouth overflows with praise to You
>   and proclaims Your magnificence all day long.

⁹Do not set me aside when I am old;

 do not abandon me when I am worn out.

¹⁰For my enemies *often* voice evil against me;

 those who desire to kill me plot together *in secret*.

¹¹They say, "God has abandoned him;

 let's go after him *right now* and seize him.

 There's no one around to rescue him."

¹²God, stay close by me.

 Come quick, O my God, and help me!

¹³May my enemies be covered in shame and *then* die;

 may those who seek to harm me

 be overwhelmed with contempt and disgrace.

¹⁴But I will keep hope alive,

 and my praise to You will grow exponentially.

¹⁵I will bear witness to Your merciful acts;

 throughout the day I will speak of all the ways You deliver,

 although, *I admit,* I do not know the entirety of either.

¹⁶I will come with *stories of* Your great acts, *my* Lord, the Eternal One.

 I will remind them of Your justice, only Yours.

PSALM 71 │ **As we mature,** our desires and friends change. It is interesting that God is always constant. This psalm tracks life from the mother's womb through childhood and youth and into the gray-haired years. While we may fear of aging, God sees each of us as the same unique person during each phase of life.

The words echoed in this psalm hit most of us sooner or later: "Do not set me aside when I am old or abandon me when I am worn out." It is obvious in this psalm that all, no matter the age, are of value to God. Although the psalmist asks God to not abandon him in his old age, the truth is that God continually disciplines, refines, and polishes the believer throughout life.

God sees the inside person and does not focus on the age of the container. Consider that aging gracefully could mean we are fully supported and satisfied by grace. It could mean we have more of God than ever before. With that in mind, we can humbly embrace the notion of being "full of years" so that we can live "full of grace."

¹⁷You have taught me since I was young, O God,
    and I still proclaim the wonderful things You have done.
¹⁸Now as I grow old and my hair turns gray,
    I ask that You not abandon me, O God.
Allow me to share with the generation to come
    about Your power;
Let me speak about Your strength *and wonders*
    to all those yet to be born.
¹⁹God, Your justice stretches to the heavens,
    You who have done mighty things!
    Who is like You, O God?

²⁰You have made me see hard times: I've experienced many miserable days,
    but You will restore me again.
You will raise me up
    from the deep pit.
²¹You will greatly increase my status
    and be my comfort *once again.*

²²I will praise You with *music played on* a harp
    because You have been faithful, O my God.
I will sing praises to You with the lyre,
    O Holy One of Israel.
²³I will shout for joy
    as I sing Your praises;
    my soul *will celebrate* because You have rescued me.
²⁴All day long I will declare how Your justice saved me,
For those who have plotted to bring me harm
    are now ashamed and humiliated.

PSALM 72

A SONG OF SOLOMON.

¹True God, bestow Your *honest* judgments upon the king
    and *anoint* the king's son with Your righteousness.

²May he be honest and fair in his judgments over Your people
and offer justice to the burdened and suffering.
³*Under his reign,* may *this land of* mountains and hills know peace
and experience justice for all the people.
⁴May the king offer justice to the burdened *and suffering,*
rescue the *poor and* needy,
and demolish the oppressor!

⁵[May the people fear You]* for as long as the sun shines,
as long as the moon rises *in the night sky,* throughout the generations.
⁶May the king be like the *refreshing* rains, which fall upon *fields of freshly*
mown grass—
like showers that *cool and* nourish the earth.
⁷May good and honest people flourish for as long as he reigns,
and may peace fill the land until the moon no longer rises.

⁸May the king rule from one sea to the next,
and *may his rule extend* from the *Euphrates* River to the far reaches of
the earth.
⁹Let the desert wanderers bow down before him
and his enemies *lay prostrate and* taste the dirt.
¹⁰Let the kings of Tarshish and the island kings
shower him with gifts
And the kings of Sheba and Seba bring him presents *as well.*
¹¹Let every king *on earth* bow down before him
and every nation be in his service.
¹²For he will rescue the needy when they ask for help!
He will save the burdened and *come to the aid of* those who have no
other help.
¹³He offers compassion to the weak and the poor;
he will *help and* protect the lives of the needy!
¹⁴He will liberate them from *the fierce sting of* persecution and violence;
in his eyes, their blood is precious.

¹⁵May he live *a long, long time*
and the gold of Sheba be given to him.

72:5 Greek manuscripts read "He will endure."

May the people constantly lift up prayers for him,
 and may they call upon God to bless him always.
¹⁶Let grain grow plentifully in this land *of promise,*
 let it sway *in the breeze* on the hilltops,
 let it grow *strong* as *do the cedars of* Lebanon,
And may those who live in the city *bloom and* flourish
 just as the grass of the fields *and meadows.*
¹⁷May his name live on forever
 and his reputation grow for as long as the sun gives light.
May *people from* all nations find in him a blessing;
 may all peoples declare him blessed.

¹⁸May the Eternal God, the God of Israel, be blessed,
 for He alone works *miracles and* wonders!
¹⁹May His glorious name be blessed forever
 and the whole earth be filled with His *eternal* glory!
Amen. Amen.

²⁰The prayers of *King* David, Jesse's son, are ended.

PSALM 73

A SONG OF ASAPH.

¹Truly God is good to *His people,* Israel,
 to those with pure hearts.
²*Though I know this is true,* I almost lost my footing;
 yes, my steps were on slippery ground.
³You see, *there was a time when* I envied arrogant men
 and thought, "The wicked look pretty happy to me."

⁴For they seem to live *carefree lives,* free of suffering;
 their bodies are strong and healthy.
⁵They don't know trouble as we do;
 they are not plagued *with problems* as the rest of us are.

⁶They've got *pearls of* pride strung around their necks;
they clothe their bodies with violence.
⁷ *They have so much more than enough.*
Their eyes bulge because they are so fat with possessions.
They have more than their hearts could have ever imagined.
⁸*There is nothing sacred, and no one is safe.* Vicious sarcasm drips from their lips;
they bully and threaten to crush *their enemies.*
⁹They even mock God *as if He were not above*;
their *arrogant* tongues boast throughout the earth; *they feel invincible.*

¹⁰Even God's people turn and are carried away by them;
they watch and listen, yet find no fault in them.
¹¹*You will hear* them say, "How can the True God *possibly* know anyway?
He's not even here.
So how can the Most High have any knowledge *of what happens here?*"
¹²Let me tell you *what I know* about the wicked:
they are comfortably at rest while their wealth is growing *and growing.*
¹³*Oh, let this not be me!* It seems I have scrubbed my heart to keep it clean
and washed my hands in innocence.
And for what? Nothing.
¹⁴For all day long, I am being punished,
each day awakening to *stern* chastisement.

¹⁵If I had said *to others* these kinds of things *about the plight of God's good people,*
then *I know* I would have betrayed the next generation.
¹⁶Trying to solve this *mystery* on my own exhausted me;
I couldn't bear to look at it any further.
¹⁷So I took my questions to the True God,
and in His sanctuary I realized *something so chilling and final*: their
lives have a *deadly* end.
¹⁸*Because* You have certainly set the wicked upon a slippery slope,
You've set them up to slide to their destruction.

¹⁹*And they won't see it coming.* It will happen so fast:

first, a flash of terror, and then desolation.

²⁰It is like a dream from which someone awakes.

You will wake up, Lord, and loathe what has become of them.

²¹*You see,* my heart overflowed with bitterness *and cynicism*;

I felt as if someone stabbed me in the back.

²²But I didn't know *the truth*;

I have been acting like a stupid animal toward You.

²³But *look at this*: You are still holding my right hand;

You have been all along.

²⁴*Even though I was angry and hard-hearted,* You gave me good advice;

when it's all over, You will receive me into Your glory.

²⁵*For all my wanting,* I don't have anyone but You in heaven.

There is nothing on earth that I desire other than You.

PSALM 73 | **Life Just Isn't Fair.** Those who ignore God and are carefree about spiritual things and sin seem to prosper. "The wicked look pretty happy to me . . . they seem to live carefree lives . . . their bodies are strong . . . they don't know trouble . . . they are so fat with possessions . . . they have more than their hearts could ever have imagined." So what is up with all this? Why do the rich get richer and the poor seem to slide backwards? It just isn't right. The psalmist confesses that all of this good he has been doing is for naught: "And for what? Nothing."

Sometimes we hold stubbornly to our own truth, creating our world to suit our moods or our actions. Almost everyone has fond memories of the days when they were poor with simple, quiet lives. In spite of this, most of us continue to struggle to reach for more "stuff." Finally, when our eyes are opened again and our hardened hearts are melted, we discover we've moved away from the True God and we see our foolishness. Regret looms heavily and remorse shows us where we've been, but God keeps holding the light of truth.

The end of this brings us back to God's perspective. "You will bring an end to all who refuse to be true to You. But the closer I am to You, my God, the better . . . life with You is good." The goodness of life is not in things, but true joy comes out of our spirit. It doesn't come from others or from things. It comes from within when we are connected to God.

²⁶*I admit how* broken I am in body and spirit,
>   but God is my strength, and He will be mine forever.

²⁷It will happen: whoever shuns You will be silenced forever;
>   You will bring an end to all who refuse to be true to You.
²⁸But the closer I am to You, my God, the better *because life with You is good.*
>   O Lord, the Eternal One, You keep me safe—
>   I will tell everyone what You have done.

PSALM 74

A CONTEMPLATIVE SONG* OF ASAPH.

¹O True God, why have You *turned Your back on us and* abandoned us
>   forever?
>   Why is *Your anger seething and* Your wrath smoldering against the
>   sheep of Your pasture'?
²Remember the congregation *of people* You acquired long ago,
>   the tribe which You redeemed to be Your very own.
>   *Remember* Mount Zion, where You *have chosen to* live!
³*Come,* direct Your attention to Your sanctuary;
>   our enemy has demolished everything and left it in complete ruin.

⁴Your enemies roared *like lions* in Your sacred chamber;
>   they have claimed it with their own standards as signs.
⁵They acted like lumberjacks swinging their axes
>   to cut down a stand of trees.
⁶They hacked up all the *beautifully* carved items,
>   smashed them *to splinters* with their axes and hammers.
⁷They have burned Your sanctuary to the ground;
>   they have desecrated the place where Your *holy* name lived in honor;
⁸They have plotted in their hearts, "We will crush them and bring them to
>   their knees!"
>   Then they scorched all of the places in the land where the True God
>   met His people.

74:title Hebrew, *maskil*

⁹We no longer receive signs,

there are no more prophets who remain,

and not one of us knows how long *this situation will last.*

¹⁰O True God, how much longer will the enemy mock us?

Will this insult continue against You forever?

¹¹Why do You stand by and do nothing?

Unleash Your power and finish them off!

¹²Even so, the True God is my King from long ago,

bringing salvation *to His people* throughout the land.

¹³You have divided the sea with Your power;

You shattered the skulls of the creatures of the sea;

¹⁴You smashed the heads of Leviathan

and fed his remains to the people of the desert.

¹⁵You broke open *the earth* and springs burst forth and streams filled *the crevices*;

You dried up the great rivers.

¹⁶The day and the night are both Yours—

You fashioned the sun, moon, *and all the lights that pierce the darkness.*

¹⁷You have arranged the earth, set all its boundaries;

You are the Architect of *the seasons*: summer and winter.

¹⁸Eternal One, do not forget that the enemy has taunted You

and a company of fools has rejected Your name.

¹⁹We are Your *precious* turtledoves; don't surrender our souls to the wild beasts.

Do not forget the lives of Your poor, *afflicted, and brokenhearted ones* forever.

²⁰Be mindful of Your covenant *with us,*

for the dark corners of the land are filled with pockets of violence.

²¹Do not allow the persecuted to return without honor;

may the poor, *wounded,* and needy sing praises *to You;*

may they bring glory to Your name!

²²O True God, rise up and defend Your cause;

remember how the foolish man insults You every hour of the day.

[23]Do not forget the voices of Your enemies,
the commotion and chaos of Your foes, which continually grow.

PSALM 75

FOR THE WORSHIP LEADER. A SONG OF ASAPH TO *THE TUNE*
"DO NOT DESTROY."*

[1]We thank You, O True God.
Our *souls are overflowing with* thanks! Your name is near;
Your people *remember and* tell of Your *marvelous* works and wonders.

[2]*You say,* "At the time that I choose,
I will judge and do so fairly.
[3]When the earth and everyone living upon it spin into chaos,
I am the One who stabilizes and supports it."*

[pause]*

[4]"I *discipline* the arrogant by telling them, 'No more bragging.'
I discipline the wicked by saying, 'Do not raise your horn *to
demonstrate your power.*
[5]Do not thrust your horn into the air, *issuing a challenge,*
and never speak with insolence *when you address Me.'"*

[6]There is no one *on earth* who can raise up another *to grant honor,*
not from the east or the west, not from the desert.
There is no one. God is the only One.
[7]God is the *only* Judge.
He *is the only One who* can ruin or redeem a man.
[8]For the Eternal One holds a full cup of wine in His hand—
a chalice well stirred and foaming *full of wrath.*

75:title Hebrew, *al-tashheth,* meaning is uncertain.
75:3 Literally, "steady its pillars"
75:3 Literally, selah, likely a musical direction from a Hebrew root meaning "to lift up"
75:4 The horn was symbol of power, and a raised horn indicated a challenge.

He pours the cup out,
 and all wicked people of the earth drink it up—every drop of it!
⁹But I will tell *of His great deeds* forever.
 I will sing praises to Jacob's True God.

¹⁰I will cut off the horns of *strength raised by* the wicked,
 but I will lift up the horns *of strength* of the righteous.

PSALM 76

FOR THE WORSHIP LEADER. A SONG OF ASAPH *ACCOMPANIED BY STRINGS.*

¹The One known in Judah is the True God;
 in Israel, His name is great.
²He has made Salem* His home;
 indeed, He rests in Zion.
³There He destroyed the instruments of war:
 flaming arrows, shields, and swords.

[pause]*

⁴You *rise and* shine *like the dawn.*
 You are more majestic than the mountains where game runs *wild.*
⁵The strong-hearted *enemies* were plundered;
 they were buried in slumber.
Even the *noble* warriors
 could not raise a hand *to stop You.*
⁶O True God of Jacob, with *just* Your rebuke
 both horse and rider fell into a deep sleep.

⁷You are feared; yes, You.
 And who can stand before You
 when Your anger flares?

76:2 Jerusalem
76:3 Literally, selah, likely a musical direction from a Hebrew root meaning "to lift up"

⁸You decreed judgment from the heavens.
>   The earth *heard it and* was petrified with fear, completely still,
⁹When the True God arose for judgment
>   to deliver all the meek of the earth.

[pause]

¹⁰For the wrath of man will end in praise of You,
>   and whatever wrath is left You will wrap around Yourself *like a belt.*
¹¹Make vows to the Eternal One, your God,
>   and do all you promised;
> Let all the nations around you bring gifts
>   to the God who arouses *fear and* awe.
¹²He squashes the *arrogant* spirit of the rulers
>   and inspires fear in *the hearts of* the kings of the earth.

PSALM 77

FOR THE WORSHIP LEADER, JEDUTHUN. A SONG OF ASAPH.

¹I cry up to *heaven,*
>   "My God, True God," and He hears.
²In my darkest days, I seek the Lord.
>   Through the night, my hands are *raised up,* stretched out, *waiting;*
> And though they do not grow tired,
>   my soul is uneasy.
³I remember the True God and become distraught.
>   I think *about Him,* and my spirit becomes weak.

[pause]*

⁴You hold my eyes *wide* open.
>   I am troubled beyond words.
⁵My mind drifts to thoughts of yesterdays
>   and yesteryears.

77:3 Literally, selah, likely a musical direction from a Hebrew root meaning "to lift up"

⁶I call to mind my music; *it keeps me company* at night.
   Together with my heart I contemplate;
   my spirit searches, *wondering, questioning*:
⁷"What will the Lord do? Reject us for good?
   Will He never show us His favor again?
⁸Has His loyal love *finally* worn down?
   Have His promises reached an end?
⁹Has the True God forgotten how to be gracious?
   In His anger, has He withdrawn His compassion?"

[pause]

¹⁰"I can't help but be distraught," I said,
   "for the power of the Most High that was once for us is now
      against us."

PSALM 77 | **"My darkest days,"** the psalmist writes, thinking there is no hope of going back. He becomes pathetic, "I am troubled . . . my mind drifts . . . my spirit searches, wondering, questioning." How is it that in bad times we question the reality of God when we know that we are the ones who should be questioned? The same story happens over and over again. Good times become bad times—dark times. There is always the same question: Will we come back to God? What kind of question is that anyway? When we think about it, we realize that the really good times are the times we acknowledge God's presence in our lives, and the really bad times are always the ones when we try to go it alone without Him.

When we sense that our actions have created an abyss between us and God's love, our hearts begin to cry. We fear that maybe we've drifted so far from what God wants us to be that He has walked out of the door of our lives forever. "Has the True God forgotten how to be gracious?" Of course not.

With the psalmist we can see the light: "I will remember the actions the Eternal One has taken . . . I will reflect . . . I will study all You have performed." Even now, it is from His great reservoir of compassion that the Eternal One continues to hold our eyes open; He wants us to recognize the truth of what we've done to ourselves.

We don't ever need to wonder if God has run out of grace; we can only wonder at ourselves for having created the dark spaces between us in the first place.

¹¹I will remember the actions the Eternal One has taken,
    reminisce on Your ancient wonders.
¹²I will reflect on all of Your work;
    indeed, I will study all You have performed.
¹³O God, Your way is *so different, so distinct,* so divine.
    No other god compares with our God.
¹⁴You, God, and Your works evoke wonder.
    You have proved Your strength to the nations.
¹⁵You used Your great power to release Your people:
    with a strong arm, You freed Jacob's children, and Joseph's.

[pause]

¹⁶The waters saw You, O True God.
    The seas saw You and swelled in sorrow.
    Even the deep trembled.
¹⁷Water poured from the clouds,
    and the sky boomed out *in response*
    as Your arrows *of lightning* flashed this way and that.
¹⁸The sound of Your thunder whirled within the wind
    as Your lightning lit up the world.
    Yes, the whole earth trembled and shook.
¹⁹Your way ran through the sea,
    Your path *cut* through great waters,
    and still no one can spot Your footprints.
²⁰You led Your people as a flock
    tended by the hands of Moses and Aaron.

PSALM 78

A CONTEMPLATIVE SONG* OF ASAPH.

¹O my people, listen to me!
    Hear my instruction; soak up every word of what I am about to tell
        you.

78:title Hebrew, *maskil*

²I will open my mouth in parables;
   I will speak of ancient mysteries—
³Things that we have heard about, things that we have known,
   things which our ancestors declared to us *again and again*.
⁴We will not keep these things secret from their children;
   rather, we will tell the coming generation
All about the praise that is due to the Eternal One.
   We will tell them all about His strength, *power,* and wonders.

⁵He gave His *holy* law to Jacob,
   His teaching to the people of Israel,
Which He instructed our fathers
   to pass down to their children
⁶So that the coming generation would know them *by heart,*
   even the children who are not yet born,
So that they might *one day* stand up and teach them to their children,
   ⁷*tell them* to put their confidence *and hope* in God,
And never forget the *wondrous* things He has done.
   They should obey His commandments *always*
⁸And avoid following in the footsteps of their parents,
   a hard-headed and rebellious generation—
A generation of uncultivated hearts,
   whose spirits were unfaithful to God.

⁹The sons of Ephraim were *master* archers, armed with all the necessary
      equipment,
   yet when the battle hour arrived, they ran away.
¹⁰They were not loyal to their covenant with God;
   they *turned away and* refused to walk in it;
¹¹They did not remember all the *wondrous* things He had done,
   even the great miracles He had revealed to them.
¹²He did miraculous things in the presence of their ancestors
   as they made their way out of Egypt, through the fields of Zoan.
¹³He split the sea and made them pass through it;
   He made the waters to rise, forming a wall *of water*.
¹⁴Every day He led them with a cloud;
   every night, with a fiery light.

¹⁵He cracked open rocks in the wilderness
>> and provided them with all the water they needed, *as plentiful* as the
>> depths of the ocean.
¹⁶He caused streams to burst forth from the rock,
>> waters to rush in like a river.

¹⁷Even after *witnessing all of these miracles,* they still chose to sin against
>> God,
>> to act against the *will of the* Most High in the desert!
¹⁸They tested God in their *stubborn* hearts
>> by demanding whatever food they happened to be craving.

PSALM 78 | **Never Forget.** Not all psalms are songs of praise or poems of repentance. Some are great hymns of the acts of God that teach and inspire. Psalm 78 is a major historical work that brings to light the culture of Israel. This psalm opens by telling us it holds parables and ancient mysteries. The truths of the psalm are to instruct Israel and to be passed down from one generation to another.

The purpose is to "never forget the wondrous things [God] has done." The miracles His people experienced while in Egypt and in the desert are to be remembered. How God opened the sea, brought water from rock, left bread on the ground, and rained meat from the sky. That generation ended in terror and "they vanished like a breath." "They were not consistently faithful to Him." The psalm tells us, "Over and over again, they tested God's patience." After He brought them into the promised land, they began to worship pagan idols and abandoned the True God. But after all this, He chose David to shepherd His people because of "honor and integrity of his heart." From this one life, the nation is saved.

"Honor" and "integrity" seem like ideas from a bygone era; yet we have a longing for them to exist, and it seems God does too. He took the shepherd boy, David, and made him a king because he had an upright heart. In fact, He called all of His leaders because of this common thread: each had a heart for Him.

God's men and women operated with the intention of integrity. Even when they fell down, they rose up again because His hand continued to lead them and remind them of their true calling. Today, we are still called by God to bring honor and integrity of heart to Him and to others. We are called to lead in wisdom. Let us learn from this psalm of history with its lesson about a pure heart. God keeps His word; we had better keep ours.

¹⁹Then they challenged God:

> "Can God fill a table *with food* in the *middle of the* desert?
²⁰He split open the rock, and water gushed out;
> streams *and rivers* were overflowing!
But can He also provide us with bread?
> Can He supply meat to His sons and daughters?"

²¹When the Eternal One heard these words, He was furious;
> His fiery anger erupted against Jacob;
> His wrath grew against Israel.
²²*This all happened* because they did not trust God;
> they did not have faith in His power to save them.
²³Nevertheless, He gave instructions to the clouds in the sky
> and swung open heaven's doors;
²⁴He showered them with manna to soothe their *hungry* bellies
> and provided them with the bread of heaven.
²⁵(*In that day* mortals ate the bread of heavenly messengers.)
> God provided them with plenty of food.
²⁶He stirred up the east wind and blew it through the sky.
> With His might, He whipped the south wind *into a storm*;
²⁷Like dust *from the sky,* He caused meat to fall on them.
> Birds, like sand on the seashore, *fell to the earth*.
²⁸They landed all about the camp,
> all around their tents.
²⁹*God's* people feasted *on the food-blessings,* and their stomachs were filled;
> He gave them exactly what they desired.
³⁰But before their bellies were soothed,
> while their mouths were still full of food,
³¹God's wrath came at them *like a tidal wave*
> and swallowed some of the *bravest,* strongest among them
> and quieted the youth of Israel.

³²Even after all this, they continued to sin
> and still did not trust *in Him or* in the incredible things He did.
³³So He *abruptly* ended their time; they vanished like a breath;
> He ended their years suddenly, with terror.

³⁴After He took *some of* their lives,
     those *left* turned back and sought God wholeheartedly.
³⁵*After all they had endured,* they remembered that God, the Most High,
     was their Rock, their Redeemer,
³⁶But *even then* they tried to deceive Him with their words
     and fool Him with a web of lies.
³⁷They were not consistently faithful to Him,
     and they were untrue to their covenant with Him.
³⁸Yet by His great compassion,
     He forgave them
     and decided not to put an end to them.
  Most of the time, He held back His anger
     and did not unleash His wrath *against them.*
³⁹He was mindful that they were human, *frail and fleeting,*
     like a wind *that touches one's skin* for a moment, then vanishes.
⁴⁰Oh, how often they disobeyed Him in the wilderness
     and frustrated Him *during their time* in the desert!
⁴¹Over and over again, they tested God's patience
     and caused great pain for Israel's Holy One.
⁴²They failed to be mindful of His great strength.
     They forgot all about the day He saved them from the enemy,
⁴³When He displayed *all sorts of* signs *and wonders* in Egypt,
     and all the amazing things He did in the region of Zoan*
⁴⁴When He transformed their rivers into blood
     so that they could not drink from their streams.
⁴⁵He sent armies of flies to bite and torment them
     and *hordes of* frogs to *ruin and* devastate them;
⁴⁶He handed over *all of* their crops to grasshoppers
     and the fruit of all their labor to locusts;
⁴⁷He sent *violent* hailstorms, which smashed all their vines,
     and ruined their sycamore-fig trees with biting frost.
⁴⁸He handed over *all of* their cattle to the hailstorms as well
     and struck *all* their herds with lightning.

78:43 Hebrew, *Avaris*

⁴⁹He poured His burning wrath upon them—
>> anger, resentment, and trouble—
>> sending a company of heavenly warriors to destroy them.
⁵⁰He carved out a road for His wrath;
>> He did not spare any from *the sting of* death
>> but handed them over to the *fangs of the* plague.
⁵¹He killed all the firstborn of Egypt,
>> the first products of their manhood in the tents of Ham, *the*
>>> *Egyptians' ancestor.*
⁵²But then He guided His people like sheep *to safety*
>> and led them like a flock into the desert *to freedom*;
⁵³He took them on a safe route so that they would not be afraid,
>> and He allowed the *hungry* sea to swallow *all of* their enemies.
⁵⁴He led them to His sacred land—
>> to this *holy* hill, which He had won by *the power of* His right hand.
⁵⁵He forced out the other nations *which were living there* before them,
>> and He redistributed the lands as an inheritance to His people;
>> He settled the tribes *and families* of Israel *peaceably* in their tents.

⁵⁶Even after *all this,* they disobeyed the Most High God
>> and tested *His patience*
>> and did not live by His commands.
⁵⁷Rather, they regressed to their fathers' ways and lived faithlessly—*disloyal*
>>> *traitors!*
>> They were as undependable *and untrustworthy* as a defective bow,
⁵⁸For they triggered His wrath by setting up high places,
>> *altars to strange gods in His land;*
>> they aroused His jealousy by bowing down to idols *in the shadow of*
>>> *His presence.*
⁵⁹God boiled with wrath when He witnessed what they were doing;
>> He totally rejected Israel.
⁶⁰He deserted His own sanctuary at Shiloh,
>> the tent where He had lived in the midst of *His* people.
⁶¹He handed His strength over to captivity;
>> He put His splendor under the enemy's control.

⁶²He handed His people over to the sword,
  and He was filled with anger toward His chosen ones; *He was burning
    with wrath!*
⁶³*A great* fire consumed all the young men,
  and the virgin girls were without *the joy of their* wedding songs.
⁶⁴Priests met their doom by the *blade of a* sword,
  and widows *had no tears to cry*; they could not weep.
⁶⁵Then the Lord awoke like a man who has been asleep,
  like a warrior who has been overcome with wine.
⁶⁶He forced all His enemies back;
  He *defeated them,* weighing them down with everlasting disgrace.

⁶⁷He even rejected the tent of Joseph *as His home*
  and showed no favor toward the tribe of Ephraim.
⁶⁸Instead, He favored the tribe of Judah—
  Mount Zion, the place He adored.
⁶⁹He built His sanctuary like the *mountain* heights;
  like the earth, He created it to last forever.
⁷⁰He chose His servant David,
  and called Him out of the sheep pastures.
⁷¹From caring for the ewes, who *gently* nurse their young,
  He called him to shepherd His people Jacob
  and *to look after* Israel, His inheritance.
⁷²David shepherded them with the *honor and* integrity of his heart;
  he led them *in wisdom* with *strong and* skillful hands.

Psalm 79

A SONG OF ASAPH.

¹O God, the nations *around us* have raided the land that belongs to You;
  they have defiled Your holy house
  and crushed Jerusalem to a heap of ruins.
²Your servants are dead;

birds of the air swoop down to pick at their remains.
Scavengers of the earth eat what is left of Your saints.
³The enemy poured out their blood; *it flowed* like water
all over Jerusalem,
and there is *no one left,* no one to bury *what remains of* them.
⁴The surrounding peoples taunt us.
We are nothing but a joke to them, people to be ridiculed.

⁵How long *can this go on,* O Eternal One? Will You stay angry *at us*
forever?
Your jealousy burning like wildfire?
⁶Flood these outsiders with Your wrath—
they have no knowledge of You!
Drown the kingdoms *of this world*
that call *on false gods and* not on Your name.
⁷For these *nations* devoured Jacob, *consumed him,*
and turned his home into a wasteland.

⁸Do not hold the sins of our ancestors against us,
but send Your compassion to meet us quickly, *God.*
We are in deep despair.
⁹Help us, O God who saves us,
to the *honor and* glory of Your name.
Pull us up, deliver us, and forgive our sins,
for Your name's sake.
¹⁰Don't give these people any reason to ask,
"Where is their God?"
Avenge the blood spilled by Your servants.
Put it on display among the nations before our very eyes.

¹¹May the *deep* groans *and wistful sighs* of the prisoners reach You,
and by Your great power, save those condemned to die.
¹²Pay back each of our invaders personally, seven times
for the shame they heaped on You, O Lord!
¹³Then we, Your people, the sheep of Your pasture,
will *pause and* give You thanks forever;
Your praise will be told by our generation to the next.

PSALM 80

FOR THE WORSHIP LEADER. A SONG OF ASAPH TO *THE TUNE*
"THE LILIES."*

¹Turn Your ear *toward us,* Shepherd of Israel,
     You who lead *the children of* Joseph like a flock.
 You who sit enthroned above heaven's winged creatures,* radiate
               Your light!
²In the presence of Ephraim, Benjamin, and Manasseh,
        arouse Your *strength and* power,
        and save us!

³Bring us back *to You,* God.
        Turn the light of Your face *upon us* so that we will be rescued *from this
           sea of darkness.*

⁴O Eternal God, Commander of *heaven's* armies,
        how long will You remain angry at the prayers of Your sons and
           daughters?
⁵You have given them tears for food;
        You have given them an abundance of tears to drink.
⁶You have made us a source of trouble for our neighbors—
        our enemies laugh to each other *behind our backs.*
⁷O God, Commander of *heaven's* armies, bring us back *to You.*
        Turn the light of Your face upon us so that we will be rescued *from
           this sea of darkness.*

⁸You took us *like* a grapevine dug from *the soil of* Egypt;
        You forced out the nations and transplanted it *in Your land.*
⁹You groomed the ground around it,
        planted it so it would root deep into the earth, and it covered all the
           land.

80:title Hebrew, *shoshannim,* white lily-like flowers, perhaps the melody to which the song is sung
80:1 Literally, cherubim

¹⁰*As it grew,* the mountains were blanketed by its shadow;
the mighty cedars were covered by its branches.
¹¹The plant extended its branches to the *Mediterranean* Sea,
and spread its shoots all the way to the *Euphrates* River.
¹²*God,* why have You pulled down the wall *that protected it*
so that everyone who wanders by can pick its *sweet grapes?*
¹³The *wild* boar of the forest eats it all,
and the creatures of the field feast upon it.

¹⁴O God, Commander of *heaven's* armies, come back *to us.*
Gaze down from heaven and see *what has happened.*
Keep watch over this vine, *and nourish it.*
¹⁵Look after the saplings which You planted with Your *own* right hand,
the child whom You have raised *and nurtured* for Yourself.
¹⁶Your enemies have chopped it down and burned it with fire;
may they be destroyed by the sight of Your rebuke.
¹⁷Let Your *protective* hand rest on the one *who is* at Your right hand,
the child of man whom You have raised *and nurtured* for Yourself.
¹⁸Then we will not turn away from You.
Bring us back to life! And we will call out for You!

¹⁹O Eternal God, Commander of *heaven's* armies, bring us back *to You.*
Turn the light of Your face upon us so that we will be rescued *from this sea of darkness.*

PSALM 81

FOR THE WORSHIP LEADER. *A SONG* OF ASAPH *ACCOMPANIED BY THE HARP.*[*]

¹Sing with joy to God, our strength, *our fortress.*
Raise your voices to the True God of Jacob.
²Sing and strike up a melody; sound the tambourine,
strum the sweet lyre and the harp.

81:title Hebrew, *gittith,* a winepress or a musical instrument from Gath

³Blow the trumpet to announce the new moon,
  the full moon, the day of our feast.*
⁴For this is prescribed for Israel,
  a rule ordained by the True God of Jacob.
⁵A precept established by God in Joseph
  during His journey in Egypt.

I hear *it said in* a language foreign to me:
⁶"I removed the burden from your shoulders;
  I removed *heavy* baskets from your hands.
⁷You cried out to Me, *I heard* your distress, and I delivered you;
  I answered you from the secret place, *where clouds* of thunder *roll.*
  I tested you at the waters of Meribah.

[pause]*

81:3 Deuteronomy 16:13-15
81:7 Literally, selah, likely a musical direction from a Hebrew root meaning "to lift up"

PSALM 81 **"Why would a loving God allow sin?"** The answer is found in this psalm, "I freed them to follow their hard hearts." God has given us a pretty impressive power in giving us the freedom to choose our own paths. We can actually ask Him to back away and leave us to make our decisions on our own. When we choose to forge our own path without Him, though, we often stumble on the cracks of our own ignorance. Here the glorious works of God are recited, and what God asks in return is faithfulness. But we often choose not to hear that part of the message.

We, like the Israelites, can actually go so far down a wrong way we become destructive to ourselves and others. Does that mean God no longer cares? On the contrary, because He cares so much, He will sometimes leave us to live with the consequences. When we think He doesn't care, it is really because we have stopped listening to His voice. When we have struggled in our own efforts to the point where we don't know what else to do and are ready to hear from Him, He'll bring us back into His fold.

Here God tells us, "If only My people would hear My voice and Israel would follow My direction! Then I would not hesitate." God is ready to help; are we willing to accept His help?

[8]"O My people, hear Me; I will rebuke you.

> Israel, *Israel!* If you would only listen to Me.

[9]Do not surround yourselves with other gods

> or bow down to strange gods.

[10]I am the Eternal One, your True God.

> I *liberated you from slavery,* led you out from the land of Egypt.
>
> If you open your mouth wide, I will fill it.

[11]"But My *own* people did not hear My voice!

> Israel refused to obey Me.

[12]So I freed them to follow their hard hearts,

> to do what they thought was best.

[13]If only My people would hear My voice

> and Israel would follow My direction!

[14]Then I would not hesitate to humble their enemies

> and defeat their opposition Myself.

[15]Those who hate the Eternal One will *cower in His presence,* pretending to submit,

> they *secretly* loathe Him, yet their doom is forever.

[16]But you—I will feed you the best wheat

> and satisfy you with honey out of the rock."

PSALM 82

A SONG OF ASAPH.

[1]The True God stands *to preside* over the *heavenly* council.

> He pronounces judgment on the *so-called* gods.

[2]*He asks:* "How long will you judge dishonestly

> and be partial to the wicked?"

[pause]*

[3]"Stand up for the poor and the orphan;

> advocate for the rights of the afflicted and those in need.

82:2 Literally, selah, likely a musical direction from a Hebrew root meaning "to lift up"

⁴Deliver the poor and the needy;
>   rescue them from their *evil* oppressors."

⁵These *bullies* are ignorant; they have no understanding *of My ways*.
>   So as they walk in darkness,
>   the foundations of the earth tremble.

⁶I said, "*Though* you are gods*
>   and children of the Most High,
⁷You will die no differently than any mortal;
>   you will fall like one of the princes."

⁸Rise up, O True God; judge *the rulers of* the earth,
>   for all the nations are Yours.

Psalm 83

A song of Asaph.

¹O True God, do not be quiet *any longer*.
>   Do not stay silent or be still, O God.
²Look now, Your enemies are causing a commotion;
>   those who hate You are rising up!
³They are conniving against Your people,
>   conspiring against those You cherish.
⁴They say, "Join us. Let's wipe the entire nation off the face of the earth
>   so no one will remember Israel's name."
⁵They are all in it together, thinking as one,
>   and making a pact against You:
⁶The people of Edom and Ishmael;
>   the Moabites and the Hagrites;
⁷Gebal, Ammon, and Amalek;
>   Philistia with the residents of Tyre.

82:6 John 10:34

⁸And the *powerful* Assyrians have joined the alliance
to *add their strength and* support the descendants of Lot: *Moab and
Ammon.*

[pause]*

⁹Do to these nations what You did to Midian,
to Sisera and Jabin at the raging waters of Kishon.
¹⁰They were destroyed at En-dor;
they became like dung, *fertilizer* for the ground.
¹¹Make their rulers like Oreb and Zeeb,
all their princes like Zebah and Zalmunna,
¹²Who schemed, "We should own the meadows of the True God,
let's take them!"

¹³O my God, blow them away like a tumbleweed,
scatter them like dust in a whirlwind.
¹⁴As a wildfire charges through the forest
or a flame *sprints* up the mountainside,
¹⁵Send Your raging winds to chase them, *hunt them down,*
and terrify them with Your storm.
¹⁶Redden their faces in shame
so that they will *turn and* seek Your *holy* name, Eternal One.
¹⁷May they face disappointment and anxiety forever;
may they be ashamed and die.
¹⁸May they know that *You and* You alone,
whose name is the Eternal One,
are the Most High, *the Supreme Ruler* over all the earth.

83:8 Literally, selah, likely a musical direction from a Hebrew root meaning "to lift up"

Psalm 84

FOR THE WORSHIP LEADER. A SONG OF THE SONS OF KORAH
ACCOMPANIED BY THE HARP.*

¹How lovely is *Your temple,* Your dwelling place *on earth,*
   O Eternal One, Commander of *heaven's* armies.
²How I long *to be there*—my soul is spent,
   wanting, *waiting to walk in* the courts of the Eternal One.
My whole being sings joyfully.
   to the living God.
³Just as the sparrow seeks her home,
   and the swallow finds in her own nest
   a place to lay her young,
I, too, seek Your altars, my King and my God,
   Commander of *heaven's* armies.
⁴How blessed are those who make Your house their home,
   who live with You;
   they are constantly praising You.

84:title Hebrew, *gittith,* a winepress or a musical instrument from Gath

---

PSALM 84 **"One Day in the Courts of Your Temple."** Not many of us have as our goal in life to be a doorkeeper. The psalmist was one of the sons of Korah who served as porters or doorkeepers in the temple of God. The glorious praise of this psalm comes from one who is used to standing at the entrance to the temple for many days at a time. After years of service we hear the confession of a porter, "Just one day in the courts of Your temple is greater than a thousand anywhere else." This is a confession of fact. The psalmist wouldn't trade anything for being close to God: "I would rather serve as a porter at my God's doorstep than live in luxury in the house of the wicked."

Does this reflect your desire? Do you want to be a porter on God's doorstep? Would you trade a thousand days for just one chance to be close to the God of the universe? If you said "yes," let's see what that might mean.

[pause]*

5Blessed are those who make You their strength,
for they treasure *every step of* the journey [to Zion].*

6On their way through the valley of Baca,
they *stop and* dig wells to collect *the refreshing* spring water,
and the early rains fill the pools.

7They journey from place to place, gaining strength *along the way*;
until they meet God in Zion.

8O Eternal God, Commander of *heaven's* armies, listen to my prayer.
O *please* listen, God of Jacob.

[pause]

9O True God, look at our shield, *our protector,*
see the face of Your anointed *king, and defend our defender.*

10Just one day in the courts of Your temple is greater
than a thousand anywhere else.
I would rather serve as a porter at my God's doorstep
than live *in luxury* in the house of the wicked.

84:4 Literally, selah, likely a musical direction from a Hebrew root meaning "to lift up"
84:5 Hebrew manuscripts omit this portion.

You'd probably spend every moment within earshot of God's voice—always ready to do His bidding. As His servant, you'd greet each visitor at the door. Perhaps, you and they would exchange personal observations and you would lift the weight of some of their burdens. Quite possibly, you would not be invited to the table until all the guests had been seated, and you might wait a good long time before you were actually served, but you would be in the service of the Eternal Lord.

And speaking of those in service of God, "He doesn't deny any good thing to those who live with integrity." Of course, if it's really more important for you to get your way or for you to have a seat up front, you can go to the house of the wicked and receive instant gratification; at least for now.

¹¹For the Eternal God is a sun and a shield.
>   The Eternal grants favor and glory;
>He doesn't deny any good thing
>   to those who live with integrity.
¹²O Eternal One, Commander of *heaven's* armies,
>   how fortunate are those who trust You.

PSALM 85

FOR THE WORSHIP LEADER. A SONG OF THE SONS OF KORAH.

¹O Eternal One, *there was a time when* You were gracious to Your land;
>   You returned Jacob's descendants from their captivity.
²You forgave the iniquity of Your people,
>   covered all of their sins.

[pause]*

³*There was a time when* You restrained all of Your *fierce* wrath,
>   when You cooled Your hot anger.

⁴O God of our salvation, bring us back again—*as You did before*—
>   and put away Your anger toward us.

85:2 Literally, *selah*, likely a musical direction from a Hebrew root meaning "to lift up"

PSALM 85 | **Seeds of Goodness.** This psalm gives us insight into a difficult period for Israel. They have returned from the Babylonian captivity to restore worship in a temple much inferior to what their fathers left. After years of hardship, they are asking if God will always be angry with them. They seek to return to His good graces.

Although our situation is much different from theirs, we also may be concerned that truth, justice, mercy, and peace are out of reach. We sometimes fear that we have so discouraged the exercise of these four characteristics in ourselves that nothing can bring them back again. But as in the reconstruction of Jerusalem, God stands ready.

⁵Will You be mad at us forever?

Will You continue to be angry with our children and theirs?

⁶Will You not bring us back to life once more

so that we, Your people, will find joy *and pleasure* in You?

⁷O Eternal One, show us Your unfailing love;

give us *what we truly need*: Your salvation.

⁸I will hear what the True God—the Eternal One—will say,

for He will speak peace over His people,

peace over those who faithfully follow Him, [but do not let them

abuse His gift and return to foolish ways].*

⁹Without a doubt, His salvation is near for those who revere Him

so that *He will be with us again and all* His glory will fill this land.

¹⁰Unfailing love and truth have met *on their way*;

righteousness and peace have kissed one another.

¹¹Truth will spring from the earth *like a plant,*

and justice will look down from the sky.

¹²Yes, the Eternal One will plant goodness *in the earth,*

and our land will yield great abundance.

¹³Justice will come before Him,

marking out a path, setting a way for His feet.

85:8 Greek manuscripts read "to those who turn to Him in their hearts."

As the psalmist says, "love and truth have met . . . righteousness and peace have kissed . . . truth will spring from the earth . . . justice will look down . . . the Eternal One will plant goodness." The parched ground of our souls can bloom again because God has planted them with the seeds of goodness and abundance. He has enriched the soil and even now sets His feet upon the path.

We who long for God's mercy and want to grow in Him must continue then to plant those seeds, expecting Him to bring in the harvest.

As believers, we can't doubt; His salvation is near, and we must embrace it.

Psalm 86

A prayer of David.

¹O Eternal One, lend an ear *to my prayer* and answer me,
>   for I am weak and wanting.
²Safeguard my soul, for I remain loyal to You.
>   Save me, Your servant, who trusts in You, my God.
³O Lord, please be merciful to me,
>   as all day long I cry out to You.
⁴Bring joy into the life of Your servant,
>   for it's *only* to You, O Lord, that I offer my soul.
⁵O Lord, You are good and ready to forgive;
>   Your loyal love flows generously over all who cry out to You.
⁶O Eternal One, lend an ear and hear my prayer;
>   listen to my pleading voice.
⁷When times of trouble come, I will call to You
>   because *I know* You will respond to me.

⁸O Lord, You stand alone among the other gods;
>   nothing *they have done* compares to Your wonderful works.
⁹O Lord, *all the peoples of earth*—every nation You established—
>   will come to You, bowing low to worship,
>   and rightly honor Your *great* name.
¹⁰For You are great, and Your works are wondrous;
>   You are the one True God.
¹¹O Eternal One, guide me along Your path
>   so that I will live in Your truth.
> Unite my *divided* heart so that I will fear Your *great* name.
¹²O Lord, my God! I praise You with all that I am.
>   I will rightly honor Your *great* name forever.
¹³For Your loyal love for me is so great *it is beyond comparison*.
>   You have rescued my soul from the depths of the grave.

¹⁴O True God, arrogant people are after me.

A violent gang wants to kill me;

they have no interest in You *or Your ways.*

¹⁵But Lord, You are a God full of compassion, generous in grace,

slow to anger, and boundless in loyal love and truth.

¹⁶Look at me, and grant me Your favor.

Invest Your strength in *me,* Your servant,

and rescue *me,* Your handmaiden's child.

¹⁷Give me a sign so I may know Your goodness *rests on me*

and so those who hate me will be *red with* shame at the sight of it.

For You, O Eternal One, have come to my aid and offered me relief.

Psalm 87

A SONG OF THE SONS OF KORAH.

¹He laid His foundation on the sacred mountains.

²The Eternal One loves Zion's gates;

He prefers it over any other place where Jacob's *descendants* make their
homes.

³Spectacular things are said about you,

O *Jerusalem,* city of the True God.

[pause]*

⁴*God says,* "I tell of some who know Me in Egypt* and Babylon;

behold, *My people are in* Philistia, Tyre, and Ethiopia* too:

'This person was born there.'"

⁵It is said of Zion,

"This person and that person were born in her."

The Most High *God* has established that city *and makes her strong.*

87:3 Literally, selah, likely a musical direction from a Hebrew root meaning "to lift up"
87:4 Hebrew, *Rahab,* a poetic reference to Egypt
87:4 Hebrew, *Cush*

⁶When keeping track of His people, the Eternal One surely notices,
"This one was born in Zion."

[pause]

⁷Those who sing and those who dance will say *together,*
"All my fountains *of joy* are in You."

PSALM 88

FOR THE WORSHIP LEADER. A SONG OF THE SONS OF KORAH
ACCOMPANIED BY DANCE.* A CONTEMPLATIVE SONG* OF HEMAN THE
EZRAHITE.

¹O Eternal One! O True God my Savior!
I cry out to You all the time, *under the sun and the moon.*
²Let my voice reach You!
Please listen to my prayers!

³My soul is deeply troubled,
and *my heart can't bear the weight of this sorrow.* I feel so close to
death.
⁴I'm like the *poor and* helpless *who die alone,*
left for dead, as good as the *unknowable sea of* souls lying under our
feet,
⁵⁻⁶Forsaken *by Him* and cut off from His hand,
abandoned among the dead who rest in their graves.
And You have sent me to be forgotten with them,
in the lowest pits *of the earth,*
in the darkest canyons *of the ocean.*
⁷You crush me with Your anger.
You crash against me like the *relentless, angry* sea.

88:title Hebrew, *mahalath leanoth,* meaning is uncertain. Only use of this phrase in the Old Testament.
88:title Hebrew, *maskil*

[pause]*

⁸Those whom I have known, *who have been with me,*
>   You have gathered *like sheaves* and cast *to the four winds.*
They can't bear to look me in the eye, and they are horrified when they think
>   of me.
>   I am in a trap and cannot be free.
⁹My eyes grow dim, weakened by this sickness;
>   *it is taking my strength from me.*
Like a worn cloth, my hands are unfolded before You daily, O Eternal One.
¹⁰Are You the miracle-worker for the dead?
>   Will they rise *from the dark shadows* to worship You again?

[pause]

¹¹Will Your great love be proclaimed in the grave
>   or Your faithfulness *be remembered in whispers like mists* throughout
>   the place of ruin?*
¹²Are Your wonders known in the *dominion of* darkness,
>   or *is* Your righteousness *recognized* in a land where all is forgotten?

¹³But I am calling out to You, Eternal One.
>   My prayers rise before You with every new sun!
¹⁴Why do You turn Your head
>   and brush me aside, O Eternal One? *Why are You avoiding me?*
¹⁵Since the days of my youth, I have been sick and close to death.
>   My *helpless* soul has suffered Your *silent* horrors; now I am desperate.
¹⁶Your rage spills over me *like rivers of fire;*
>   Your assaults have *all but* destroyed me.
¹⁷They surround me like a flood, *rising* throughout the day,
>   closing in from every direction.
¹⁸You have taken from me the one I love and my friend;
>   even *the light of* my acquaintances are darkness.

88:7 Literally, selah, likely a musical direction from a Hebrew root meaning "to lift up"
88:11 Hebrew, *Abaddon*

Psalm 89

A contemplative song* of Ethan the Ezrahite.

¹I will sing of Your unfailing love, Eternal One, forever.
    I will speak of Your faithfulness to all generations.
²I will tell how Your unfailing love will always stand strong;
    and how Your faithfulness is established in the heavens above.
³*You said,* "I have made a covenant with My chosen one.
    I made My servant, David, this promise:
⁴"I will establish your dynasty so that you and your descendants will always
        be secure.
    Your rule will continue for generations to come.'"

[pause]*

⁵Let the heavens *join in* praising the wonderful works of the Eternal.
    The holy ones have gathered, *singing* of Your faithfulness.
⁶For there is no one above who compares to the Eternal,
    not one of heaven's creatures is like Him *in the least*.
⁷In the council of holy ones, God is *lifted high and* feared;
    His presence overwhelms all who are near Him.
⁸O Eternal God, Commander of *heaven's* armies,
    who is mighty like You?
    You are completely faithful; *that's why we trust You.*
⁹The ocean waters are at Your command.
    When *violent* waves rise up, You still them.
¹⁰You defeated Rahab, *that ancient monster of chaos,* and left it lifeless.
    You routed Your enemies and scattered them by Your great arm of
        power.
¹¹Everything in the sky above and the earth below are Yours.
    The world and all it contains are Yours, for You created them all.

89:title Hebrew, *maskil*
89:4 Literally, selah, likely a musical direction from a Hebrew root meaning "to lift up"

¹²Everything was created by You—the north, the south—
>*the mountains of* Tabor and Hermon echo joyously the song of Your name.

¹³Your arm is strong.
>Your grip is powerful. Your right hand is raised up high.

¹⁴Your rule is rooted deeply in justice and righteousness—
>unfailing love and truth lead *from the way* ahead of You.

¹⁵How happy are those who have learned how to praise You;
>those who journey *through life* by the light of Your face.

¹⁶Every hour of the day, they rejoice at *the sound of* Your name.
>They are lifted up *and encouraged* by Your righteousness.

¹⁷For You are the beauty of their strength.
>On account of Your favor, *our strength,* our horn, is increased.

¹⁸For our shield *of protection* comes from the Eternal One,
>and the Holy One of Israel *has given us* our king.

¹⁹Long ago You spoke through a vision to Your faithful followers, saying,
>"I have given help to a warrior;
>I have chosen *a hero* from among My people.

²⁰I have found David, My servant.
>With My holy oil, I have anointed him *king.*

²¹My *strong* hand will stay with him *and sustain him, regardless of trial or foe.*
>My *mighty* arm will be his strength *and shield.*

²²The *deceit of his* enemies will not outwit him.
>the wicked will not defeat him.

²³I will pound his enemies right in front of him.
>I will strike down all those who hate him.

²⁴My faithfulness and unfailing love will never leave him;
>Through My name, strength and power will be his.

²⁵I will extend his rule over the oceans,
>his right hand will control the rivers,
>*and he will rule everything in between.*

²⁶He will cry out to Me, 'You are my Father,
>my God, and the Rock of my salvation!'

²⁷I will make him My firstborn;
>no earthly king shall be greater.

²⁸My unfailing love will always be with him, *protecting him;*
  My covenant with him will never be broken.
²⁹I will ensure his family's future forever;
  his dynasty will last as long as the heavens.
³⁰If his children *turn away from Me and* forsake My law,
  if they refuse to walk according to My judgments,
³¹If they disobey My instructions
  and ignore My commandments,
³²Then I will use the rod to punish their sins
  and stripes to deal with their iniquity.
³³And yet My unfailing love of him will remain steadfast *and strong.*
  I will not be unfaithful to My promise.
³⁴I will not violate My covenant,
  nor will I alter *even one word of* what My lips have spoken.
³⁵*These words* I have pledged in My holiness once *and for all,*
  and I will not lie to David.
³⁶*As long* as the sun *lights the day* before Me, his descendants will continue
    to rule.
  His kingdom will last forever.
³⁷His dynasty will stand firm for all time like the moon,
  the faithful witness *that stands watch* in the night sky."

[pause]

³⁸But *what now?* You have turned Your back and walked away!
  Your full fury burns against Your anointed *king.*
³⁹You made a covenant with Your servant, then renounced it,
  casting his *sacred* crown into the dust.
⁴⁰You have broken down the walls that protected Your servant;
  his defenses are reduced to *a pile of* rubble.
⁴¹Strangers now plunder all that he has left;
  he has become a laughingstock among his neighbors.
⁴²You have made his adversaries strong.
  His enemies celebrate *their victory.*
⁴³You have dulled the blade of his sword,
  and You have not helped him stand *strong* in the battle.

⁴⁴You have brought his *days of* splendor to an *abrupt* end;
> You have toppled his throne; it sits in the dust.
⁴⁵You have cut short the days of his youth
> and have covered him with shame *and despair.*

[pause]

⁴⁶How long *must we endure,* O Eternal One? Will You hide Yourself
> forever?
> How long will Your wrath burn like fire?
⁴⁷Remember my days are numbered.
> Have You created the children of Adam to live futile lives?
⁴⁸Death waits *at the gate;* who can escape and live?
> *Does the grave hold exceptions for any of us?*
> Who can deliver us from the power of the grave?

[pause]

PSALM 89 | **"Who can deliver us?"** This psalm may have come from Ethan, a Levitical musician during the time of David. A central element in the psalm is the promise God made to David that his descendants would rule forever: "I will make him My firstborn; no earthly king shall be greater. . . . His kingdom will last forever." These words have a dual application to David and to Jesus some 1,000 years later. In either case, we learn about the majesty of God and the faithfulness of His promise.

How shall we choose to journey through life? Walking in the garden by the light of God's face or wandering through a wilderness of our own creation, which leads only to darkness? Every good thing has its breath in the Eternal One. From mountain heights to ocean depths, all that we survey was divinely inspired.

Recognizing what God has done both in creation and in bringing Messiah from the Davidic line moves us emotionally. We must awaken to the truth. Only by His light can we see the beauty and the power in all He allows us to enjoy.

Toward the end of this psalm there is a clear messianic reference, "Death waits at the gate, who can escape and live? . . . Who can deliver us from the power of the grave?" God has interwoven His plans through the ages. Only those at the end of the story will experience all of the pieces coming together.

⁴⁹O Lord, where is the unfailing love You showed in times past?
  And where is *the proof of* Your faithfulness to David?
⁵⁰Remember how Your servants are ridiculed, O Lord;
  how I carry within me the insults of so many peoples.
⁵¹Your enemies are mocking me, O Eternal One,
  mocking every step Your anointed one made.

⁵²Praise the Eternal One always. Amen. Amen.

PSALM 90

A PRAYER OF MOSES, A MAN OF GOD.

¹Lord, You have always been our refuge.
  Our ancestors made You their home *long ago.*
²Before mountains were born,
  before You fashioned the earth and filled it with life,
  from ages past to distant futures, You are *truly* God.

³You turn people back to dust,
  saying, "Go back *to the dust,* children of Adam."
⁴For You a thousand years is like a day when it is over,
  a watch during the night,
  there is no difference to You.

⁵⁻⁶You release the waters *of death* to sweep mankind away in his slumber.
  In the morning, we are blades of grass,
 Growing rapidly under the sun but withering quickly;
  yet in the evening, we fade and die, *soon to be cut down.*

⁷For Your anger has consumed us.
  Your wrath *has shaken us to the core*
  and left us deeply troubled.
⁸You have written our offenses before You—
  the light of Your presence shines brightly on our secret sins,
  and we can't run or hide.

[9]For all our days are spent beneath Your wrath;
our youth gives way to old age, and then
one day our years come to an end with a sigh.
[10]We may journey through life for 70 years;
some *may live and breathe* 80 years—if we are strong.
Yet our time here is only toil and trouble;
soon our days are gone, and we fly away.
[11]Who can *truly* comprehend the power unleashed by Your anger?
Your wrath matches the fear that is due to You.
[12]Teach us to number our days
so that we may *truly live and* achieve wisdom.

[13]How long *will we wait here alone*?
Return, O Eternal One, *with mercy.*
Rescue Your servants with compassion.
[14]With every sun's rising, *surprise us* with Your love,
satisfy us with Your kindness.
Then we will sing with joy and celebrate every day we are alive.

PSALM 90 | **Days That Count.** How often children look at the older generations and think they don't want to live into retirement age! As we get older, the lost opportunities pile up, and we wish for more time. From God's perspective, our lifetime is but a brief moment. It is sad to think of all the years we waste being away from the Lord, for only time spent doing the will of God extends like His immortality endlessly into the future.

How many of us have truly learned to number our days? We walk along, day after day, mindlessly letting days slip into weeks and months and scarcely noticing that we've lost precious time we can never retrieve. Numbering our days comes down to looking at each day as unique to itself and making sure that it counts for eternity. The psalmist goes on to say, "so that we may truly live and achieve wisdom." We are told to "celebrate every day" so that God may "bring success to all we do."

God continues to show us infinite kindness. He helps us succeed in our dreams and aspirations and gives us the gift of His presence. As we recognize His patience and long to accomplish His will, we will make each day count by helping others to see His love and kindness lived out in us.

[15]You have spent many days afflicting us with pain and sorrow;
    now match those with years of *unspent* joy.
[16]Let Your work *of love* be on display for all Your servants;
    let Your children see Your majesty.
[17]And then let the *beauty and* grace of the Lord—our God—rest upon us
    and bring success to all we do;
        yes, bring success to all we do!

PSALM 91

[1]He who takes refuge in the shelter of the Most High
    will be *safe* in the shadow of the Almighty.
[2]He will say to the Eternal One, "My shelter, my *mighty* fortress,
    my God, I place *all* my trust in You."
[3]For He will rescue you from the snares set by your enemies *who entrap you*
    and from deadly plagues.
[4]*Like a bird protecting its young,* God will cover you with His feathers,
    will protect you under His *great* wings;
    His faithfulness will form a shield around you, a rock-solid wall *to*
        protect you.
[5]You will not dread the terrors that haunt the night
    or *enemy* arrows that fly in the day
[6]Or the plagues that lurk in darkness
    or the disasters that wreak havoc at noon.

[7]A thousand may fall on your left,
    ten thousand *may die* on your right,
    but these horrors won't come near you.
[8]Only your eyes will witness
    the punishment that awaits the evil,
    but you will not suffer because of it.

[9]For you made the Eternal One [your]* refuge,
    the Most High your only home.

91:9 Hebrew manuscripts read, "who is my."

¹⁰No evil will come to you;
plagues will be turned away at your door.

¹¹He will command His heavenly messengers to guard you,
to keep you safe in every way.
¹²They will hold you up in their hands
so that you will not *crash, or fall, or even* graze your foot on a stone.*
¹³You will walk on the lion and the cobra;
you will trample the lion and the serpent underfoot.

¹⁴"Because he clings to Me in love,
I will rescue him *from harm*;
I will set him above danger.
Because he has known Me by name,
¹⁵He will call on Me, and I will answer.
I'll be with him through hard times;
I'll rescue him and grant him honor.
¹⁶I'll reward him with many *good* years *on this earth*
and let him witness My salvation."

91:11-12 Matthew 4:6; Luke 4:10-11

PSALM 91 | **Protection!** If we watch the news or simply the headlines on the news broadcast, we probably feel anything but safe! We've become an isolated generation, hiding behind computer screens, shopping online, living vicariously so that we don't have to risk our personal safety, and yet this psalm offers a promise to those who step out of the comfort zone.

It would be foolish to say that bad things never happen to believers, but it is also true that only things God can use for good happen to those who are His. Terrible things do come into our lives (the writer lists snares, deadly plagues, disasters, lions, and snakes), but he also says, "heavenly messengers . . . will hold you up in their hands." We are told God knows us by our names and will be with us through "hard times."

Bad things will happen to us, but God will walk through them with us. He will guard and protect us from ruin. He will use the bad for good. We can trust Him for the good.

PSALM 92

¹How good it is to give thanks to the Eternal One
    and to praise Your name with song, O Most High;
²To speak of Your unfailing love in the morning
    and *rehearse* Your faithfulness as night *begins to fall.*
³*How good it is to praise* to the sound of strings—lute and harp—
    the stirring melodies of the lyre.
⁴Because You, O Eternal One, thrill me with the things You have done,
    I will sing with joy in light of Your deeds.

⁵Your works are marvelous, O Eternal One!
    Your thoughts are unfathomable.
⁶But a weak-minded man can't understand this;
    foolish people are unable to see
⁷That evil men sprout like grass
    and wicked men flourish,
  Only so that they will be doomed forever.
⁸But You, O Eternal One, are above all, forever.
⁹As for Your enemies, O Eternal One,
    Their fate is obvious: those who hate You will not survive;
    those who practice evil will be broken *in pieces.*

¹⁰But You have made me strong as a wild ox,
    anointed me with the refreshing oil *of Your blessing.*
¹¹And I have seen with my own eyes my enemies defeated;
    I have heard with my own ears my attackers cut down.

¹²Those who are devoted to God will flourish like *budding* date-palm trees;
    they will grow *strong and tall* like cedars in Lebanon.
¹³Those planted in the house of the Eternal One
    will thrive in the courts of our God.

¹⁴They will bear fruit into old age;
  even in winter, they will be green and full of sap
¹⁵To display that the Eternal One is righteous.
    He is my rock, and there is no *shadow of* evil in Him.

PSALM 93

¹The Eternal One reigns, clothed in majesty;
    He is dressed *in power*; He has surrounded Himself with strength.
He has established the world, and it will never be toppled.
²Your throne was established from the beginning of the world, *O God,*
    and You are everlasting.

PSALM 93 | **Hope in Our Unchanging God.** The Hebrew word *Yahweh* is normally translated in English as "LORD." Literally, it means "One Who Is Eternal." Thus, it appears here as "the Eternal One." Now we have a hard time with "eternal." In a world of diminishing resources, tentative relationships, and fast food chains, it is difficult for us to realize what it means for something to be everlasting. As we age, we begin to understand that life is finite, but can we ever grasp the Infinite? The One who is everlasting can never be surprised or toppled, even perhaps in spite of what humanity might do. What we do seems so insignificant in comparison.

Truth from One who is constant in the way the Eternal One is (He is the same yesterday, today, and forever) can never be relative and can never evolve. Such truth simply is. Because our understanding of things is often less than true, only in light of God's perspective can we understand the fullness about the truth of anything. Here the psalmist says, "Your teachings are true; Your decrees are sure." They never change.

Our God's strength endures and His power is absolute. He is firmly established. Therefore, worldly change cannot overwhelm us because worldly change is tentative. The Eternal One who does not change gives us hope, for in Him we have life everlasting!

³The waters have risen, O Eternal One;
    the sound of pounding waves *is deafening.*
    The waters have roared *with power.*
⁴More powerful than the thunder of mighty rivers,
    more powerful than the mighty waves in the ocean
    is the Eternal One on high!

⁵*Your teachings are true;* Your decrees sure.
    Sacredness adorns Your house,
    O Eternal One, forevermore.

PSALM 94

¹O Eternal God of vengeance,
    O God who sets things right, shine upon us.
²Rise, O Judge *who presides* over the earth,
    and *pronounce Your sentence* upon the proud.
    Give them what they deserve!
³How long, O Eternal One, how long
    will the guilty revel *in their prosperity*?

⁴Arrogance pours from their mouths;
    all these troublemakers brag *of their exploits.*
⁵They have broken Your people to pieces, O Eternal One,
    and brought ruin to Your future generations.
⁶They slay a widow, kill a newcomer,
    and murder an orphan.
⁷Then they say, "The Eternal One can't see *what we're up to*;
    the God of Jacob's people pays no attention *to us.*"

⁸Think, brainless people;
    stupid people, when will you get it?
⁹Does the God who set the ear *in its place* not hear?
    Does the God who made the eye not see?

¹⁰Does the God who teaches the nations
     and guides humanity to knowledge,
     not exercise *just* correction?
¹¹The Eternal One knows the *highest* thoughts of the wise,
     and they are worthless.*

¹²How fortunate are those You discipline, O Eternal One,
     those You train by Your *divine* law;
¹³You relieve them in times of distress,
     until a grave is dug for evildoers.
¹⁴The Eternal One will not abandon His people;
     He will not turn away from those He redeemed
¹⁵Because justice is coming for those who do what is right
     and all the good-hearted will pursue it.

¹⁶Who will back me up when evildoers come against me?
     Who is willing to take my side against the wicked?
¹⁷If the Eternal One had not come to my rescue,
     my soul would have descended to the land where *death* silences
          every voice.
¹⁸When I said, "My foot is slipping!"
     Your unfailing love, O Eternal One, held me up.
¹⁹When anxiety overtakes me *and worries are many,*
     Your comfort lightens my soul.
²⁰Can wicked tyrants be Your allies?
     Will You align with rulers who create havoc with *unjust* decrees?
²¹They have joined forces against the life of the just-living, *the right-seeking,*
     and have sentenced the innocent to death.
²²But the Eternal One has been my citadel;
     my God, a sure safe haven.
²³He will fold their wickedness back upon them,
     and because they are malicious, He will silence them.
     The Eternal One, our True God, will scatter them.

94:11 1 Corinthians 3:20

PSALM 95

¹Come, let us worship in song, *a joyful offering* to the Eternal One.
  Shout. Shout with joy to the rock of our liberation.
²Come face-to-face with God, and give thanks;
  with loud and joyful voices, praise Him in songs.
³For the Eternal One is a great God,
  and a great King, *supreme* over all gods.
⁴Within His control are the very depths of the earth;
  the mountaintops too—they all belong to Him.
⁵The sea belongs to Him, for He created it—*scooped and filled* it—
  with His hands He made the dry land—*every valley and mountain.*

⁶Come, let us worship Him. *Everyone* bow down;
  kneel before the Eternal One who made us.
⁷For He is our God
  and we are His people, *the flock* of His pasture,
  His sheep *protected and nurtured* by His hand.

Today, if He speaks, hear His voice.
  ⁸"Don't harden your hearts the way they did in the bitter uprising *at Meribah*
    or like that day they complained in the wilderness *of Massah.*
⁹Your ancestors tested Me,
  wanted Me to prove Myself though they had seen *that nothing was too great for Me.*
¹⁰For 40 years I despised that *grumbling* generation
  and said, 'Their hearts are unfaithful;
  they no longer walk in My ways; *though I call, they do not listen to My voice.'*
¹¹That is why in My anger I swore,
  'They will never enter into My rest.'"

PSALM 96

¹Sing a new song to the Eternal One;

Sing *in one voice* to the Eternal, all the earth.

²Sing to the Eternal *of all the good things He's done.*

Bless His name;

broadcast the good news of His salvation each and every day.

³Enlighten the nations to His splendor;

describe His wondrous acts to all people.

⁴For the Eternal One is great *indeed* and praiseworthy;

feared *and reverenced* above all gods, the True God shall be.

⁵For all human-made, *lifeless* gods are *worthless* idols,

but the Eternal plotted the *vast* heavens, *shaped every last detail.*

⁶Honor and majesty precede Him;

strength and beauty infuse His *holy* sanctuary.

PSALM 96 | **Credit Where Credit Is Due.** How seldom we think about our chief purpose: to glorify God. He chose Israel out of all peoples and then grafted the Gentiles into the church for a special role in His plan. This psalm tells us to "sing a new song . . . broadcast the good news . . . enlighten the nations . . . describe His wondrous acts . . . give all the credit . . . credit Him . . . shout out to the nations . . . let the heavens resound." Our worship should be a testimony shouting out the wonders of our God.

If we count our blessings, crediting God for each and every amazing thing He has done in our lives, most of us would never run out of things to count. Even those of us who feel we have more than our share of sorrows might recognize that the scales are weighted highly in our favor as we add up the positive things God has done.

Today, we don't think about taking a sacrifice to God's altar to show Him that we revere Him. Indeed, we look upon sacrifice as something we have to bear rather than as something we joyfully put before God in gratitude for His kindness.

As we look at our lives today, we may add it all up again and give the credit to the One who makes each day possible, who gave us the gifts to serve as we do. All honor and glory are His!

⁷Give all credit to the Eternal One, families of the world!
 Credit Him with glory, *honor,* and strength!
⁸Credit Him with the glory *worthy* of His *magnificent* name;
 gather your sacrifice, and present it at His temple.
⁹Bow down to the Eternal, adorned in holiness;
 lay awestruck before Him, trembling, all *people of* the earth.

¹⁰Shout out to the nations, "The Eternal reigns!
 Yes, indeed, the world is anchored and will not shake loose.
 He governs all people with a fair hand."
¹¹And so, let the heavens resound in gladness! Let joy be the earth's rhythm
 as the sea and all its creatures roar.
 ¹²Let the fields *grow in* triumph, *a grand jubilee* for all that live there.
Let all the trees of the forest *dig in and* reach high with songs of joy
 ¹³before the Eternal One, for He is on His way.
 Yes, He is coming to judge the earth.
He will set the world right by His standards,
 and by His faithfulness, *He will examine* the people.

PSALM 97

¹The Eternal One reigns *powerful over all*; let the earth sing with joy;
 let the *distant* islands celebrate.
²Clouds and deep darkness encircle Him;
 righteousness and justice are the bedrock of His rule.
³Fire precedes Him;
 it burns away His opponents on all sides.
⁴With His lightning *flashing about,* He illuminates the world;
 the earth watches and trembles.
⁵Like wax *before the flame,* mountains melt when the Eternal One appears,
 the Master of the whole earth.

⁶The heavens display His *order and perfect* justice;
    all peoples witness His magnificence.
⁷Those who worship idols,
    who boast in the impotent creations of human hands, will be shamed.
    Worship Him, all you gods.
⁸Zion heard and was glad,
    and the daughters of Judah celebrated
    because they saw Your justice, O Eternal One.
⁹For You are the Eternal One, the Most High, over the entire world;
    You far exceed all gods.

¹⁰Hate evil, you lovers of the Eternal One.
    He protects the souls of those who follow Him;
    He rescues them from the devices of the wicked.
¹¹Light is sown in the just;
    as it grows, it brings joy to the pure of heart.
¹²Celebrate the Eternal God, *all you who are* faithful;
    offer thanks to His holy name.

PSALM 98

A SONG.

¹*Compose* a new song, and sing it to the Eternal One
    because of the unbelievable things He has done;
He has won the victory
    with *the skill of* His right hand and *strength of* His holy arm.
²The Eternal One has made it clear that He saves,
    and He has shown the nations that He does what is right.
³He has been true to His promises; *fresh in His mind* is His unfailing love
    for all of Israel.
Even the ends of the earth have witnessed how our God saves.

⁴Raise your voices; make a beautiful noise to the Eternal One, all the earth.
   Let your joy explode into song and praise;
⁵Make music to the Eternal One with the harp;
   sing a *beautiful* melody with the harp *and chorus.*
⁶With trumpets and horns,
   fill the air with joyful sounds to the King, the Eternal One.

⁷Let the sea *rumble and* roar, and all *the creatures* it holds *shout praise*;
   let the *whole* world and all those who live in it *join the celebration.*
⁸Let the rivers applaud
   and the mountains join in joyful song
⁹In the presence of the Eternal One because He is coming
   to judge the earth.
He is coming, and His judgment will be what is right for the world
   and just to all people.

PSALM 98 | **The Ultimate Celebration.** Have you ever experienced a monster celebration like happens when a school wins a major championship after years of losing, victory is declared in a war, or members of royalty are married? Such an event can be truly exciting. When Jesus entered Jerusalem at the beginning of the Passion Week, there was celebration, but nothing like it will take place when all the earth worships God and the Lamb at the end of this age. The psalmist says, "explode into song and praise." Our worship now is intended to look forward to that great day when the "sea rumble[s]" and "all the creatures . . . shout praise"—when even the "rivers applaud" and the "mountains join in joyful song."

Imagine the celebration as it ripples through the oceans and the mountains with the very trees clapping for joy at the coming of the Liberator, the true Creator of all living things. God invites us to join along! To raise our voices, to sing out loud, to play any handy instrument, and shout for joy at His coming, for His love will set all the captives free and cause the earth to tremble. Think of this as if all celebrations of all time happened at the same moment. Now, when we worship our King, that is what we are preparing for.

Psalm 99

¹The Eternal One is king *ruling over the universe*; let all people shake *in fear*.
>He sits on His throne, settled between winged guardians;* let the
>>planet tremble.

²The Eternal One is great in *the hearts of His people*; *He has made* Zion *His
>>sacred mountain,*
>and He reigns *majestic* over all people.

³Let them express praise *and gratitude* to Your amazing and awesome
>>name—
>because He is holy, *perfect and exalted in His power.*

⁴The King who rules with strength also treasures justice.
>You *created order and* established what is right.
You have carried out justice
>and done what is right to *the people of* Jacob.

⁵Lift up the Eternal One our God *in your heart*;
>bow down *to the earth* where He rests His feet.
>He is holy, *perfect and exalted in His power.*

⁶Moses and Aaron were two of His priests;
>Samuel was among those who called out to Him.
>They asked the Eternal One *for help,* and He answered them.

⁷He answered them from a column of cloud;
>they heeded His testimonies
>and *lived by* the laws He gave them.

⁸You answered them, Eternal One, our God;
>You were, to them, a God who forgives, yet You *did not ignore* what
>>they did wrong
>and punished them *fairly as well.*

⁹Lift up the Eternal One, our God, *in your hearts,*
>and celebrate His goodness at His holy mountain,
>for the Eternal One, our God, is holy, *perfect and exalted in His power.*

99:1 Literally, cherubim

PSALM 100

[1]Raise your voices; make a beautiful noise to the Eternal One, all the earth.
[2]Serve the Eternal One gladly;

enter into His presence singing songs of joy!

[3]Know this: the Eternal One Himself is the True God.

He is the One who made us; we have not made ourselves;

we are His people, like sheep *grazing* in His fields.

[4]Go through His gates, giving thanks;

walk through His courts, giving praise.

Offer Him your gratitude and praise His *holy* name.

[5]Because the Eternal One is good,

His loyal love *and mercy* will never end

and His truth will last throughout all generations.

PSALM 100 **It is just too hard** for us to understand the enormity of God. All of His characteristics are perfection and beyond anything we can imagine. So how are we to bless Him in return for the blessings He gives us? One clear statement in this psalm should cause all of us to pause, "Know this: the Eternal One Himself is the True God." Every other religion, ideal, political system, celebrity—whatever we substitute for God—is nothing compared to Him. He is the only True God. All others are fake and worthless next to Him. His love is loyal and unending, and His truth will last beyond everything every generation ever does. Now, with that in mind, pay careful attention.

We must celebrate the perfections of God with all that we have. We need to celebrate His love that is greater than any love we will ever experience elsewhere. We need to glorify His truth that is more pure and just than any ideal ever devised. When we worship our God, let our spirits soar with awe and appreciation. God is good to the extreme.

PSALM 101

A SONG OF DAVID.

¹I will sing of *God's unsparing* love and justice;
  to You, O Eternal One, I will sing praises.
²I will seek to live a life of integrity;
  when will You come to me?

I will walk in my house
  with an honest and true heart.
³I will refuse to look
  on any sordid thing;

I detest the *worthless* deeds of those who stray;
  evil will not get a hold on me.
⁴I will rid my heart of all perversion;
  I will not flirt with any evil.

PSALM 101 **Walking in integrity** presents a challenge. It requires choosing to embrace it. As a part of his worship, David promises to God to live a life of integrity. He will desire honesty, uprightness, and goodness with his whole heart. David shares his intentions toward this virtue, starting in his own house, pledging to turn his back on any kind of evil.

Just think how life could be if all our thoughts and conversations were wholesome and loving toward those who share a space with us. But how can we have honest hearts like David describes and still look at suggestive TV shows or at sordid content on the Internet? No doubt, constant contact with evil numbs us to its effects. That's why David says, "I will rid my heart of all perversion."

If walking with integrity has something to do with adhering to a moral code or being aboveboard in all that we do, then we do well to take this psalm to heart, and so honor God. Integrity starts at home. David says the wicked ones will not be welcome in his house.

⁵Whoever secretly slanders his neighbor,
>   I will silence;
> I will not tolerate
>   a condescending smirk, an arrogant heart.
⁶I will look for those who are loyal in the land
>   so that they may live with me *and know my pleasure.*
> Whoever walks with integrity
>   will enter my service.

⁷The one who makes a habit of deceit
>   will not be welcome in my house;
> The one who lies
>   will not remain in my presence for long.

⁸Every morning I will purge
>   all the wicked from the land
> So as to rid the city of the Eternal One
>   of those who practice evil.

PSALM 102

A PRAYER OF THE WEAK AND OPPRESSED, WHEN HE TURNS HIS
COMPLAINTS TO THE ETERNAL ONE.

¹*Hear me,* O Eternal One, hear my prayer!
>   Hear my *lonely desperate* cry for help.
²Do not hide from me
>   when my days *are filled* with anguish;
> Lend Your ear to my wailing,
>   and answer me quickly when I call.

³For my days *come and go,* vanishing like smoke,
>   and my bones are charred like *bricks of* a hearth.
⁴My heart is beaten down like grass withered *and scorched in the summer
>   heat*;
>   I can't even remember to eat.

⁵*My body is shaken* by my groans;
   my bones cling to my skin, *holding on for dear life.*
⁶I am like a *solitary* owl in the wilderness;
   I am a *lost and lonely screech* owl *at home* in the rubble.
⁷*I stare at the ceiling,* awake in my bed;
   I am alone, a *defenseless* sparrow perched on a roof.
⁸All day long my enemies chide me;
   those who mock me spit out my name as a curse.
⁹For ashes have become my bread;
   my tears fall into my drink
¹⁰Because of the depth of Your wrath.
   You have brought me up and then hurled me aside.
¹¹My days go by like a long shadow—*stretched thin and disappearing*—
   I shrivel up like grass *baked in the hot sun.*

PSALM 102 | **End of the Rope.** There seem to be two different psalms here. The first 11 verses are about the long slide to depression, while the second half is about the very character of God and its effect on the discouraged believer.

Desperation is fueled by loneliness. It's a feeling that no matter how loudly we shout, how sad and wasted we become, that nobody is really listening—not even God! In this state, we feel like we're slowly disappearing and no one will even know when we're gone. The psalmist cries out in anguish and wails for God's attention. His days are disappearing without any sign of his having been here.

This psalm smacks at the heart of that soulful, heart-wrenching feeling. Pleading night and day to be heard leaves us beaten down and weary. Even the knot at the end of our rope gives way and we can barely hold on. The psalmist's bones are dry and worn out; his heart is beaten down.

Distrust is the culprit when we can't eat, are getting bony, and are simply clinging to dear life. In stark contrast to the paranoia and fear of one who is disillusioned, we have God who is the same yesterday, today, and forever and who must be trusted, must be believed, and must be sought with our whole heart. Only then can He lead us out of the way of quiet desperation. God is the solid rock and the source of our recovery. The psalm ends with a promise, "The children of those who serve You will enjoy a good, long life."

¹²But You, O Eternal One, remain forever,
    and Your name endures to all generations.
¹³You will rise up *once again* and remember Your love for Zion;
    it is time to have mercy on Your city;
    yes, it is the *divinely* appointed time.
¹⁴Your *faithful* servants take pleasure in her *every* stone;
    they *even* delight in the dust *of her streets.*
¹⁵*Days are coming when* nations will tremble at the name of the Eternal One;
    all the rulers of the earth *will bow down to* Your glory.
¹⁶For the Eternal One will *return to* rebuild *His city,* Zion;
    He will be seen in His splendor.
¹⁷He will listen to the prayer of the impoverished
    and welcome their prayers.

¹⁸Let this record be kept for posterity
    so that people not yet born may praise the Eternal One.
¹⁹*Tell them that* He looked down from holy heights, *His heavenly sanctuary;*
    the Eternal One looked down from heaven and closely watched the
        earth,
²⁰Hearing the prisoners' groans—
    releasing those awaiting execution—
²¹That the name of the Eternal One would resound in Zion,
    and His praise would be proclaimed in Jerusalem
²²When the peoples gather
    and the nations' *leaders assemble* to worship the Eternal One.

²³Along my way He has sapped my strength;
    He has shortened my days *here on earth.*
²⁴I said, "O my True God, don't take me away
    in the middle of my life;
 Unlike me, Your years continually unfold
    throughout all generations."

²⁵In the beginning, You laid the foundation of the earth
    and set the skies above us with Your own hands.
²⁶But *while* they will someday pass away, You remain *forever;*
    When they wear out like old clothes,

You will *roll them up and* change them into something new, and they will
pass away.

²⁷But You are the same, *You will never change;* Your years will never
come to an end.*

²⁸The children of those who serve You will enjoy a *good,* long life;
their offspring will stand strong before You.

Psalm 103

A song of David.

¹O my soul, *come,* praise the Eternal One
with all that is in me—*body, emotions, mind, and will—every part of
who I am—*
Praise His holy name.
²O my soul, *come,* praise the Eternal One;
sing a song from a grateful heart;
sing and never forget all the good He has done.
³Despite all your *many* offenses, He forgives *and releases you.*
More than any doctor, He heals your diseases.
⁴He reaches *deep* into the pit to deliver you from death.
He crowns you with unfailing love and compassion *like a king.*
⁵*When your soul is famished and withering,*
He fills you with good *and beautiful* things, satisfying you as long as
you live.
He makes you *strong* like an eagle, restoring your youth.

⁶When people are crushed, *wronged, enslaved, raped, murdered,*
the Eternal One is just; He makes the wrongs right.
⁷He showed Moses His ways;
He allowed His people Israel to see His *wonders and* acts *of power.*
⁸The Eternal One is compassionate and merciful.
When we cross all the lines, He is patient *with us.*

102:25-27 Hebrews 1:10-12

When we struggle against Him, He lovingly stays with us—
 changing, convicting, prodding;
⁹He will not constantly criticize,
 nor will He hold a grudge forever.
¹⁰*Thankfully,* God does not punish us for our sins and depravity as we
 deserve.
 In His mercy, He tempers justice with peace.
¹¹*Measure* how high heaven is above the earth;
 God's *wide,* loving, kind heart is greater for those who revere Him.
¹²*You see,* God takes *all* our crimes—*our seemingly inexhaustible sins*—and
 removes them.
 As far as east is from the west, *He removes them* from us.
¹³An *earthly* father expresses love for his children;
 it is no different *with our heavenly Father;*
The Eternal One shows His love for those who revere Him.
¹⁴For He knows what we are made of;
 He knows our frame is frail, and He remembers we came from dust.

PSALM 103 | **Sometimes we need a "do-over."** Our bad choices, our selfish behaviors, our craziness needs to be stopped, and new choices need to be made. Good news! We are so fortunate that God doesn't judge quickly. He is more interested in restoration than in punishment. That's why the God of the universe allows us another opportunity. He watches our stupidity, waits for us to recognize it, and then He reaches down into the pit where we find ourselves and delivers us. He puts us back on to the path. Why? . . . because He's compassionate and merciful and wants us to discover His truth. What a great mentor, teacher, counselor in that He "lovingly stays with us," not criticizing nor holding a grudge!

God's desire is that we strive to be more like Him. Admitting and turning away from our weakness helps us see Him more clearly. It frees Him to remove far away from us the debris and devastation of life, and even more importantly, to move those things far away from Him. Having all our crimes moved as far as the east is from the west gives us room to grow and try again. God's unfailing love is forever, and He offers to guide us through the temptations we face until we are able to stand on our own.

¹⁵The children of Adam are like grass; their days *are few*;
　　they flourish for a time like flowers in a meadow.
　　　It is a beautiful thing that quickly passes.
¹⁶As the wind blows over the field and bloom is gone,
　　it doesn't take much to blow us out of the memory of that place.
¹⁷But the unfailing love of the Eternal One is always and eternal
　　for those who reverently run after Him.
　　He extends His justice *on and on* to future generations,
¹⁸To those who will keep His bond of love
　　and remember to walk in the guidance of His commands.

¹⁹The Eternal One has established His throne up in the heavens.
　　He rules over every seen and unseen realm and creature.
²⁰Adore the Eternal One! *Give Him praise,* you heavenly messengers,
　　you powerful *creatures who listen to*
　　and act on His every word.
²¹Give praise to the Eternal One, all armies *of heaven*—
　　you servants who stand ready to do His will.
²²Give praise to the Eternal One, all that He has made
　　in all corners of His creation.
O my soul, *come,* praise the Eternal One!

PSALM 104

¹Call Him good, my soul, *and praise* the Eternal One.
　　I am here to declare my affection for You, Eternal One, my God, You
　　　are indeed great—
You who are wrapped in glory and dressed in greatness.
　　²For covering, You choose light—Your clothes, *sunset and moonrise.*
For a tent, You stretch out the heavens; *for Your roof, You pitch the sky.*
　　³Your upper chamber is built on beams that lie in the waters overhead,
And the clouds, Your chariot;
　　You are held aloft by the wind.

⁴You make Your messengers like the winds;
the breeze whispers Your words,
Your servants are like the fire and flame.

⁵You made the earth,
and You made its frame stable forever.
Never will it be shaken.
⁶You wrapped it in a gown of waters—
ancient mountains under layers of sky.
⁷But when You reprimanded those waters, they fled;
the thunder of Your voice sent them running away.
⁸⁻⁹They hammered out new depths, heaved up new heights,
and swallowed up whatever You commanded.
At first, they covered the earth,
but now You have bound them,
and they know their appointed place.

¹⁰You send *fresh* streams that spring up in the valleys,
in the cracks between hills.
¹¹Every animal of the *open* field makes its journey there for drink:
wild donkeys lap *at the brooks' edges.*
¹²Birds build their nests by the streams,
singing among the branches.
¹³*And the clouds, too, drink up their share,*
raining it back down on the mountains from the upper reaches of
Your home,
Sustaining the whole earth with what comes from You.
And the earth is satisfied.

PSALM 104 | **We're living on a dying planet,** according to most scientists. In other words, it won't be able to sustain life indefinitely. Then there are those who say anyone who speaks out for ecological issues is misguided and weak. Obviously, they have never read Psalm 104.

This psalm celebrates the wondrous planet we are privileged to share. Its writer is beside himself in praise for the heavens, wind, waters, mountains, and

¹⁴⁻¹⁵Thus You grow grain for bread, *grapes for wine,* grass for cattle.
>All of this for us.
And so we have bread to make our bodies strong,
>wine to make our hearts happy,
Oil to make our faces shine.
>Every good thing we need, Your earth provides;
>*our faces grow flush with Your life in them.*
¹⁶The forests are Yours, Eternal One—*stout hardwoods* watered deeply,
>*swollen with sap—*
>like the *great* cedars of Lebanon You planted,
¹⁷Where *many* birds nest.
>There are fir trees for storks,
¹⁸High hills for wild goats,
>stony cliffs for rock badgers.
For each place, a resident,
>*and for each resident, a home.*
¹⁹The moon *strides through her phases,* marking seasons as she goes.
>The sun hides at his appointed time,
²⁰And with the darkness You bring, so comes night—
>when the prowling animals of the forest move about.
²¹*It is then that* lions seek the food You, the True God, give them,
>roaring after their prey.
²²At sunrise, they disappear
>and sleep *away the day* in their dens.

---

streams that God made from scratch. This is not a recycled earth. Everything is a creative masterpiece.

The reality is that an honest believer can't fail to recognize the grandeur of the creation show. No matter what your political agenda, the glory of creation demonstrates the greatness of our God. "There is so much here, O Eternal One, so much You have made."

²³*Meanwhile,* the people take *to the fields and to the shops and to the roads,*
>   to all the places that people work, until evening *when they rest.*

²⁴There is so much here, O Eternal One, so much You have made.
>   By the wise way in which You create,
>   *riches and* creatures fill the earth.
²⁵*Of course,* the sea is vast and stretches *like the heavens beyond view,*
>   and numberless creatures inhabit her.
>   From the tiny to the great, they swarm beneath her waves.
²⁶Our ships skim her surface
>   while the monsters of the sea play beneath.

²⁷And all of these look to You
>   to give them food when the time is right.
²⁸When You feed, they gather what You supply.
>   When You open Your hand, they are filled with good *food.*
²⁹When You withdraw Your presence, they are dismayed.
>   When You revoke their breath, the life goes out of them,
>   and they become, again, the dust *of the earth from which You formed*
>   *them at the start.*
³⁰When You send out Your breath, life is created,
>   and the face of the earth *is made beautiful* and is renewed.

³¹May the glorious presence of the Eternal One linger *among us* forever.
>   And may He rejoice in *the greatness of* His own works—
³²He, who rattles the earth with a glance;
>   He, who sets mountains to smoking with a touch.
³³I will sing to the Eternal One all of my life;
>   I will call my God good as long as I live.
³⁴May the thoughts of my mind be pleasing to Him,
>   for the Eternal One has become my happiness.
³⁵But may those who hate Him, who act against Him,
>   disappear from *the face of* this *beautiful* planet.
> As for the Eternal One, call Him good, my soul.
> [Praise the Eternal One!]*

104:35 Greek manuscripts place this portion before Psalm 105.

PSALM 105

¹*Come,* offer thanks to the Eternal One; invoke His *holy* name.
   Tell other people about the things He has done.
²Sing songs of praise to Him;
   tell *stories* of all His miracles.
³Revel in His holy name.
   May the hearts of the people who seek the Eternal One celebrate and
      experience *great* joy.
⁴Seek the Eternal One and His power;
   look to His face constantly.
⁵Remember the wonderful things He has done,
   His miracles and the wise decisions He has made,
⁶O children of Abraham, His servant;
   O children of Jacob, His chosen people!

⁷He is the Eternal One, our True God;
   His justice extends to every corner of the earth.
⁸He keeps His covenant *promises* forever
   and remembers the word He spoke to a thousand generations—
⁹The covenant He made with Abraham
   and His *sworn* oath to Isaac, *his son.*
¹⁰Then God confirmed it to Jacob—decreed it so—
   to Israel He promised a never-ending covenant,
¹¹Saying, "I will give you the land of Canaan
   as your part; it will be your inheritance."

¹²When *God's* people were only a few in number—
   indeed, very few—they were strangers in a foreign land.
¹³They roamed from place to place,
   from one kingdom to another.
¹⁴God didn't allow anyone to tyrannize them;
   He rebuked kings in order to protect His people:
¹⁵"Do not lay a hand on My anointed people;
   do not do any harm to My prophets."

¹⁶He ordered famine to grip the land and
    cut them off from their supply of bread.
¹⁷*But long before,* He had sent a man ahead of them:
    Joseph, who had been sold into slavery.*
¹⁸*At first,* his masters shackled his feet with chains,
    placed his neck into a collar of iron.
¹⁹That was until the Eternal One's promises came to pass;
    His word tested Joseph *and proved him worthy.*
²⁰The king sent *out the order* to release him *from prison*;
    the ruler *of Egypt* liberated him *from the chains.*
²¹Then he put Joseph in charge of the *royal* household,
    made him ruler of all the royal possessions,
²²*Allowed him* to imprison the royal officials whenever he saw fit
    and impart wisdom to the elders *in the land.*

²³Then, *when the time was right,* Israel also went to Egypt;*
    Jacob resided as an alien in the land of Ham.
²⁴And *while they were there,* the Eternal One made His people prosperous;
    He made them stronger than their enemies.
²⁵He turned the Egyptians' hearts against His people
    to cheat and scheme against His servants.

²⁶Then, He sent His servant Moses
    and Aaron, the men He had chosen.
²⁷They did all the signs He planned for them to do among the Egyptians,
    and they performed miracles in the land of Ham.
²⁸He sent darkness to cover the land;
    they did not stray from His word.
²⁹At His command, their waters turned to blood;
    their fish began to die.
³⁰Throngs of frogs covered the land,
    invading even in the chambers of their kings.
³¹At His command, a swarm of flies arrived,
    and gnats came over all their land.

105:17 Genesis 37; 39–50
105:23 Exodus 1–15

³²He caused hail to fall instead of rain;
  lightning flashed over all their land.
³³He struck their vines and their fig trees;
  He destroyed the trees over all their land.
³⁴At His command, locusts came;
  young locusts *marched* beyond number,
³⁵And they ate up all the plants that grew
  and all the fruits over their land.
³⁶He also brought death to the firstborn in all their land,
  the first offspring of each man.

³⁷Then He brought His people out *of slavery, weighed down* with silver and
    gold;
  and of all His tribes, not one of them stumbled,
  not one was left behind.
³⁸Egypt was glad to see them go,
  for Pharaoh's people had been overcome with fear of them.
³⁹He spread out a cloud to cover *His people*
  and sent a fire to light *their way* at night.
⁴⁰They asked, and He sent them *coveys of* quail,
  satisfying their hunger with the food of heaven.
⁴¹He split the rock and water poured out;
  it flowed like a river through the desert.
⁴²For He remembered His holy covenant
  with Abraham, His servant.

⁴³That's why He rescued His people joyously
  and why His chosen ones celebrated with shouts and singing.
⁴⁴*When the time was right,* He gave them land from other nations
  so that they might possess the works of their hands,
⁴⁵So that they would be able to keep His commands
  and obey His laws.
  Praise the Eternal One!

¹Praise the Eternal One!
>   Thank Him because He is good
>   and His loyal love will never end.
²Who could *find words to* tell of the Eternal One's mighty deeds
>   or give Him all the praise *He deserves*?
³Blessed are those who work for justice,
>   who always do *what they know to be* right!

⁴Remember me, O Eternal One, when You show kindness to Your people;
>   don't forget me when You are saving them.
⁵That way I can know how good it is to be Your chosen people;
>   that way I can celebrate the joy of Your nation;
>   that way I can join those who belong to You in *unending* praise.

⁶Like our ancestors, we have sinned;
>   we have done wicked things.
⁷When our ancestors were leaving Egypt,
>   they did not consider Your marvelous acts.
> They forgot Your overwhelming kindness to them
>   and instead rebelled at the Red Sea.*
⁸Nevertheless, God saved them for the honor of His name
>   so He could show His power *to the world*.
⁹He gave the order, and *the waters of* the Red Sea* dried up,
>   and He led the people across the sea floor as though it were the
>   wilderness.
¹⁰That's how He liberated them from their enemies
>   and rescued them from the hand of their oppressors.
¹¹*After that* the sea *surged and* covered their foes,
>   and every one of them drowned *in its waters*.
¹²When God's people *saw what He did,* they believed what He said
>   and they sang praises to Him.

106:7 Literally, Sea of Reeds
106:9 Literally, Sea of Reeds

¹³But it didn't take long for them to forget what He had done.

They moved on without waiting for His instructions,
¹⁴So our ancestors became very hungry in the wilderness

and the rabble grumbled and complained, testing God's patience in the
desert.
¹⁵Although He granted their request,

He *also* sent a disease that caused them to waste away.

¹⁶While they were camped *in the desert,* some began to be jealous of Moses
and Aaron, the holy priest of the Eternal One.
¹⁷The earth opened up, and *a deep fissure* swallowed Dathan
and buried Abiram's group.

PSALM 106 | **Trust!** If you put your level of trust in God, in another human being, and in yourself on some scale, how would the meter read? In whom do you really trust? The history of Israel is one very long list of wonderfully kind acts of God followed by immediate rejoicing of the people followed by sudden amnesia followed by disbelief. Even after God's people had been safely gathered beyond the Red Sea, eaten quail and manna in the wilderness, and witnessed God's glorious provision, they still abandoned their trust in Him. At the place where they should have triumphantly passed over the finish line into the promised land, they quit. They forgot the God of their hearts and their experience.

If you only trust God as far as you can see Him, pray for greater vision so that you won't fall right at the finish line. Don't let the things of this world trip you up; instead, trust God and God alone. Just look at the two opposites in this psalm: One describes the long history of God's unbroken chain of mercies, and the other gives the parallel history of Israel's unbroken chain of forgetfulness and rebellion. The psalmist confesses a continuing state of disloyalty for the entire nation and closes with a plea for God to bring His people back together from their long exile of being scattered throughout the surrounding nations.

This psalm is also a picture of the individual believer who is overcome with doubt and then wanders far away from communion with God. We each must confess our own doubt and rebellion, recognizing the unfailing love of our God. "Save us, O Eternal One our God, and gather us who are scattered among all the nations."

¹⁸A blaze ignited where they were gathered;
    the fire consumed the wicked *mob*.

¹⁹The people made a *golden* calf in Horeb
    and bowed to worship an image they had made.
²⁰They traded the glory *of God*
    for the likeness of an ox that eats grass.
²¹They forgot about God, their True Savior,
    who had done great things *for them* in Egypt—
²²Miracles in the land of Ham
    and amazing deeds at the Red Sea.*
²³Therefore, He declared *in His anger* that He would wipe them away.
    If Moses, His chosen one,
  Had not pleaded *for the people*,
    His anger would have destroyed them.

²⁴At the *edge of the* beautiful land *God had promised them,*
    they didn't trust His words, so they refused to enter.
²⁵They complained *when they were gathered* in their tents;
    they ignored the voice of the Eternal One.
²⁶Because of their attitude, He swore,
    "I'll leave you where you fall in the desert.
²⁷I'll scatter your children—*whoever is left*—
    throughout the nations all over the earth."

²⁸Then they aligned themselves with the god of Peor,
    and they ate sacrifices that had been made to lifeless *gods*.
²⁹Through their actions, they stirred up His anger,
    and a plague broke out in their midst.
³⁰Then Phinehas took a stand and intervened,
    so the plague was stopped.
³¹And God *saw what he did and* considered him righteous,
    a man to *be honored by* all generations forever.

106:22 Literally, Sea of Reeds

³²Again they stirred up His anger at the waters of Meribah,
  and serious trouble came to Moses because of them;
³³Because they stood against the Spirit,
  Moses spoke rashly with them.

³⁴*Later, after they entered the promised land,* they did not eradicate the
    peoples,
  as the Eternal One had ordered them to do,
³⁵But they mixed *and married* with the *outsider* nations,
  adopted their practices,
³⁶And worshiped their idols,
  which entrapped them.
³⁷They even offered their sons
  and daughters as sacrifices to the demons.
³⁸The *promised* land was corrupted by the innocent blood
  they offered to the idols of Canaan,
  The blood of their *very own* sons and daughters.
³⁹They became impure because of their *unfaithful* works;
  by their actions, they prostituted themselves *to other gods.*

⁴⁰Therefore the Eternal One's anger was ignited against His people;
  He came to despise *the people of* His inheritance.
⁴¹So He handed them over to the control of foreign nations,
  to be ruled by people who hated them.
⁴²Their enemies *exploited them,* victimized them,
  and restrained them by *abusive* power.
⁴³He delivered them over and over again;
  however, they *were slow to learn and* deliberately rebelled.
  Their sins humbled them *and nearly destroyed them.*
⁴⁴Nevertheless, He saw their great struggle, *took pity on them,*
  and heard their prayers;
⁴⁵H*e* did not forget His covenant *promises* to them
  but reversed *their fortune and released them* from their punishment
  because of His loyal love.
⁴⁶He changed the hearts of all who held them captive
  so that they would show compassion on them.

⁴⁷Save us, O Eternal One, our God,
>and gather us who are scattered among all the nations,
>That we may give thanks to Your holy name
>>and celebrate Your *amazing* greatness with praise.

⁴⁸Blessed be the Eternal One, the God of Israel,
>from everlasting to everlasting.
>And let everyone say, "Amen!"
>>Praise the Eternal One!

PSALM 107

¹Erupt with thanks to the Eternal One, for He is good
>and His loyal love lasts forever.
²Let all those redeemed by the Eternal One—
>those rescued from *times of deep* trouble—join in *giving thanks.*
³He has gathered them across the earth,
>from east and west,
>from [north and south].*

⁴Some drifted around in the desert
>and found no place where they could live.
⁵Their bellies growled with hunger; their mouths were dry with thirst;
>their souls grew weak and weary.
⁶In their distress, they called out to the Eternal One,
>and He saved them from their misery.
⁷*He showed them the best path; then* He led them down the right road
>until they arrived at an inhabited town.
⁸May they *erupt with praise and* give thanks to the Eternal One
>in honor of His loyal love
And all the wonders He has performed for humankind!
⁹He has quenched their thirst,
>and He has satisfied their hunger with what is good.

107:3 Hebrew manuscripts read "and the sea."

¹⁰Some people were *locked up* in dark *prisons,* confined in gloom *as bleak as death*.

They were captives bound by *iron* chains and misery,

¹¹All because they had rebelled against the directives of the True God
and had rejected the wisdom of the Most High.

¹²So they suffered the heaviness of *slave* labor;

when they stumbled *and fell,* there was no one to help *them up*.

¹³In their distress, they called out to the Eternal One;

He saved them from their misery.

¹⁴He rescued them from the darkness, delivered them from the deepest
gloom *of death*;

He shattered their *iron* chains.

¹⁵May they *erupt with praise and* give thanks to the Eternal One
in honor of His loyal love

PSALM 107 | **Life can get pretty stormy** at times. One minute, things
are relatively calm; the next minute it's crisis after crisis. The winds of life blow,
causing hardship, knocking us off balance, and frustrating our direction and plans.
When that happens, the psalmist advises understanding the cycle of sin, prayer,
and restoration. Four times in this psalm the pattern is followed: First, some
believers drift away from God into a desert with no water or food and they grow
weary. But "in their distress, they [call] out to the Eternal One, and He [saves]
them from their misery." The saving is followed by thanksgiving and restoration.
Then a second group is oppressed and put into prison or slave labor. They call out,
are freed, thank God, and are restored. Again, a third group rebels and becomes
deathly ill. They call out, are healed, thank God, and are restored. Finally, a fourth
group runs away to the sea and is caught in a violent storm. They call out, the sea
is calmed, thank God, and they are restored.

The Eternal One sees all their crises and has a grip on every person and
every situation. He alone knows how to save from prison or from the storm and
is able to provide what is needed for people to continue along the path with Him.
It may be impossible to avoid life's ups and downs and unexpected wild rides,
but one thing can be depended on. The One who watches over His world and His
people will set things right. "Is there anyone wise? If so, may the wise take notice
of these things and reflect upon the loyal love of the Eternal One."

And all the wonders He has performed for humankind!
¹⁶He has broken down the bronze gates
      and severed the iron bars *that imprisoned them.*

¹⁷Some people became fools infected by their rebellious ways,
      and sickness followed because of their sins.
¹⁸*Afflicted and weak,* they refused any sort of food
      as they approached the gates of death.
¹⁹In their distress, they called out to the Eternal One,
      and He saved them from their misery.
²⁰He gave the order and healed them
      and rescued them from *certain* death.
²¹May they *erupt with praise and* give thanks to the Eternal One
      in honor of His loyal love
   And all the wonders He has performed for humankind!
²²Let them present to Him thanksgiving sacrifices
      and tell *stories* of His *great* deeds through songs of joy.

²³Some set out to sea in ships,
      traveling across mighty seas in order to trade *in foreign lands.*
²⁴They witnessed the *powerful* acts of the Eternal One,
      marveled at the great wonders He revealed over the deep *waters.*
²⁵For He spoke and summoned a violent wind
      that whipped up the waves of the sea.
²⁶*Relentless* waves lifted *the ships* high in the sky, then drove them down to
            the depths;
      the sailors' courage dissolved into misery.
²⁷They staggered and stumbled around like drunkards,
      and they had no idea what to do.
²⁸In their distress, they called out to the Eternal One,
      and He saved them from their misery.
²⁹He commanded the storm to calm down, *and it became still.*
      A hush came over the waves of the sea,
³⁰The sailors were delighted at the quiet,
      and He guided them to their port.
³¹May they *erupt with praise and* give thanks to the Eternal One
      in honor of His loyal love

And all the wonders He has performed for humankind!

³²Let them glorify Him in the assembly of His people
 and worship Him in the presence of the elders.

³³God transforms *wild, flowing* rivers into *dry, lonely* deserts,
 lively springs of water into thirsty ground.
³⁴He turns lush gardens into lifeless wastelands,
 all because of the wickedness of those who reside there.
³⁵Yet He transforms a *dry, lonely* desert into pools of *living* water,
 parched ground into lively springs.
³⁶And He allows those who are hungry to live there
 so that they might build a livable city.
³⁷There they sow fields and plant vineyards
 and gather up an abundant harvest.
³⁸*He anoints them* with His blessings, and they greatly increase in number.
 He does not allow their herds to dwindle.

³⁹When His people lessen *in number* and are humbled
 through persecution, suffering, and brokenheartedness,
⁴⁰He pours out contempt on *those responsible* leaders
 and then makes them drift around in an uncharted wasteland.
⁴¹But He raises the poor away from their suffering
 and multiplies their families like a flock.
⁴²The righteous see God's actions, and they take delight *in what He does,*
 but the unrighteous don't dare to speak.
⁴³*Is there anyone wise? If so,* may the wise take notice of these things
 and reflect upon the loyal love of the Eternal One.

PSALM 108

A SONG OF DAVID.

¹My heart is committed, O God:
 I will sing;
I will sing praises *with great affection*
 and pledge my whole soul to the singing.

²Wake up the harp and lyre, *and strum the strings;*
   I will stir the sleepy dawn *from slumber*!
³I will *stand and* offer You my thanks, Eternal One, in the presence of
      others;
   I will sing of Your greatness among the nations *no matter where I am.*
⁴For Your amazing love soars *overhead* far into the heavens;
   Your truth rises up to the clouds
Where passing light bends.

⁵O God, that You would be lifted up above the heavens *in the hearts of Your
      people*;
   until the whole earth knows Your glory.
⁶*Reach down and* rescue those whom You love;
   pull us to safety by Your *mighty* right hand, and answer me.
⁷God's voice has been heard in His holy sanctuary:
   "I will celebrate.
   I will allocate Shechem and the Succoth Valley *to My people.*
⁸Gilead belongs to Me, and so does Manasseh;
   Ephraim is the helmet that protects My head;
   Judah is the scepter through which I rule;
⁹Moab is the washpot in which I clean Myself;
   I will throw My shoe over Edom *in conquest*;
   Philistia will soon hear My *victory* shout."

¹⁰But who will take me into the fortified city?
   Who will lead me into Edom?
¹¹Have You not turned Your back on us, O God?
   Will You *stay away and* not accompany our armies, O God?
¹²Help us against our enemy; *we need Your help!*
   It's useless to trust in the hand of man *for liberation.*
¹³Only through God can we be successful.
   It is God *alone* who will defeat our enemies *and bring us victory!*

PSALM 109

FOR THE WORSHIP LEADER. A SONG OF DAVID.

¹O True God of my *every* praise, do not keep silent!
²My enemies have opened their wicked, deceit-filled mouths *and blown*
their foul breath on me.
They have slandered me with their twisted tongues
³And unleashed loathsome words that swirl around me.
Though I have done nothing, they attack me.
⁴Though I offer them love and keep them in my prayers, they accuse me;
⁵Though I treat them well, they answer me with evil;
Though I give them love, they reply with *a gesture of* hatred.

⁶*Here's what they say:* Find some evil scoundrel to go after him.
Let's get some accuser *to level charges* against him.
⁷At his trial, let's make sure he is found guilty
so that even his prayers become evidence *that convicts him.*
⁸Let his days be few, *his life cut short;*
let another take over his position.
⁹*Lay waste to his family—*
let his children become orphans and his wife a widow.
¹⁰Let his children wander *the streets—his legacy, homeless* beggars
scavenging for food,
[driven out of]* the rubble *and slums* where they live.
¹¹Let the bankers take what is his;
strangers help themselves to *what little is left of* all he's earned.
¹²Let there be no one around to offer him compassion,
nor anyone to give his fatherless children *warmth or* kindness.
¹³Let his family line come to an end—
no future generations to carry on his name!
¹⁴Let the sins of his fathers be remembered before the Eternal One,
and the sins of his mother never be erased.

109:10 Hebrew manuscripts read "sought among."

¹⁵Let their offenses always be before the Eternal One
>   so that the memory of this family is long forgotten by *all the people of*
>   the earth,
¹⁶Because it never occurred to him to show compassion;
>   instead, he oppressed the poor, afflicted,
>   and brokenhearted and sent them to their death.
¹⁷He loved to invoke a curse—so let his curses come back to him.
>   He preferred not to speak a blessing—so let all blessings be far
>   from him.
¹⁸He wrapped himself with cursing, *draped around him* like a cape;
>   may it flood his body like water
>   and *seep* into his bones like oil.

| PSALM 109 | **Unfounded Accusations.** Have you ever been in a situation where someone has decided to hate you and has been out destroy your reputation? Maybe you are one of the fortunate ones who have avoided this. But many have not.

David certainly had his detractors in Saul, in his own son Absalom, and eventually in many Israelites who were jealous of his success and wanted a different king. Their words became bitter and hurtful. Even without cause, David's enemies made up things to injure him.

Unfounded accusations can cause great confusion and sadness to the heart, especially when they come from people we love. Gossip takes victims. Falsehoods are perpetuated through careless, unsubstantiated comments. The list is long in this psalm of how David's enemies sought to destroy him. In verse 20, though, David turns a corner. He calls upon God to reward his enemies by making the false accusations leveled against him come true in their own lives. He calls out for help and God restores. David became well loved, especially by God about whom he said, "He always stands in support."

As we, like David, resist the urge to spread the news about the failings or misfortunes of others and instead offer them the grace God extends to us, we give them the opportunity to rise and move forward. Good can come from unfair persecution when all those involved see the hand of God working in the one who is persecuted. Instead of continuing the cycle of jealousy and harm, a new pattern of praise and kindness can be established.

¹⁹Let those curses wrap around him like a cloak *on a cold night,*
　　like a belt tightly knotted around him every day.
²⁰Let the Eternal One so reward my accusers,
　　all those who speak and plot evil against me.
²¹But You, my Master, the Eternal One,
　　treat me with kindness for the sake of Your name, *the good of Your*
　　　　reputation;
　　because Your unfailing love is so good, O deliver me!
²²*You see,* I am poor and needy,
　　and my heart is broken inside me.
²³My life is fading away like a shadow *that vanishes* in the evening;
　　I am like a locust easily brushed off *the shoulder.*
²⁴*I can barely stand;* my knees are weak from not eating;
　　I am *haggard and drawn,* just skin and bones.
²⁵I have become a person of contempt to my accusers;
　　whenever they see me, they *taunt me,* shaking their heads *in*
　　　　disapproval.

²⁶Help me, Eternal One, my God; *come to my rescue!*
　　Save me through Your unfailing love.
²⁷Let everyone know that You are the source *of my salvation*
　　that You, Eternal One, have done this *mighty work.*
²⁸Let them utter a curse, *if they will,* but You will speak a blessing;
　　[when they come to attack,]* let them know *utter* shame.
　　Then Your servant will celebrate *and praise You!*
²⁹Let my enemies be clothed with disgrace *and humiliation*;
　　let them be dressed in a robe of their own shame.
³⁰I will continually give thanks to the Eternal One
　　with *the praises of* my mouth;
　　I will praise Him in the company of many.
³¹For He *always* stands in support of the *afflicted and* needy,
　　to rescue their souls from those who judge *and condemn* them.

109:28 Greek manuscripts omit this portion.

PSALM 110

A SONG OF DAVID.

¹The Eternal One said to my Lord,
  "Sit here at My right hand,
  in the place of honor and power,
And I will gather your enemies together,
  lead them in on hands and knees;
  you will rest your feet on their backs."

²The Eternal One will extend your reach as you rule
  from *your throne on* Zion.
  You will be out in enemy lands, ruling.
³Your people will come as volunteers that day;
  no conscripts, no mercenaries will be found among them. They will be a
  sight to see:

PSALM 110 **The Priest-King.** Psalm 110, the most quoted psalm in the New Testament, contains a verse that is rather difficult to explain. Its writing is attributed to David who speaks of the Messiah as one coming from his own lineage. Like many prophecies, there is an immediate application and a future fulfillment. In this case, the immediate application would be to David or one of his heirs. If that is the case, then who is the "Lord" in the first verse? Jesus in Matthew 22:41-46 raises this question to the Pharisees.

The solution in the psalm is a king who is a priest (which is not allowed in Israel) from the order of Melchizedek, mentioned twice in the Old Testament and explained in Hebrews as Jesus Himself. The first part of verse 4 adds to the mystery where David says, "The Eternal One has sworn an oath and cannot change His mind."

Despite the debate over what the contemporaries of David understood this psalm to mean, the New Testament sees this as a prophecy about Jesus and His

On that day, you will lead your army, noble in their holiness.
As the new day dawns and dew settles *on the grass,*
    your young *volunteers* will make their way to you.
⁴The Eternal One has sworn an oath
    and cannot change His mind:
"You are a priest forever—
    in the *honored* order of Melchizedek."

⁵The Lord is at Your right hand;
    on the day that his fury comes *to its peak,* he will crush kings.
⁶*You will see* the dead *in heaps at the roadside,*
    corpses spread far and wide *in valleys and on hillsides.*
Rulers and military leaders will lie among them *without distinction.*
    This will be his judgment on the nations.
⁷There is a brook along the way.
    He will *stop there and* drink;
And when he is finished,
    he will raise his head.

---

role as prophet, priest, and king. One wonderful truth that relates to this psalm is God's promise that Jesus' sacrifice would result in salvation and that no one other than Jesus could possibly fill this complex role; no other option will come forward for God to consider. He with great certainty, in His plan, gave us a Savior forever.

Some might try to convince you that God will choose to provide a better plan, but the psalmist's words and their New Testament interpretation rule out any other possibility. Jesus is the only option that provides the necessary righteousness.

The final verse is also difficult, but it does complete the story. Jesus is uniquely qualified to be a king/priest, and His work to save is completed on the cross. When He is finished there, He cries out. When the "Lord" in Psalm 110 finishes, he raises up his head. It is a similar gesture to that in the passion of Jesus and signals completion. God promised deliverance, He sent the priest of the order of Melchizedek, and with the sacrifice on the cross, the story of redemption is complete.

¹Praise the Eternal One.
  I will thank Him with all my heart
      in the presence of the right-standing and with the assembly.
²The works of the Eternal are *many and* wondrous!
      They are examined by all who delight in them.
³His work is *marked with* beauty and majesty;
      His justice has no end.
⁴His wonders are reminders that
      the Eternal is gracious and compassionate *to all*.
⁵He provides food to those who revere Him.
      He will always remember His covenant.
⁶He has shown the mighty strength of His works to His people
      by giving the land of *foreign* nations to them.
⁷*All* His accomplishments are truth and justice;
      all His instructions are certain.

Psalm 111 A Hebrew acrostic poem

PSALM 111 **"Reverence for the Eternal** is the first step toward wisdom." What a profound truth. When we find ourselves confused and need understanding, it is helpful to recognize that our confused state often begins with thinking we are wiser than is really the case. The root of knowledge, the blessing of understanding, becomes ours only as we fear and revere God. He is all-powerful, all-knowing, and everlasting. He holds the forces of life and death, of creation and destruction, of the world as we know it, in His hand. He rules. We exist at His good pleasure. How can we possibly have true wisdom without recognizing the place God has in the whole scheme of things?

It is this reverence that causes us to bow our heads in prayer and raise our hands in unending praise. It is this fear that keeps us wanting to learn more about how to stay within the will of the One who loves us and who made a way for us to come back into His sacred presence. This fear, this reverence, this awe is what reminds us to keep looking up from our knees. The psalmist summarizes, "All those who worship Him have a good understanding."

⁸His precepts will continue year in and year out,
>   performed *by His people* with honesty and truth.
⁹He has redeemed His people,
>   guaranteeing His covenant forever.
>   His name is holy and awe-inspiring.
¹⁰Reverence for the Eternal is the first step toward wisdom.
>   All those who worship Him have a good understanding.
>   His praise will echo through eternity!

Psalm 112*

¹Praise the Eternal One!
>   How blessed are those who revere the Eternal One,
>   who *turn from evil and* take great pleasure in His commandments.
²Their children will be a *powerful* force upon the earth;
>   this generation that does what is right *in God's eyes* will be blessed.
³His house will be stocked with wealth and riches,
>   and His *love for* justice will endure for all time.
⁴When *life is* dark, a light will shine for those who live rightly—
>   those who are merciful, compassionate, and strive for justice.
⁵Good comes to all who are gracious and share freely;
>   they conduct their affairs with *sound* judgment.
⁶Nothing will ever rattle them;
>   the just will always be remembered.
⁷They will not be afraid when the news is bad
>   because they have resolved to trust in the Eternal One.
⁸Their hearts are confident, and they are fearless,
>   for they *expect to* see their enemies *defeated*.
⁹They give freely to the poor;
>   their righteousness endures for all time;*
>   their *strength and* power is established in honor.

Psalm 112 A Hebrew acrostic poem
112:9 2 Corinthians 9:9

[10]The wicked will be infuriated when they see *the good man honored*!
They will clench their teeth and dissolve to nothing;
and when they go, their wicked desires will follow.

PSALM 113

[1]Praise the Eternal One!
All of you who call yourselves the children of the Eternal One, *come and*
praise His name.
Lift Him high to the high place in your hearts.

[2]At this moment, and for all the moments yet to come,
may the Eternal's name ascend *in the hearts of His people.*
[3]*At every time and in every place—*
from *the moment* the sun rises to *the moment* the sun sets—
May the name of the Eternal One be high *in the hearts of His people.*

PSALM 113 | **No Longer Invisible.** It is hard to read this psalm without beginning to sing praise to God. This psalm sets the tone from the beginning, "From the moment the sun rises to the moment the sun sets—May the name of the Eternal One be high in the hearts of His people." God knows the desires of our hearts. In fact, He knows us better than anyone because He sees us from the inside out. Sometimes we may feel that we're invisible in this world—that no one sees the real person inside. But the psalmist says if we've had to suffer from a poverty of material things, isolation, or poor health, we'll find ourselves dining with the powerful. The ones who haven't recognized when we were right there in front of them will sit next to us in a way that assures they can't miss us—we will no longer be invisible.

The psalmist has a special word at the end for women who have longed to have babies around whom to wrap their arms and hearts, but have been barren. They will find themselves surrounded with little ones. They will bask in a happiness they never before experienced.

Why? The Eternal One knows our needs and our wants, and He loves us. He plans only for our good. Let us "lift Him high to the high place in [our] hearts."

⁴The Eternal One is seated high above every nation.
His glory fills the skies.

⁵To whom should we compare the Eternal One, our God?
No one.
From His seat, high above,
⁶He deigns to observe the earth and her *thin* skies,
stooping even to see her goings on, far beneath His feet.
⁷He gathers up the poor from their dirt *floors,*
pulls the needy from the trash heaps,
⁸And places them among heads of state,
seated next to the rulers of His people *where they cannot be ignored.*
⁹Into the home of the childless bride,
He sends children who are, for her, a cause of happiness *beyond*
measure.
Praise the Eternal One!

PSALM 114

¹When the time came for Israel to leave Egypt—
for Jacob's family *to be free* of those who spoke another language—
²God chose to make Judah His sacred place,
and Israel became His realm.

³*And creation raised its head and took notice:*
the waters of the sea witnessed *God's actions* and ran away;
the Jordan, too, turned around and ran back *to where it came from.*
⁴*All of* the mountains leapt with *the strength of mighty* rams,
and all of the hills *danced* with *the joy of little* lambs.

⁵Why do you retreat, O sea?
Why do you roll back *your waters,* O Jordan?
⁶Why, O mountains, do you leap with *the strength of* rams?
Why, O hills, *do you dance with joy* like *little* lambs?

⁷Shudder and quake, O you earth, at the sight of the Lord.
    The God of Jacob comes,
⁸Who turns rock into pools of *refreshing* water
    and flint into fountains of *life-giving* streams!

PSALM 115

¹Not for us, O Eternal One; this glory is not for us—but for Your name
    because of Your loyal love and truth.
²Why should the nations ask,
    "Where is their God *now*?"

³Our God is in heaven
    doing whatever He chooses.
⁴Those nations worship idols of silver and gold,
    crafted by human hands:
⁵They have *given their gods* mouths, but they cannot speak;
    eyes, but they cannot see.
⁶They have *provided their idols with* ears, but they cannot hear;
    noses, but they cannot smell.
⁷They have *fashioned* hands, but the idols cannot *reach out and* touch;
    feet, but they cannot walk.
    Their idols cannot make a sound in their *finely crafted* throats.
⁸The people who make idols will become *useless* like them,
    like all who trust in idols.

⁹O Israel, put your trust in the Eternal.
    He is their helper and defender.
¹⁰O family of Aaron, put your trust in the Eternal.
    He is their helper and defender.
¹¹All who fear *and know* the Eternal, put your trust in Him.
    He is their helper and defender.

¹²The Eternal One has remembered us, and He will bless us.
    He will bless the people of Israel.
    He will bless the *priestly* family of Aaron.

¹³The Eternal One will bless those who *worship and* stand in awe of Him,
from the least to the greatest.

¹⁴May the Eternal One prosper your family,
growing both you and your descendants.
¹⁵May the blessings of the Eternal One,
maker of heaven and earth, be on you.

¹⁶The heavens above belong to the Eternal One,
and yet earth *in all of its beauty* has been given to humanity by Him.

| PSALM 115 | **Trusting in Little Gods.** Since man was created, it has been the same problem. Most people tend to be consumed by someone or something. It could be a hobby that eats up most of our time. It could be an ideal that captures our imagination and affects how we evaluate things or determines what success looks like to us. It could be someone or something we think will bring us lasting satisfaction. In more primitive societies, it is idols that have that kind of deity attributed to them. In our world, it is much more complex. No matter how sophisticated the result is, these obsessions become our gods; and we become, in a way, their servants. What little gods have we created for ourselves? We all have our idols. We may serve our bank accounts or Wall Street. We may devote ourselves to our own talents or to our intelligence or to another person's success. In the end, what we serve is what we trust. Some of us may think we don't trust anything. But we all have our little gods. In Psalm 115, we are told these gods can't speak, see, hear, smell, touch, walk, or make a sound. They are useless. But still, we put our trust in them.

The reality is that there is only one secure place to put our trust and service, and that is in the One who sees us and who walks with us. Only the Eternal One can respond to our needs, provide for our well-being, and direct our steps. The psalmist points to Israel, to Aaron (the priest), and to all who fear God. In each case, he declares, the Eternal is "their helper and defender." And He is our hope and protection in this world.

To misplace trust—to set it aside in accounts that can only fade away—is to lose hope. The psalmist encourages us to turn quickly and build an everlasting trust account with the One who has already proven Himself to be worthy. He tells us to stand in awe of God who does have all the senses and who speaks and acts on our behalf. If you are going to have a god, choose the real God who is forever.

¹⁷The dead do not praise the Eternal,
> nor do any who descend into the silent *grave.*

¹⁸But we will *praise and* bless You—our Eternal One—
> today and forever.

Praise the Eternal One!

PSALM 116

¹I love the Eternal One; for not only does He hear
> my voice, my pleas for mercy,

²But He leaned *down when I was in trouble and brought* His ear close to me.
> So as long as I have breath, I will call on Him.

³*Once* I was wound in the wrappings of death;
> the terror of *dying and* the grave had a grip on me;
> *I could not get away,* for I was entombed in distress and sorrow.

⁴Then I called on the name of the Eternal One:
> "O Eternal One—I am begging You—save me!"

⁵The Eternal One is full of grace and *naturally* just;
> our God is compassionate *and merciful.*

⁶And the Eternal One watches over the naive.
> Whenever I was knocked down, He *reached down and* saved me.

⁷O my soul! Return *and relax. Come* to your *true* rest,
> for the Eternal One has showered you with His favor.

⁸*God,* You *alone* rescued my soul from *the grips of* death,
> my eyes from weeping,
> and my feet from slipping.

⁹I will come before the Eternal One
> *as long as I journey* in the land of the living.

¹⁰I believed *Your promise*; therefore I spoke,
> "I am in deep trouble."

¹¹In my confusion I blurted out,
> "All people are liars!"

¹²How will I pay back the Eternal One
      for all His graciousness toward me?
¹³I will raise the cup of deliverance
      and call out the name of the Eternal One.
¹⁴I will fulfill the promises I made to the Eternal One
      here *as a witness* to all His people.

¹⁵Precious in the eyes of the Eternal One
      are the deaths of those who follow after Him.
¹⁶O Eternal One, *You know* I am Your servant.
      I am Your servant, a child of Your maidservant, *devoted to You;*
      You have cut me loose from the chains *of death* that bind me.
¹⁷And I *come, eager to* offer a sacrifice of gratitude
      and call on the name of the Eternal One.
¹⁸I will fulfill the promises I made to the Eternal One
      here as a witness to all His people

| PSALM 116 | **Does God Hear Us?** Even in our troubles and distress does He really hear? The psalmist cries out, "I am in deep trouble." And later he declares, "I am Your servant."

It may seem to be a silly analogy, but have you ever wanted to be on a team and not been picked? It is rough on the old ego. When we sign up to join a team of any kind, we do so because we want to be a part of that team's success. In fact, it excites us to know that we can actually contribute to victory. The same thing is true when we sign up for God's team. When we become His servants, we are on His team, and our task is to do His will. We are set in motion to give our best to Him. He can call us in when He needs our special set of skills to make something happen. We're His servants, and we are happy to serve.

The psalmist is reflecting on the kind of joy we have as we serve God with gratitude. Some of us may be grateful and amazed at having been chosen for the team, and we're delighted when He calls us in for special service according to our abilities. The psalmist tells us we are "a witness to all His people." His use of our talent witnesses to His sovereignty and grace. Serving God is a privilege and an honor for which we give Him thanks and praise! Our service if done with a pure heart is praise to Him in it's simplest form.

¹⁹In the courts of the Eternal One's temple,
    among the people *of God's city,* O Jerusalem.
  Praise the Eternal One!

PSALM 117

¹Praise the Eternal One, all nations.
    Raise your voices, all people.*
²For His unfailing love is great, and it is *intended* for us,
    and His faithfulness *to His promises* knows no end. *It will last forever.*
  Praise the Eternal One!

PSALM 118

¹Give thanks to the Eternal One because He is *always* good.
    He never ceases to be loving and kind.

²Let *the people of* Israel proclaim:
    "He never ceases to be loving and kind."
³Let *the priests of* Aaron's line proclaim:
    "He never ceases to be loving and kind."
⁴Let the people who fear the Eternal One proclaim:
    "He never ceases to be loving and kind."

⁵When trouble surrounded me, I cried out to the Eternal One;
    the Eternal answered me and brought me to a wide, open space.
⁶The Eternal One is with me *and wants what is best for me,* so I will not be
    afraid of anything.
    After all, if God is on my side, how can anyone hurt me?
⁷The Eternal One is on my side, a champion for my cause;
    so when I look at those who hate me, victory will be in sight.

117:1 Romans 15:11

^{8}It is better to put your faith in the Eternal One *for your security*
   than to trust in people.
^{9}It is better to put your faith in the Eternal One *for your security*
   than to trust in princes.

^{10}All *these* nations surround me, *squeezing me from all sides;*
   with the name of the Eternal One, I will destroy them.
^{11}They *rose up against me,* squeezed me from all sides, yes, from all sides;
   with the name of the Eternal One, I will destroy them.
^{12}They surrounded me like *a swarm of* bees;
   they were destroyed *quickly and* thoroughly—
Flaring up like a pile of thorns—
   with the name of the Eternal One, I will destroy them.
^{13}I was pushed *back,* attacked so that I was about to fall,
   but the Eternal One was there to help me *keep my balance.*

PSALM 118 | **Rejected Stone.** One of the best-known quotes from Psalms is, "The stone that the builders rejected has become the very stone that holds together the entire foundation." The cornerstone is the key stone where all the stress of the different planes of the foundation are tied together, providing stability and strength. Anything we build needs a firm foundation. Whether we're building a physical structure or a family or a business, we need to know what it stands on and what it stands for. We need to know exactly what holds it all together. If we don't, we run the risk of having it collapse.

As with most prophecies, this one has two applications: In the New Testament, this analogy is directly applied to Jesus, but the immediate application here is to Israel as the cornerstone. Babylon went to great trouble to capture Israel and then later rejected her.

All people build their lives on something: living out private dreams, personal talents, or maybe a special belief. If we look at our lives as the building, the concept of the cornerstone becomes very important. Money, talent, intelligence, friends . . . all those things are nice building blocks for our lives, yet none of them can assure the success of the foundation. The apostle Peter tells us Jesus is our cornerstone, the foundation of our faith and all we do that stands firm. In Him, we are connected to God the Father, we are intertwined with other members of the body of Christ, we receive our salvation from sin, and we find our model of what the ideal person is to be like.

¹⁴The Eternal One is my strength, and He is the reason I sing;
He has been there to save me *in every situation.*

¹⁵In the tents of the righteous *soldiers of God,*
there are shouts of joy and victory. *They sing:*
"The right hand of the Eternal has shown His power
¹⁶The mighty arm of the Eternal is raised *in victory;*
the right hand of the Eternal has shown His power."
¹⁷I will not die. I will live.
I will live to tell about all the Eternal One has done.
¹⁸The Eternal One *has taught me many lessons;*
He has been strict and severe,
but even in His discipline, He has not allowed me to die.

¹⁹Open *wide* to me the gates of justice
so that I may walk through them
and offer praise *and worship* to the Eternal One.

²⁰This is the gate of the Eternal One;
the righteous *children of God* will go through it.

²¹I will praise You because You answered me *when I was in trouble.*
You have become my salvation.
²²The stone that the builders rejected
has become the very stone that holds together the entire foundation.
²³This is the work of the Eternal One,
and it is marvelous in our eyes.*
²⁴This is the day the Eternal God has made;
let us celebrate and be happy today.
²⁵O Eternal One, save us, we beg You.
O Eternal One, we beg You, bring us success!

²⁶He who comes in the name of the Eternal One will be blessed;*
we have blessed You from the house of the Eternal.
²⁷The Eternal One is the True God;
He shines His light on us.

118:22-23 Matthew 21:42; Mark 12:10-11
118:26 Matthew 21:9; 23:39; Mark 11:9; Luke 13:35; 19:38; John 12:13

Let the feast begin.

>Bring the sacrifice, and tie it to the horns of the altar.

[28]You are my God, and I give You thanks;

>You are my God, and I praise You.

[29]Give thanks to our Eternal Lord; He is always good.

>He never ceases to be loving and kind.

PSALM 119[*]

Aleph

[1]Happy are the people who walk with integrity,

>who live according to the teachings of the Eternal One.

[2]Happy are the people who keep His decrees,

>who pursue Him wholeheartedly.

[3]These are people who do nothing wrong;

>they *do what it takes to* follow His ways.

[4]You have given *us* Your precepts

>so we would be careful about keeping them.

[5]Oh, that *every part of* my life would remain in line

>with what You require!

[6]Then I would feel no shame

>when I fix my eyes upon Your commands.

[7]With a pure heart, I will give thanks to You

>when I hear about Your just *and fair* rulings.

[8]I will live within Your limits;

>do not abandon me completely!

Beth

[9]How can a young person remain pure?

>*Only* by living according to Your word.

[10]I have pursued You with my whole heart;

>do not let me stray from Your commands.

[11]Deep within me I have hidden Your word

>so that I will never sin against You.

Psalm 119 A Hebrew acrostic poem

¹²You are blessed, O Eternal One;

     instruct me in what You require.

¹³My lips have told how

     You have delivered all Your *wise* rulings.

¹⁴I have celebrated Your testimonies

     as though rejoicing over an immeasurable fortune.

¹⁵I will fix my mind on Your instructions

     and my eyes on Your path.

¹⁶I will find joy in Your ordinances;

     I will remember Your word *forever*.

Gimel

¹⁷Treat Your servant well, Lord,

     so that I may live and remain faithful to Your word.

¹⁸Let me see *clearly* so that I may take in

     the amazing things coming from Your law.

¹⁹I am a sojourner in the world;

     do not keep Your commands hidden from me.

²⁰My soul aches from craving

     Your wise rulings day and night.

²¹You rebuke those who are proud,

     and those who stray from Your commands are cursed.

²²Free me from the contempt and disdain *of others*

     because I keep Your decrees.

²³Even though *powerful* princes conspire against me,

     I fix my mind on what You require.

²⁴Yes, Your testimonies are my joy;

     they are like the friends I seek for counsel.

Daleth

²⁵My very being clings to the dust;

     preserve my life, in keeping with Your word.

²⁶I have admitted my ways *are wrong,* and You responded;

     now help me learn what You require.

²⁷Compel me to grasp the way of Your statutes

     so I will fix my mind on Your wonderful works.

²⁸My soul weeps, and trouble weighs me down;
>   give me strength *so I can stand* according to Your word.
²⁹Eliminate faithlessness You find in my step,
>   be gracious, and give me Your guidance.
³⁰I have decided to take the path of faith;
>   I have focused my eyes on Your regulations.
³¹I cling to Your decrees; O Eternal One,
>   do not let me face disgrace!
³²I will chase after Your commandments
>   because You will expand my understanding.

He

³³O Eternal One, show me how to live according to Your statutes,
>   and I will keep them always.
³⁴Grant me understanding so that I can keep Your law
>   and keep it wholeheartedly.
³⁵Guide me to walk in the way You commanded
>   because I take joy in it.
³⁶Turn *my head and* my heart to Your decrees
>   and not to sinful gain.
³⁷Keep my eyes from gazing upon worthless things,
>   and give me *true* life according to Your plans.
³⁸Verify Your word to Your servant,
>   which will lead me to worship You.
³⁹Take away the scorn that I dread
>   because Your actions are *just and* good.
⁴⁰Look and see—I long for Your guidance;
>   restore me in Your righteousness.

Vav

⁴¹May Your unfailing love find me, O Eternal One.
>   Keep Your promise, and save me;
⁴²When that happens, I will have a *good* response for anyone who taunts me
>   because I have faith in Your word.
⁴³Do not take Your message of truth from my mouth
>   because I wait *and rely* on Your just decisions.

⁴⁴Therefore I will follow Your teachings,
forever and ever.
⁴⁵And I will live a life of freedom
because I pursue Your precepts.
⁴⁶I will even testify of Your decrees before royalty
and will not be humiliated.
⁴⁷I will find my joy in Your commands,
which I love,
⁴⁸And I will raise my hands to Your commands, which I love,
and I will fix my mind on what You require.

Zayin

⁴⁹Do not forget Your promise to Your servant;
through it You have given me hope.
⁵⁰This brings me solace in the midst of my troubles:
that Your word has revived me.
⁵¹Those who are proud cruelly ridicule me,
but I keep to the steady path of Your teachings.
⁵²I have considered Your ancient rulings, O Eternal One,
and their memory brings me comfort.
⁵³Burning anger *rises in me,* has me in its grip
because the unrighteous abandon Your teachings.

PSALM 119 | **Pay Attention to God.** When we dream of what could be, normally we envision positive things like success, travel to exotic places, ideal personal relationships, fame, and, of course, fortune. Seldom do we dwell on the possibility of failure or major trials. We may be missing some real gems in overlooking negatives, for some of them may turn out to be of far greater value than the good or fun things that we imagine. Do you really believe there is value in troubles? When we're in the midst of them, it's hard to believe there is, but the psalmist says trouble helps us grow in understanding. Without them, we might not be as ready to seek God's help, and we might not understand as fully how much we need His word.

⁵⁴As I journey *through this life,*
   Your statutes are my song.
⁵⁵O Eternal One, through the night, I *stop to* recall Your name.
   That's how I live according to Your teachings.
⁵⁶This has become my practice:
   to keep Your ordinances.

Heth
⁵⁷The Eternal One is mine. *He's all I need.*
   I have *promised to* keep Your words.
⁵⁸I sought Your blessing wholeheartedly.
   Show grace to me as You promised.
⁵⁹I carefully charted out my paths
   to align my steps with Your decrees.
⁶⁰I did not procrastinate and hurried
   to follow Your commands.
⁶¹The wicked have entangled me in their nets,
   but I have not forgotten Your teaching.
⁶²In the middle of the night, I wake to thank You
   because Your rulings are *just and* right.
⁶³I am a friend of anyone who fears You
   and of those who follow Your precepts.
⁶⁴The earth is filled with Your unfailing love, O Eternal One;
   teach me to observe what You require.

We like to believe we exercise good judgment and that important decisions are based on good, solid information. Sometimes we reap the benefit of our research, but at other times we totally miss the boat. We don't seek God's word or good counsel, or we're simply too much in a hurry to wait for the right direction. We act and we fail and yet we still feel surprised at the outcome. The reality is that God is in control. Often when we take a shortcut, God brings us back around so that we don't miss the point of the experience.

Knowledge and good judgment can only be a part of our decision-making pattern if we slow down and pay attention to God. Trials help bring us back on the right path. God directs us toward the end that falls within His purpose. Let's be thankful for the guidance.

Teth

⁶⁵You have handled Your servant well,

O Eternal One, as You promised.

⁶⁶Help me to learn good judgment and knowledge

because I believe Your commandments.

⁶⁷Before I had trouble, I strayed *from the true path, the path of righteousness,*

but now I live according to Your word.

⁶⁸You are *truly* good, and Your acts are too;

teach me what You require.

⁶⁹The proud smear me with their lies;

I will keep Your instructions wholeheartedly.

⁷⁰Their hearts are dull and callous;

I am delighted to study Your teaching.

⁷¹It is a good thing that I was humbled

because it helped me learn Your limits.

⁷²Your teachings are more valuable to me

than a fortune in gold and silver.

Yodh

⁷³Your *strong* hands formed me and established me;

give me understanding so I can learn Your commands.

⁷⁴Let those who fear You see me and rejoice

because I hope in Your word.

⁷⁵I know, O Eternal One, Your rulings are right,

and when You humbled me, You did so out of faithfulness.

⁷⁶Now let Your unfailing love be my comfort,

in keeping with Your promise to Your servant.

⁷⁷Shower me with Your compassion so that I may live

because I find great joy in Your law.

⁷⁸Let the proud be humiliated,

for they sabotage me with a lie;

still I will fix my mind on Your directives.

⁷⁹Let those who fear You and know Your testimonies

come back *and find* me.

⁸⁰Let my heart be *whole, my record* according to what You require

so that I will not be humiliated.

Kaph

81My soul is exhausted awaiting Your rescue
      yet I keep hoping in Your word.
82My eyes are strained as I look for what You promised,
      saying, "When will You *come to* comfort me?"
83Even though I *have shriveled up* like a wineskin *left* in the smoke,
      I still remember what You require.
84How long must Your servant wait?
      When will You carry out justice *and punish* those who persecute me?
85Those proud souls do not live according to Your commands,
      and they have dug pits to entrap me.
86*Indeed,* all Your commands are trustworthy,
      but my enemies have harassed me with their lies; help me!
87They have nearly ended my life on earth,
      but as for me, I never abandoned Your statutes.
88According to Your unfailing love, spare my life
      so that I can live according to the decrees of Your mouth.

Lamedh

89Forever, O Eternal One,
      Your word stands in heaven, firm *and resolute*.
90Your faithfulness endures to every generation;
      You founded the earth, and it remains.
91Everything remains today in keeping with Your laws,
      for all things exist to serve You.
92If I had not found joy in Your guidance,
      then I would have died from my misery.
93I will never forget Your precepts,
      for through them You have given me life.
94I belong to You, *Lord;* save me
      because I have taken care to live by Your principles.
95The wicked lie in wait, *anxious* to kill me;
      I will set my mind on Your statutes.
96I have seen the limit of all perfection,
      but Your commands are all-encompassing.

Mem

⁹⁷Oh, how I love Your law!

I fix my mind on it all day long.

⁹⁸Your commands make me wiser than my enemies

because they are always with me.

⁹⁹I have more discernment than all my teachers

because I *study and* meditate on Your testimonies.

¹⁰⁰I comprehend more than those who are my elders

because I have kept Your precepts.

¹⁰¹I have kept my feet from walking the paths of evil

so that I may live according to Your word.

¹⁰²I have not neglected Your lessons,

for You, *God,* have been my teacher.

¹⁰³Your words are sweet to my taste!

Yes, they are sweeter than honey in my mouth!

¹⁰⁴I gain understanding from Your instructions;

that's why I hate every deceitful path.

Nun

¹⁰⁵Your word is a lamp for my steps;

it lights the path before me.

¹⁰⁶I have taken an oath and confirmed it:

I pledge to do what You say is right and just.

¹⁰⁷I have suffered terribly, O Eternal One;

give me the life You promised.

¹⁰⁸Please accept the words I offer willingly, O Eternal One,

and instruct me in *the ways of* Your justice.

¹⁰⁹My soul is continually in danger,

but I do not forget Your teachings.

¹¹⁰The wicked have laid a trap for me,

but I have not drifted away from Your instructions.

¹¹¹Your decrees are forever mine,

for they bring joy to my life.

¹¹²I have committed myself to do what You require

forever and ever, to the very end.

Samekh

113I despise those who waver back and forth,
>but I love Your teachings.

114You are my hiding place and my shield *of protection*;
>I hope in Your word.

115Away from me, reprobates!
>I am committed to observing the commands of my God.

116Support me in keeping with Your promise, *O God,* so that I may live;
>do not let my hope turn into shame.

117Help me so that I will be safe,
>and I will respect Your laws continually.

118You have rejected all those who stray from Your commands
>because their fraudulent lifestyles are *cunning and* empty.

119You have discarded all the wicked from the land, *skimmed them off* like
>dross;
>that's why I love Your testimonies.

120My body shakes because of my fear of You,
>and I am in awe of Your *wise* rulings.

Ayin

121I have lived with fairness and integrity;
>do not leave me at the mercy of my tormenters.

122Provide security *and protection* for Your servant's welfare;
>do not let the proud oppress me.

123My eyes are strained as I look for Your salvation
>and for Your righteous promise *to be fulfilled.*

124Treat Your servant in a manner that shows Your unfailing love,
>and help me to learn Your decrees.

125I am Your servant; impart to me understanding
>so that I may fully grasp *the depths of* Your statutes.

126It is time for the Eternal One to *step in and* do something
>because some have broken Your law.

127Indeed, I love Your commands
>more than gold, even more than the highest quality gold.

128It's true that I regard all Your guidance to be correct *and good*;
>I despise every deceptive path.

Pe

129 Your decrees inspire wonder;
>   because of that, my soul *desires to* keep them.
130 When Your words are unveiled, light shines forth;
>   they bring understanding to the simple.
131 My desire for Your commands
>   left me *waiting,* open-mouthed and panting.
132 Acknowledge me and show me Your grace
>   as is Your habit toward all those who love Your name.
133 Guide my steps in *the ways of* Your word,
>   and do not let any sin control me.
134 Rescue me from *the torment of* my human oppressors
>   so that I may live according Your decrees.
135 Let Your face shine upon Your servant,
>   and help me to learn what You require.
136 My eyes shed rivers of tears
>   whenever people fail to keep Your teaching.

Tsadhe

137 You are *good and* just, O Eternal One,
>   and Your rulings are right.
138 You have set out Your decrees in justice,
>   and they can be trusted.
139 I am overwhelmed by my passion
>   because my enemies have forgotten Your words.
140 Your promise is tested *and true;*
>   that's why Your servant loves it.
141 I may be insignificant *to some* and hated *by others,*
>   but *at least* I do not forget Your precepts.
142 Your righteousness will last forever,
>   and Your law is truth.
143 Trouble and distress have overtaken me,
>   but Your commandments bring me great joy.
144 Your decrees are right *and true* forever;
>   grant me understanding so that I may live.

Qoph

¹⁴⁵I called to You wholeheartedly: "Answer me, O Eternal One!"
    I will respect, I will follow Your statutes.
¹⁴⁶I cried out to You: "Rescue me,
    and I will live according to Your decrees."
¹⁴⁷I wake before the dawn and call for help;
    I hope in Your words.
¹⁴⁸My eyes do not shut before each watch of the night
    so that I can fix my mind on Your word.
¹⁴⁹Listen to my voice, in keeping with Your unfailing love.
    Preserve my life, O Eternal One, according to Your just rulings.
¹⁵⁰Those who wish me harm are moving closer *to me*;
    they are far away from Your teaching.
¹⁵¹But You are near me, O Eternal One,
    and all You have commanded is true.
¹⁵²I learned a long time ago
    that You established Your decrees to last forever.

Resh

¹⁵³Give attention to my misery and rescue me
    because I have not forgotten Your teaching.
¹⁵⁴Fight for me, and set me free;
    give me life in keeping with Your promise.
¹⁵⁵Salvation is far from the wicked
    because they do not live in pursuit of Your precepts.
¹⁵⁶Your mercies are *tender and* great, O Eternal One;
    grant me life in keeping with Your ordinances.
¹⁵⁷I have many oppressors and foes;
    still I do not swerve from Your decrees.
¹⁵⁸I observe the faithless and detest them
    because they turn away from Your word.
¹⁵⁹Reflect, *O God,* on how I love Your precepts;
    give me life, O Eternal One, in keeping with Your unfailing love.
¹⁶⁰The entirety of Your word is truth,
    and every one of Your right rulings will surely last forever.

Shin

161 Princes persecute me without reason,

but my heart remains *true and is* awed by Your words.

162 I celebrate because of Your promise,

like someone who discovers great treasure.

163 I despise and abhor lies,

but I love Your law.

164 Seven times every day I praise You

because of Your right rulings.

165 Those who love Your law have an abundance of peace,

and nothing *along their paths* can cause them to stumble.

166 I wait for Your salvation, O Eternal One,

and I live out Your commands.

167 My soul is faithful to Your decrees,

and my love for them is extraordinary.

168 I live according to Your precepts and decrees

because everything I do is right before Your eyes.

Tav

169 Let my cry come before You, O Eternal One.

Grant me understanding in keeping with Your word.

170 Let my plea come before You;

liberate me in keeping with Your word.

171 Praise will pour from my lips

because You help me learn what You require.

172 My tongue will sing of Your word

because every command of Yours is right.

173 Let Your hand be poised to help me

because I have chosen *to live by* Your precepts.

174 I long for Your salvation, O Eternal One.

Meanwhile, Your teaching brings me great joy.

175 Let my soul live on so that I may praise You,

and let Your precepts guide me.

176 I have wandered *down the wrong path* like a lost sheep; come find *me,* Your servant,

because I do not forget Your commands.

Psalm 120

¹When I was in *deep* trouble, I called out to the Eternal One,
  and He answered my call.
²*I prayed:* "Protect me, Eternal One,
  from lips that lie
  and tongues poisoned with deceit."

³*Liars,* what will be your prize?
  And what will come your way,
  O you tongues *poisoned* with deceit?
⁴*Here's what you can expect:* the archers' arrows honed sharp
  as well as the red-hot coals of the broom wood.

⁵Sorrow is mine, for I am *a foreigner* wandering in Meshech;
  I am *a stranger* drifting among the tents of Kedar!
⁶My soul has roamed much too long
  among people who despise peace.
⁷I am for peace; *I ask for peace,*
  but even as I open my mouth,
  they are ready to fight.

Psalm 121

A SONG FOR THOSE JOURNEYING *TO WORSHIP*.

¹I look up at the *vast size of the* mountains—
  from where will my help come *in times of trouble*?
²The Eternal Creator of heaven and earth *and these mountains*
  will send the help I need.

³*He holds you firmly in the place you need to be.*
>He will not let you fall.
>He who keeps you will *never take His eyes off you and* never drift off to
>>sleep.
⁴*What a relief!* The One who watches over Israel
>never leaves for rest or sleep.

⁵The Eternal One keeps you safe,
>*so close to Him that His shadow* is a *cooling* shade to you.
⁶Neither bright light of sun
>nor dim light of moon will harm you
>*because the Lord is standing with you.*

⁷The Eternal One will keep you safe
>from all of life's evils,
⁸From your first breath to the last breath you breathe,
>from this day and forever.

PSALM 121 | **How often do we forget** to include God in our thinking? Right now, at this very moment, God is watching over us. He was watching us as we worked and played yesterday, and He'll be back at it again tomorrow because, the psalmist observes, God never grows weary of seeing our efforts to grow. He'll be there to guard us when the moon sweeps across our faces and when the sun awakens us to a new day. We are His and He walks beside us through every obstacle course we encounter, every bad hair day, every confused moment when we are simply learning who we are. He's not asleep on the job.

We can praise Him for keeping us safe and for allowing us to rest so peacefully in His refreshing shadow. Isn't it a comfort to know He's always with us? From our first breath until we take our last breath, from this day forward into eternity He is always there.

PSALM 122

A SONG [OF DAVID]* FOR THOSE JOURNEYING *TO WORSHIP*.

¹I was so happy when my fellow pilgrims said,
> "Let's go to the house of the Eternal One!"
²*We have made the journey, and now* we are standing
> within your gates, O Jerusalem.

³Jerusalem! *What a magnificent* city! Buildings
> so close together, so compact.
⁴*God's people belong here.* Every tribe of the Eternal
> makes its way *to Jerusalem*—
Just as God decreed for Israel
> to *come together and* give thanks to the Eternal One.
⁵*In Jerusalem, justice is the order of the day* because there sit the judges
> and kings, the descendants of David.

⁶Ask heaven to grant peace to Jerusalem:
> "May those who love you prosper.
⁷*O Jerusalem,* may *His* peace fill this entire city!
> May this citadel be *quiet and* at ease!"
⁸It's because of *people*—my family, friends, *and acquaintances*—
> that I say, "May peace permeate you."
⁹And because the house of Eternal One, our God, is here, *know this:*
> I will *always* seek your good!

122:title Some manuscripts omit this portion.

Psalm 123

A SONG FOR THOSE JOURNEYING *TO WORSHIP*.

¹I raise my eyes to *fix my gaze on* You,
 for Your throne resides in the heavens.
²Just as the eyes of servants
 closely watch the hand of their masters,
 Just as a maid carefully observes
 the slightest gesture of her mistress,
 In the same way we look to *You,* Eternal One,
 waiting for our God to pour out His mercy upon us.

³O Eternal One, show us Your mercy. We beg You.
 We are not strangers to contempt *and pain.*
⁴We have suffered more than our share
 of ridicule and contempt from *self-appointed* critics who live easy lives
 and pompously display their own importance.

PSALM 123 **The life of a servant,** at the time when this psalm was written, was totally dependent on the graces of the master. With no recourse beyond the word of the master and with all support for living coming from him, the servant would watch the master closely for clues as to what was required next.

As beloved servants of God, we seek His approval for the work we do. We look to Him to guide our efforts, to help us see any places we have gone wrong, or simply to assure us all is well. The result of work well done brings satisfaction and

PSALM 124

A SONG OF DAVID FOR THOSE JOURNEYING *TO WORSHIP.*

[1]If the Eternal One had not been with us—
    sing, Israel, sing—
[2]If the Eternal One had not been with us
    when the villains came for us,
[3]When their anger flamed around us,
    they would have swallowed us up alive!
[4]*Their hatred was like a flood:*
 the waters *were rising and* would have engulfed us;
    the streams *were rushing past and* would have overcome us.
[5]The furious waters would have broken over us.
    Battered and overwhelmed, we surely would have drowned!

[6]Blessed be the Eternal One
    who did not leave us
    to be torn by their fangs!
[7]*Our souls cry out:* "We escaped *with our lives* like a bird
    from the fowler's snare!
 The snare was broken,
    and we escaped *with our lives*!"

[8]Our help has come in the name of the Eternal One,
    the Maker of heaven and earth!

joy and seems to accomplish what God has asked us to do. If we can hardly wait to seek His face because we feel so good about what we've done for Him, that's probably a fair measure.

No matter how we feel, though, it's important to continue going to God. He cares for us and is merciful to us, and time spent in His presence is the best way to know Him and to learn His will for our lives. Even our lives are a gift from Him.

PSALM 125

A SONG FOR THOSE JOURNEYING *TO WORSHIP*.

¹All who have faith in the Eternal One stand as Mount Zion:
    unmoved, enduring, eternal.
²Just as the mountains around Jerusalem *embrace her,*
    the Eternal One, too, wraps around those who belong to Him—
    for this moment and for every moment to come.
³For wickedness will not *get the upper hand;*
    it shall not rule the land where righteous people live
 Lest good people go bad
    and do what is wrong.
⁴Be good, Eternal One, to those who are good,
    to those who are filled with integrity.
⁵The Eternal will send all the wicked away
    along with those who *pervert what's good and* twist it in their own
        crooked way.
    May peace be with Israel.

PSALM 125 **Two Sides of a Mountain.** Throughout Scripture, mountains play a key role. They provide a buffer from surrounding nations; they greatly influence weather patterns, making one side of a mountain a lush garden and the other side a desert. They are the location of many places of worship, and they provide protection from attack. Living in a place surrounded by mountains or in a dwelling nestled at the base of a mountain gives a sense of being protected and embraced by it. There is a sense that outside society can't penetrate the security found in the mountains. A mountain is a beautiful symbol of strength and endurance.

Comparing a mountain with God's enduring love for all who have faith in Him, the psalmist paints a picture of One who holds and protects His children every moment of every day. A final benefit of living on a mountain is the different perspective on the world it provides. The height allows you to see far into the distance. Looking down on life from on high helps us understand God's view. When we observe the vastness of His creation and understand the complexity of the world He sustains, we are humbled by His greatness.

PSALM 126

A SONG FOR THOSE JOURNEYING *TO WORSHIP*.

¹*Remember* when the Eternal One brought back the exiles to Zion?
　　It was as if we were dreaming—
²Our mouths were filled with laughter;
　　our tongues were spilling over into song.
The word went out *across the prairies and deserts,*
　　across the hills, over the oceans wide, from nation to nation:
"The Eternal One has done remarkable things for them."
³*We shook our heads. All of us were stunned*—the Eternal One has done
　　　remarkable things for us.
　　We were beyond happy, *beyond joyful.*

⁴And now, Eternal One, *some are held captive and poor.*

PSALM 126 | **Overwhelming joy** filled the Jews as they returned to the promised land from exile in Babylon. The psalmist describes it as if they were dreaming and the joy became laughter and then turned to singing and finally tears of deep-seated appreciation. God has done remarkable things. Oh, those were wonderful days.

Joyful memories are like beautiful paintings. Every time we look at them, consider them, let our hearts and minds wander through them, we're happy again. When we talk about them, they actually become real again right before our eyes. More than that, they take on a shape and an importance that help offset whatever hardships life has brought our way since then.

A special memory gives us hope, reminding us we can feel that kind of incredible joy again. This psalm invites us to search our memories and to remember glorious moments when we, too, were happier because of something wonderful that only the Eternal One could have brought together for us. But the joy is far more than good feelings. The acts of God are a factual proof that He is the One of Eternity who is the Almighty. It is not feeling but truth that causes us to spill over into emotions. Our joy springs out of the reality that is our God.

Release them, and restore our fortunes
as the dry riverbeds of the South *spring to life when the rains come
at last.*
⁵Those who walk the fields to sow, *casting their seed* in tears,
will one day tread those same long rows, amazed by what's appeared.
⁶Those who weep as they walk
and plant *with sighs*
Will return singing with joy,
when they bring home the harvest.

PSALM 127

A SONG OF SOLOMON FOR THOSE JOURNEYING *TO WORSHIP.*

¹Unless the Eternal One builds the house,
those who labor *to raise it* will have worked for nothing.

PSALM 127 **"Unless the Eternal One builds the house"** is not about home construction or monetary success. This psalm is about creating people of quality—our children, grandchildren, and all who are touched by them. No amount of child psychology will make up for a family without God.

"It is pointless to get up early" tells us that planning and work apart from the redemptive activity of God are useless. It turns out that neither our success nor our children's is about having an Ivy League education or being born on the right side of the tracks. Success (ours and our children's) is about one thing and one thing only. We have to put all our plans, all our hopes, and all our power into the hands of the Eternal One. We have to commit our families to His will and to His love for us. Nothing else matters!

Children are a gift entrusted to parents and must be treasured as belonging to Him. Our main objective as parents is not to provide a good home but a godly home in which they can grow and become even more valuable to God's kingdom. Then we will be able to return these precious jewels to Him as the worthy servants returned with interest the talents they had been given (see Jesus' parable in Matthew 25:14-30). In the meantime, our labors will be rewarded as our children eventually mature and in turn care for us.

Unless the Eternal One stands watch over the city,
    those who guard it have wasted their time.
2*God provides for His own.* It is pointless to get up early,
    work hard, and go to bed late
Anxiously laboring for food to eat;
    for God provides for those He loves, even while they are sleeping.

3Know this: children are a gift from the Eternal One;
    the fruit of the womb is His reward.
4Your sons born in your youth are *a protection,*
    like arrows in the hand of a warrior.
5Happy is the man who has
    his quiver full, *for they will help and protect him when he is old.*
He will not be humiliated when he is accused at the gate,
    for his sons will stand with him against his enemies.

PSALM 128

A SONG FOR THOSE JOURNEYING *TO WORSHIP.*

1Those who stand in awe of the Eternal One—
    who follow wherever He leads, *committed in their hearts*—experience
      His blessings!

PSALM 128 **To show that you love God** and are loyal to Him, go where
He leads, work hard, and you will prosper.

    Now, it is important to note how you are to prosper. You will have many
children who will bloom like flowers from seed. They will bring you blessing
throughout your life. And you, in turn, will be a blessing through future generations.
In our day, this doesn't seem like such a good deal. But we have to consider why
we would think that. You see, we have become accustomed to measuring our
personal blessing in the accumulation of material things, but God takes the long
view on blessing. The psalmist is talking about blessings that are real and lasting:

²*God will use* your hard work to provide you food.
   You will prosper *in your labor,* and it will go well for you.

³Your wife will be like a *healthy* vine producing plenty of fruit,
   a spring of life in your home.
Your children will be like *young* olive shoots;
   you will watch them bud and bloom around your table.
⁴Such are the blessings the Eternal lavishes
   on those who stand in awe of Him!

⁵May the Eternal One *continue to* pour out *His love* on you,
   showering down blessings from *His holy mountain*, Zion.
May you see Jerusalem prosper
   all your days.
⁶May you have the privilege of seeing your grandchildren *as they grow.*
   May peace flourish in Israel!

(continued from previous page)

values, children, family, neighbors, community—all drawn together in awe of God and the richness of His mercy poured into people. There is no mention of wealth; the prosperity relates to the necessities of life and the value of relationships.

Most of us strive after possessions and still more possessions. But God wants to bless us with deep, abiding relationships with Himself and with people who revere Him. The quality of these relationships and the freedom from material obsessions provide a quality of blessing that God promises will give us peace. He will lead us in His path, give us good, hard work, a family at peace, and it will go well. So what isn't good about that plan?

Blessing after blessing has been bestowed upon us, giving us room to grow and explore and become all that God designed us to be. We can start now and start anywhere to count those blessings: family, friends, talents and gifts, restful sleep, inspired moments, hugs . . . the list is never-ending. We are challenged to see God's gracious and generous hand in our lives today and to embrace the outpouring of His generous Spirit.

Psalm 129

¹"*This is not the first time* my enemies assaulted me;

    they have often attacked me since I was young."

So let Israel now proclaim,

²"*This is not the first time* my enemies assaulted me;

    they have attacked me since I was young,

    and yet they have not been able to overpower me.

³The plowers plowed over me;

    they plowed their furrows *deep and* long down my back."

⁴The Eternal One is just.

    He's severed the bindings of the wicked *so they can't hurt me anymore.*

⁵May all who despise Zion

    hang their heads in shame. *May all who despise Zion* recoil and run away.

⁶Let them grow like grass upon rooftops

    that withers *and dies in the sun* long before it has time to grow,

⁷Unfit to be harvested by the worker,

    not worthy of the effort to carry off to the binder.

⁸*Unwanted, uncared for*—no passersby *to greet them, no one* to say,

    "May the favor of the Eternal One be upon you;

We bless you in His name."

Psalm 130

¹From the depths *of disaster* I appeal to You, O Eternal One:

    ²Lord, hear my cry!

Attune Your ears

    to my humble prayer!

³If You, Eternal One, recorded each offense,

Lord, who *on earth* could stand *innocent*?

⁴But with You forgiveness exists;

that's why *true* respect of You might flow.

⁵So I wait for the Eternal One—my soul awaits *rescue*—

and I put my hope in His *transforming* word.

⁶My soul waits for the Lord *to break into the world*

more than *night* watchmen *expect* the break of day,

even more than night watchmen *expect* the break of day.

⁷O Israel, *ground your* hope in the Eternal One.

For in the Eternal One lives *the most* loyal love,

and with Him comes *the most* abundant redemption.

⁸He will ransom Israel

from all the sinful acts *that stole you away*.

PSALM 130 **Have you ever had a day** so awful that you couldn't wait for it to end so you could start all over? This psalm expresses that kind of feeling. The writer says his soul waits for the new day like the watchman looking for the end of his watch. Two things are happening here: first, the watchman is tired and wants to go home to his bed. Second, attack often comes with the dawn when everyone is either still asleep or tired from guard duty. It is a time of anxious waiting. The psalmist was anxious, tired, and ready for a new start.

Sometimes it is easier to start over again than to straighten out a bad situation. But what if *we* are the bad situation? Trying to salvage the remaining good from things deemed useless or worn out isn't easy. Only the Eternal One can go through the refuse that we become over time, digging through the scraps of us to still find a nugget worth holding on to. Indeed, His mercy and His salvation are what restore souls and give them value once again.

The psalmist confesses numerous offenses and resulting forgiveness. He is counting on the "loyal love" of the Eternal One and on His "abundant redemption." These both sound really good, don't they? He is calling out "from the depths of disaster." And he rests on the saving grace of God "from all the sinful acts."

Weary and worn as we are, God can still make something of us. We wait for the Lord to find us in all our brokenness and cement us together once more with His stubborn love and abundant grace.

PSALM 131

A SONG OF DAVID FOR THOSE JOURNEYING *TO WORSHIP*.

[1]O Eternal One, my heart is not occupied with proud thoughts;
 my eyes do not look down *on others*;
I don't *even begin to* get involved in matters too big, *matters of faith, state,
 business,*
 or the many things that defy my ability *to understand them.*
[2]*Of one thing I am certain:* my soul has become calm, quiet, *and contented
 in You.*
 Like a weaned child resting upon his mother, *I am quiet.*
 My soul is like this weaned child.

[3]O Israel, stake your trust *completely* in the Eternal One—
 from this very moment and into the vast future.

PSALM 132

A SONG FOR THOSE JOURNEYING *TO WORSHIP*.

[1]Eternal One, *don't let* the suffering of *our father* David *be forgotten*—
 for his sake, remember!
[2]Remember the pledge he made, *how he poured out his heart* to the Eternal
 One,
 the promise he made to the Mighty One of Jacob:
[3]*He said,* "I will not go inside my house
 or lie down in my bed;
[4]I will not even rest my eyes—
 I will not *take comfort in* sleep—
[5]Until I find a *dwelling* place for You, the Eternal One,
 a *holy* residence dedicated to the Mighty One of Jacob."

⁶We heard rumors of the holy ark in Ephrathah,*
    and *later* we found it in the field of Jaar.*

⁷Let us journey to His dwelling place;
    let us worship at His footstool.

⁸Eternal One, arise and go to Your new home—
    You and the ark of Your strength.
⁹Let every priest *join the march* wearing righteousness,
    and let songs of joy erupt from *the hearts and mouths of* Your
        godly ones.
¹⁰For the well-being of Your anointed servant,
    do not turn Your back on David.

¹¹The Eternal One made His own promise, sworn in truth to David,
    an oath which He *cannot,* will not break:
"I will continue your dynasty, *David;*
    one of your descendants will sit on your throne.

132:6 Ephrathah is the region where Bethlehem is located, Micah 5:2.
132:6 Jaar is a shortened form of Kirjath-jearim, 1 Samuel 7:1.

PSALM 132 | **Walking with God?** When did we lose the sense of walking with God? For most of us, what we do is more like passing Him on the street from time to time. This psalm is about the close communion that David had with God and the promises they made to one another. The really interesting thing is that these personal promises have affected generations unborn at the time the promise was made. The writer of this psalm is remembering back to the day as if these promises were still in effect during his lifetime.

David promised that nothing would stop him from preparing a home for God. God heard David's promise but forced a generation's delay in its completion. Although loved by God, David was kept from building God's temple because of his immoral behavior. God did allow him to gather the materials and to make the plans, but David's son Solomon actually built the house. God also made a promise to David that has affected all people. He established David's dynasty forever, and from David's descendants would come the Messiah—the Christ who would bring redemption for all.

¹²If your children obey My covenant
     and follow the statutes which I shall teach them,
And if they remain faithful, their children will also
          sit upon your throne—forever."

¹³For the Eternal One selected Zion;
     He desired it as His *holy place of* residence.
¹⁴"This is *My sanctuary,* My resting place, forever *and ever;*
     I will remain here, for this is what I have desired.
¹⁵I will bless Zion with an endless supply of all she needs;
     I will satisfy *the bellies of* her hungry with bread.
¹⁶I will clothe her priests with salvation,
          and songs of joy will erupt from *the hearts and mouths of* her godly
          people.

¹⁷"From there I will make the strength of David's *kingdom* grow
     and prepare a lamp for My anointed one.
¹⁸I will clothe his enemies with *a garment of* shame;
     but as for David's son, his crown will shine *brightly like the sun.*"

Here's a reminder for those who aren't sure they want to stand on the Lord's side. We see what God promises to David and therefore to us as we walk in His ways. He promises to keep us strong so we can grow. Since God holds in His hands everything that means anything to us, we can see He wants us to be enriched and blessed. The lesson here is that God keeps His word, and He expects the same from us.

The Eternal One promises to prepare a lamp to light our way, and He leads us to the places we need to go. If getting His direction, growing stronger, and thriving in the work God calls us to do pleases us, then these are life-giving promises. Because God cares about the path we take, He also sheds light on the alternative faced by those who reject what He offers: a garment of shame to wear. We choose where we want to stand. You see, we are meant to walk with God as David did. We are to follow His light on the path He has for us. But, we are never alone.

Psalm 133

A SONG OF DAVID FOR THOSE JOURNEYING *TO WORSHIP*.

¹How good and pleasant it is
　　when brothers *and sisters* live together in peace!
²It is like the finest oils poured on the head,
　　sweet-smelling oils flowing down to cover the beard,
Flowing down the beard of Aaron,
　　flowing down the collar of his robe.
³It is like the gentle rain of *Mount* Hermon
　　that falls on the hills of Zion.
Yes, from this place, the Eternal One spoke the command,
　　from there He gave His blessing—life forever.

Psalm 134

A SONG FOR THOSE JOURNEYING *TO WORSHIP*.

¹Praise the Eternal One, all you who serve Him—
　　who *stand ready to* serve in the house of the Eternal through the
　　night.

PSALM 134 | **Giving genuine, heartfelt praise** is sometimes hard.
Maybe because it's not about us and in truth it's not even about how we feel. It's
about the person who merits praise.

Think back on a moment when you delivered high praise for a job well done
or a kindness bestowed. Now consider the accolades you might give a celebrity
or perhaps a president or king or a person in leadership in the church. Then focus
your attention toward the One who is worthy above *all* names, *all* kings, and *all*
persons who have ever lived and deliver heartfelt praise.

²Lift up your hands toward His sanctuary,
and praise the Eternal One.

³May the Eternal One grant you His blessing from Zion,
God, the weaver of heaven and earth.

PSALM 135

¹Praise the Eternal One!
Praise *and glorify* the name of the One who always has been and
always will be;
praise Him, servants of the Eternal One;
²*Join in the chorus,* all you who minister in the Eternal's temple;
in the courts of our God's temple,
³Glorify the Eternal, for He is good!
Sing praises, and honor His name for it is delightful.
⁴For the Eternal One made His choice; He selected Jacob as His own;
He claimed Israel as His possession.

⁵Now I know this: the Eternal One is great; *His power is unmatched.*
Our Master is above any *so-called* god.
⁶He does whatever He pleases,
in heaven, on earth,
in the seas, and in all the *ocean* depths.

Praise God in your sacred place, but better yet, praise God in everyday
situations—in everything you do. All of us are called to serve God if we belong to
Him. Our genuine, dedicated service is an act of praise. In following God's direction
and giving back to Him our time and energy, we are acknowledging that He is our
Lord and we are His servants. The One who weaves the tapestry of life deserves
praise every way we can give it!

⁷He draws up the clouds that rise over the whole earth,

> He causes rain and the lightning *to strike,*
>
> and He summons the wind from His storehouses.

⁸He took the lives of Egypt's firstborn,

> human and beast alike.

⁹O Egypt, He worked wonders and signs

> before your eyes,
>
> *signs* against Pharaoh and Pharaoh's servants.

¹⁰He destroyed nation after nation

> and killed mighty kings:

¹¹Sihon, the Amorite king;

> Og, the king of Bashan;
>
> and even all the kingdoms of Canaan.

¹²He *conquered* their land *and* gave it as an inheritance—

> an inheritance for His people, Israel.

¹³Eternal One, Your name is everlasting.

> Your legacy, Eternal One, will be known through all the ages.

¹⁴For the Eternal One will judge His people,

> He will show compassion to those who serve Him.

¹⁵The nations have idols of silver and gold,

> crafted by human hands!

¹⁶They shaped mouths for them, but they cannot speak;

> they carved eyes into them, but they cannot see;

¹⁷They placed ears on them, but they cannot hear;

> they cannot breathe, *not even a puff of air* from their mouths!

¹⁸The artisans who made them

> are just like them,
>
> and so are all who *mistakenly* trust in them, *no exceptions.*

¹⁹House of Israel, praise the Eternal One;

> house of Aaron, praise the Eternal One;

²⁰House of Levi, praise the Eternal One;

> all those who revere the Eternal One, praise Him!

²¹Blessed be the Eternal One from Zion,
>   the One who has made Jerusalem His home.
> Praise the Eternal One!

PSALM 136

¹*Let your heart overflow with* praise to the Eternal One, for He is good,
>   for His faithful love lasts forever.
> ²Praise the True God *who reigns* over all other gods,
>   for His faithful love lasts forever.
> ³Praise the Lord *who reigns* over all other lords,
>   for His faithful love lasts forever.

⁴To Him who alone does marvelous wonders,
>   for His faithful love lasts forever.
> ⁵Who created the heavens with skill *and artistry,*
>   for His faithful love lasts forever.
> ⁶Who laid out dry land over the waters,
>   for His faithful love lasts forever.
> ⁷Who made the great *heavenly* lights,
>   for His faithful love lasts forever.
> ⁸The sun to reign by day,
>   for His faithful love lasts forever.
> ⁹The moon and stars to reign by night,
>   for His faithful love lasts forever.

¹⁰To Him who struck down the firstborn of the Egyptians,
>   for His faithful love lasts forever.
> ¹¹Who set Israel free from Egyptian masters,
>   for His faithful love lasts forever.
> ¹²With *fierce strength,* a mighty hand, and an outstretched arm,
>   for His faithful love lasts forever.

¹³To Him who split the Red Sea* in two *and made a path between the divided waters,*
> for His faithful love lasts forever.

¹⁴Then allowed Israel to pass *safely* through *on dry ground,*
> for His faithful love lasts forever.

¹⁵*To Him* who crushed Pharaoh and his army in *the waters of* the Red Sea,*
> for His faithful love lasts forever.

¹⁶Who guided His people through the desert,
> for His faithful love lasts forever.

¹⁷Who struck down mighty kings,
> for His faithful love lasts forever.

¹⁸Who slaughtered famous kings,
> for His faithful love lasts forever.

136:13 Literally, Sea of Reeds
136:15 Literally, Sea of Reeds

PSALM 136 **Objects of His Affection.** Can't we just imagine a choir singing the response to this beautiful psalm? Knowing we are the recipients of God's eternal love and kindness is really pretty mind-boggling. After all, we continue to refuse His loving grace, though He strives to show us He is present with us in a myriad of ways. Sometimes we deny that He is the author of our good, the One who caused all of it to happen.

This song was a great celebration of Israel as they recited perfections of God and reviewed the saving acts of God they had experienced. After each perfection or work, they sang out "for His faithful love lasts forever." Since all of us struggle with how to worship God alone, try this little exercise. Write out the things about God that make you stand in awe, and list the things He has done in your life. Then pray or sing the items on your paper, repeating after each item, "You are faithful and Your love for me lasts forever." If you will do this, you will never be quite the same again.

God provides every opportunity, every blade of grass, every bit of food. He provides in spite of us and because of us. We are His objects of affection. We're loved more than we can imagine and certainly more than we deserve.

We can praise God with poetry or song; we can sing unending refrains; we can lift our hearts to the King of the universe. We can and we should because all honor and glory are His! He is faithful and His love lasts forever.

¹⁹Sihon, the king of the Amorites,
    for His faithful love lasts forever.
²⁰And Og, the king of Bashan,
    for His faithful love lasts forever.
²¹*To Him* who gave the conquered land as an inheritance,
    for His faithful love lasts forever.
²²*Who made the land* a heritage to Israel, His servant,
    for His faithful love lasts forever.

²³*To Him* who remembered us when we were nearly defeated,
    for His faithful love lasts forever.
²⁴Who rescued us from our enemies,
    for His faithful love lasts forever.
²⁵Who provides food for every living thing,
    for His faithful love lasts forever.

²⁶*Let your heart overflow with* praise to the True God of heaven,
    for His faithful love lasts forever.

PSALM 137

¹By the rivers of Babylon,
    we sat and wept
    when we thought of Zion, *our home, so far away.*
²On *the branches of* the willow trees,
    we hung our harps *and hid our hearts from the enemy.*
³And the men that surrounded us
    made demands that we *clap our hands and* sing—
Songs of joy *from days gone by,*
    songs from Zion, *our home.*
Such cruel men taunted us—*haunted our memories.*

⁴How could we sing a song about the Eternal One
    in a land so foreign, *while still tormented, brokenhearted, homesick?*
    Please don't make us sing this song.

5-6O Jerusalem, even still, don't escape my memory.
>*I treasure you and your songs, even as I hide my harp from the enemy.*
And if I can't remember,
>may I never sing *a song* again—
>may my hands never play well again—
For what use would it be if I don't remember Jerusalem
>as my source of joy.

7Remember, Eternal One, how the Edomites, *our brothers, the descendants*
>*of Esau,*
>*stood by and* watched as Jerusalem fell.
Gloating, they said, "Destroy it;
>tear it down to the ground,"
>*when Jerusalem was being demolished.*
8O daughter of Babylon, you are destined for destruction!
Happy are those who pay you back for how you treated us
>*so you will no longer walk so proud.*
9Happy are those who dash your children against the rocks
>*so you will know how it feels.*

PSALM 138

A SONG OF DAVID.

1To You, *Eternal One,* I give my whole heart, *a heart filled* with praise, *for I*
>*am grateful;*
>before the gods, my heart sings praises to You *and You alone.*
2I bow *before You,* looking to Your holy temple,
>and praise Your name, for Your unfailing love and Your truth;
>for You have placed Your name and Your word over all things *and all*
>times.
3On the day *I needed You,* I called, and You responded
>and infused my soul with strength.

⁴May all the kings of the earth praise You, O Eternal One,
    because they have heard the words You have spoken.
⁵*They will marvel* at the Eternal's ways, and they will sing,
    for great is the glory of the Eternal One.
⁶Although the Eternal One is greatest of all, He is attentive to the needy
    and keeps His distance from the proud *and pompous*.

⁷Whenever I walk into trouble,
    You are there to bring me out.
You hold out Your hand
    to protect me against the wrath of my enemies,
    and hold me safely in Your right hand.
⁸The Eternal One will finish what He started in me.
    Your faithful love, O Eternal One, lasts forever;
    Do not give up on what Your hands have made.

PSALM 138 | **Gaining Perspective.** Sometimes the pattern of life becomes so familiar that we lose sight of what is happening. We begin to take things and people for granted. We go for months without telling our children how proud we are of them or telling our spouses we love them and they are unique in all the world. Worse even than that, we forget about the love God has for each of us individually. David wrote, "On the day I needed You, . . . You responded." He later said, "Whenever I walk into trouble, You are there to bring me out."

We walk into trouble without even knowing it sometimes. Not all the enemies are defined for us. It's only God's protection that keeps us walking in and out of events that could devastate us if we were totally on our own. The Eternal One started a work in us, and He will see it through. His presence then is not just something we hope for, but something we need, and even more, something He provides because He loves us.

As we consider all the times we've been aware of trouble in our lives, we recognize that many of those troubles have been temporary, ultimately enriching us and helping us grow. We also think about the troubles that never actually touched our lives or the ones that were averted by our watchful God. His mercy toward us is everlasting! We can trust Him to "finish what He started" in us.

PSALM 139

FOR THE WORSHIP LEADER. A SONG OF DAVID.

¹O Eternal One, You have explored my *heart* and know *exactly* who I am;
²You even know *the small details like* when I take a seat and when I stand
up again.
Even when I am far away, You know what I'm thinking.
³You observe my wanderings and my sleeping, *my waking and my dreaming,*
and You know everything I do in more detail *than even I know.*
⁴You know what I'm going to say *long before I say it.*
It is true, Eternal One, that You know everything *and everyone.*
⁵You have surrounded me *on every side,* behind me and before me,
and You have placed Your hand *gently* on my *shoulder.*
⁶It is the most amazing feeling to know *how deeply* You know me, *inside
and out;*
the realization of it is so great that I cannot comprehend it.

⁷Can I go anywhere apart from Your Spirit?
Is there anywhere I can go to escape Your *watchful* presence?

⁸If I go up into heaven, You are there.
If I make my bed in the realm of the dead, You are there.
⁹If I ride on the wings of morning,
if I make my home in the most isolated part of the ocean,
¹⁰Even then You will be there to guide me;
Your right hand will embrace me, *for You are always there.*
¹¹Even if I *am afraid and* think *to myself,* "There is no doubt that the
darkness will swallow me,
the light around me will soon be turned to night,"
¹²*You can see* in the dark, for it is not dark to Your eyes.
For You the night is just as bright as the day.
Darkness and light are the same to Your eyes.

¹³For You shaped me, inside *and out.*

You knitted me together in my mother's womb *long before I took my first breath.*

¹⁴I will offer You my grateful heart, for I am Your *unique* creation, filled with wonder and awe.

You have approached even the smallest details with excellence; Your works are wonderful;

PSALM 139 **Celebrating the work of God in creation** is the theme of several psalms. What power and majesty it took to make the heavens and the earth! Psalm 139 is unique in that it points to God's fingerprint in the minute details of creation. The focus is on the meticulous knowledge God has of everything created, "You even know the small details like when I take a seat and when I stand up. . . . You know what I'm thinking . . . what I'm going to say long before I say it. . . . You know everything."

For most of us, this is truly amazing but also a little frightening. God is with us in our thoughts, even before we verbalize them. It can also be encouraging. We have a connection with the Eternal. Our Creator never leaves us to fend for ourselves, no matter where we go on this planet. He promises to be with us even after we leave it. He sees us in our happiest moments and in the depths of our despair. He sees us and knows us as we are created "in the heart of the earth" and before we are "born from its womb." God can certainly understand us. We are connected.

That connection can go both ways. The psalmist makes an interesting statement: "Your thoughts and plans are treasures to me, O God!" Think of what you are missing by not having close communion with God. The creator and sustainer of all things is open to sharing our lives and His plans and thoughts with us. That means immense wisdom and understanding is available to us.

The psalm ends with an invitation to God: "Explore me . . . put me to test . . . examine me . . . guide me down Your path forever." Most stop their development after becoming a child of God, but when we open our lives completely to Him, He explores our souls and refines what He discovers. We can invite Him to test our resolve. To be fully marked as a devoted follower, we must become an open book to God, allowing Him to clean house and to write a new ending to our story. He can be trusted to do what is best for us, and we can go deeper in our relationship with Him.

I carry this knowledge deep within my soul.

¹⁵*You see all things;* nothing about me was hidden from You
As I took shape in secret,

carefully crafted in the heart of the earth *before I was born from its womb.*

¹⁶*You see all things;* You saw me growing, changing *in my mother's womb;*
Every detail *of my life* was already written in Your book;

You established the length of my life before I ever tasted *the sweetness* of it.

¹⁷Your thoughts *and plans* are treasures to me, O God! *I cherish each and every one of them!*

How grand in scope! How many in number!

¹⁸If I could count each one of them, they would be more than all the grains of sand *on earth. Their number is inconceivable!*

Even when I wake up, I am still near to You.

¹⁹I wish You would destroy all the wicked, O God.

So keep away from me, those who are thirsty for blood!

²⁰For they say such horrible things about You,

and those who are against You abuse Your good name.

²¹Is it not true that I hate all who hate You, Eternal One?

Is it not true that I despise all who come against You?

²²Deep hatred boils within me toward them;

I am Your friend, and they are my enemies.

²³Explore me, O God, and know the real me. *Dig deeply and discover who I am.*

Put me to the test and watch how I handle the strain.

²⁴*Examine me to* see if there is an evil bone in me,

and guide me down Your path forever.

PSALM 140

FOR THE WORSHIP LEADER. A SONG OF DAVID.

¹Save me, O Eternal One, from the evil men *who seek my life.*

Shield me from *this band of* violent men.

²Their hearts devise evil! *They conspire against me;*
  they are constantly causing a storm of war.
³These snakes have sharpened their tongues;
  viper venom hides beneath their lips.*

[pause]*

⁴Keep me from the grip of these cruel *men,* O Eternal One.
  Shield me from *this band of* violent men
  whose *only* intention is to trip me up *and undermine all I do.*
⁵Those arrogant people are trying to catch me;
  they've laid their trap, hiding a net along my path;
  their traps are set, *and I am the prey.*

[pause]

⁶"Eternal One," I said, "You are my *one and only* God.
  Hear me, O Eternal, hear my humble cry *for rescue.*
⁷O Lord, Eternal One, power of my deliverance,
  You are my helmet in the day of battle.
⁸So do not fulfill the desires of these evildoers, Eternal One;
  do not advance their evil schemes, lest they brag *about their successes.*

[pause]

⁹"As for the gang leader of those who surround me,
  let their mischievous words cover them; *smother them in trouble.*
¹⁰Let hot coals fall *from heaven* upon them
  and cast them into the *roaring* fires.
  May they sink into the muddy marsh from which there is no return.
¹¹Let no liar find a home anywhere in the land;
  let evil hunt down the violent man *and do him in* quickly."

¹²I am certain the Eternal One supports the cause of the distressed;
  the poor will receive the justice *they deserve.*
¹³Indeed, the just-living will glorify Your name,
  and honorable people will be at home in Your presence.

140:3 Romans 3:13
140:3 Literally, selah, likely a musical direction from a Hebrew root meaning "to lift up"

Psalm 141

A SONG OF DAVID.

¹O Eternal One, I call upon You. Come quickly!
Listen to my voice as I call upon You!
²Consider my prayer as *an offering of* incense *that rises* before You;
when I stand with my hands outstretched *pleading toward the heavens,*
consider it as an evening offering.

³Guard my mouth, O Eternal One; *control what I say.*
Keep a careful watch on every word I speak.
⁴Don't allow my deepest desires to steer me toward doing what is wrong
or associating with wicked people
Or joining in their wicked works
or tasting any of their pleasures.

PSALM 141 **Cleaning up our act** from the outside—that aspect of us that we present to the world—isn't really difficult. A little soap and water, some hair gel, and we're on our way! But how do we go about cleaning up our innermost being? You see, the things we say reveal the condition of our souls.

It's an interesting dilemma, because what's on the inside of us is what really projects to others when we enter a room. The way we are inside is reflected in our posture, in our attitude, and in our demeanor. Most apparently, it spills out in our language so that any dirty, little secrets we have eventually become public. It is just too difficult to always guard our language—especially when the thoughts behind the language are the problem.

Inside cleanup takes work. It means surrendering our thoughts and words and actions to the Eternal One every moment, with every breath. It means praying for clean hearts and for loving friends who will hold us accountable and help guide us back to the selves God intended . . . from the inside out! We can trust God to gently scrub us clean.

⁵Let those who do right strike me down in kindness
    and correct me *in love.*
  Their kind correction washes over my head like *pure* oil; do not let me *be*
      foolish and refuse *such compassion.*
    Still my prayer is against the deeds of the wicked:
⁶Their judges will be thrown from the edges of cliffs *and crushed upon the*
      rocks below,
    and the wicked will hear my words *and realize* that what I said was
      pleasing.
⁷Just as when a farmer plows and breaks open the earth, *leaving clumps of*
      dirt scattered along the rows,
    our bones are scattered at the mouth of the grave.

⁸My gaze is fixed upon You, Eternal One, my Lord;
    in You I find *safety and* protection. Do not *abandon me and* leave me
      defenseless.
⁹Protect me from the jaws of the trap my enemies have set for me
    and from the snares of those who work evil.
¹⁰May the wicked be caught in their own nets
    while I *alone* escape unharmed.

PSALM 142

A CONTEMPLATIVE PRAYER* OF DAVID WHILE HE HID IN A CAVE.

¹I call out loudly to the Eternal One;
    I lift my voice to the Eternal begging for His favor.
²I let everything that's going wrong spill out of my mouth;
    I spell out all my troubles to Him.
³When my spirit buckled under the burdens I bear,
    You knew my way.
  They conspired to *trip me up and* trap me
    on the path where I was walking.

142:title Hebrew, *maskil*

⁴Take a look *around* and see—to the right, *to the left*—
    no one is there who cares for me.
There's no way out of here;
    no one cares about *the state of* my soul.

⁵You are the One I called to, O Eternal One.
    I said, "You're the *only* safe place I know;
    You're all I've got in this world.
⁶Oh, *let me know that You* hear my cry
    because I'm languishing and desperate;

Rescue me from those who torment me
    because *there's no way I can stand up to them*; they are much too strong
        for me.
⁷Lift my *captive* soul from this *dark* prison
    so I may render to You my gratitude;
Then Your righteous *people* will gather around me
    because You will treat me with astounding goodness."

PSALM 142 | **A Safe Place.** Desolate? Have you ever been truly alone? Not sure that anyone actually sees you or even cares that you exist? If you have felt this way or for some other reason have felt isolated, then you have probably also experienced the natural cry from the depths of your soul for connection. All of us crave acceptance, even those people we might assume have no problems. The composer of this psalm refers to the feelings we have as "languishing" and "desperate." At such times, a darkness pervades every fiber of our being in the "dark prison" that holds our souls captive.

Despite all this, the psalmist reminds us of a greater truth. Even in that dark despair, that utter loneliness, that "no one cares for me" corner, there is one safe place to turn—one ever-present, ever-loving, all-knowing safe zone. "You're the only safe place I know," he tells God. The Eternal One awaits our call, hears our cries, and reaches out to us, even when we feel utterly alone. We are His and He sees us even now. "Then Your righteous people will gather around me because You will treat me with astounding goodness."

PSALM 143

A SONG OF DAVID.

¹Eternal One, *I come before You* with my prayer. Hear me out; *I plead
with you.*
Lend an ear to my requests.
In Your faithfulness and justice, respond to my pleas.
²Be kind *and slow* to judge Your *faithful* servant.
For compared to You, no one is truly just.

³My adversary has pressed in, *drawn closer, threatened* my life;
He's crushed me, driven me underground.
He's forced me to live down *here* in the dark; it's as *if I joined* those
who died a long time ago.
⁴That's why my spirit is growing faint inside me; *I have nothing left;*
my heart is *completely empty and* desolate.

PSALM 143 | **Is your spirit just weak?** Do you feel empty, even to the
point that you are isolated and desolate? David cried out to God, "My spirit is
weak . . . let me see Your face." Honesty with God is the beginning of healing.
There is no point in putting a good face on a bad situation: God knows us too well.

At some time in your life, you have probably prayed, "Your will be done." Sure,
the phrase is in the Lord's Prayer, but have you wondered just how God's will is
done? More importantly, how do *you* do His will? David, too, sought recovery or
reenergizing: "Teach me how I should walk. . . . Teach me how to do Your will."
"How" is an interesting question and way to focus. It's not the "why" of things as
we so often ask, but it's a request for instruction, direction, further insight as to the
best way to follow God's plan.

"How" is about what *you* need to do in order for God's will to be done. The
real key to this is found near the end of the psalm: "Allow Your good Spirit to guide
me." Ask what part God wants you to play in making His will happen. Pray that the
Eternal One will help you to allow the Spirit to lead you.

⁵*And yet* I can't forget the days of old, *the days I've heard so much about;*
    I fix my mind on all You have done;
    I ponder the work of Your hands;
⁶I reach out my hands to You.
        All that I am *aches and* yearns for You, like a dry land *thirsting*
            for rain.

[pause]*

⁷Hurry and answer me, O Eternal One,
    for my spirit is weak, *my courage is gone.*
 Do not turn away; let me see Your face;
    otherwise, I'll *die and* be like all those who have gone to the grave.
⁸Make me hear of Your faithful love in the morning,
        for I trust in You.
 Teach me how I should walk,
        for I offer my soul up to You.

⁹Rescue me from my enemies, Eternal One,
        for You are my shelter *from them.*
¹⁰Teach me how to do Your will,
        for You are my God.
 Allow Your good Spirit to guide me
        on level ground, *to guide me along Your path.*

¹¹For the sake of Your name *and the good of Your reputation,*
        preserve me, O Eternal One.
    In Your righteousness, save my life from *burden and* misery.
¹²In Your loyal love, silence my enemies *for good*;
        destroy all those who take pleasure in my suffering,
        for I am Your *faithful* servant!

143:6 Literally, selah, likely a musical direction from a Hebrew root meaning "to lift up"

Psalm 144

A SONG OF DAVID.

¹Blessed be the Eternal One, my rock.

> He trains my hands for war, gives me the skills *I need* for battle.

²*He is* my unfailing love and my citadel.

> *He is* my tower of strength and my deliverer.

He is my shield of protection and my shelter;

> He holds my people in check under me.

³O Eternal One, what is man, that You even care to know him?

> or the son of man, that You are mindful of him?

⁴Humans are like a *passing* breath;

> their time *on earth* is like a shadow that passes *over us during the day
> and soon is gone.*

⁵Eternal One, stretch out an opening in the heavens, and descend.

> Touch the mountains, and make them smoke.

⁶Send forth *bolts of* lightning, and scatter my enemies.

> Shoot Your *fiery* arrows, and rout the enemy.

⁷Reach down from Your high place;

> save me out of the great waters;
> rescue me from the grasp of these foreigners

⁸Who speak only lies

> and don't have truth in their deeds.

⁹To You, my God, I will sing a new song;

> I will sing Your *sweet* praises to *the sound of* a ten-stringed harp,

¹⁰For You deliver kings *from their enemies*

> and You rescue Your servant, David, from the sword of evil.

¹¹Rescue me,

> and save me from the grasp of these foreigners

Who speak only lies

> and don't have truth in their deeds.

¹²May our sons be like healthy plants
      as they grow and mature,
And may our daughters be like the corner pillars
      that decorate a palace.
¹³May our storehouses be full
      with abundant supplies of every crop,
And may the flocks of our fields
      multiply into thousands and tens of thousands!
      ¹⁴May our cattle be *strong and* productive,
Without miscarriage, without loss,
      and may there be no riots or protests in our streets!

¹⁵Happy are the people for whom all this is true;
      happy are the people whose God is the Eternal One!

PSALM 145*

A SONG OF PRAISE BY DAVID.

¹I will lift my praise *above everything* to You, my God and King!
      I will *continually* bless Your name forever and always.
²*My praise will never cease*—I will praise You every day;
      I will lift up Your name forever.
³The Eternal One is great and deserves endless praise;
      His greatness knows no limit, recognizes no boundary. No one can
            measure or comprehend His magnificence.

⁴One generation *after another* will celebrate Your great works;
      they will pass on the story of Your powerful acts to their children.
⁵Your majesty and glorious splendor *have captivated me*;
      I will meditate on Your wonders, *sing songs of Your worth.*
⁶We confess—there is *nothing greater than You, God,* nothing mightier
            than Your awesome works.
      I will tell of Your greatness *as long as I have breath.*

Psalm 145 A Hebrew acrostic poem

⁷*The news of* Your rich goodness *is no secret*—Your people love to recall it
and sing songs of *joy to celebrate* Your righteousness.

⁸The Eternal One is gracious. He shows mercy *to His people.*
For Him anger does not come easily, but faithful love does—and it is
rich and abundant.
⁹But the Eternal's goodness *is not exclusive*—it is offered *freely* to all.
His mercy extends to all His creation.

¹⁰*All creation will stand in awe of You,* O Eternal One. Thanks will pour
from *the mouths of* every one of Your creatures;
Your holy people will bless You.
¹¹*They will not be silent;* they will talk of the grandeur of Your kingdom
and celebrate *the wonder of* Your power
¹²Until everyone on earth *who has ears to hear* knows Your valiant acts
and the splendor of Your kingdom.
¹³Your kingdom will never end;
Your rule will endure forever.

[You are faithful to Your promise,
and Your acts are marked with grace.]*

145:13 Most Hebrew manuscripts omit this portion.

PSALM 145 **God surprises you**—just when you think you have His Word
figured out. The Old Testament is supposed to be about God's chosen people and
about how He corrects and delivers them. Jesus is the Messiah who lives and
ministers mostly to God's chosen people. Then Paul and, to some degree, Peter are
moved to include the "outsiders" in the family of God. Psalm 145 blows away the
logic that this is a late New Testament concept. "The Eternal One's goodness is not
exclusive—it is offered freely to all." So what is going on here?

Though we remind ourselves of God's promise in John 3:16, "For God
expressed His love for the world in this way: He gave . . . ," we still like to think of
His goodness as being "exclusive." In fact, sometimes we go so far as to assume
that being one of His children makes us part of a special club (Israel in the Old
Testament, the church in the New Testament), and though we give voice to the

(continued on next page)

[14]The Eternal One sustains all who stumble on their way.

> For those who are broken down, *God is near.* He raises them up *in hope.*

[15]All eyes have turned toward You, *waiting in expectation;*

> *when they are hungry,* You feed them right on time.

[16]The desires of every living thing

> are met by Your open hand.

[17]The Eternal One is right in all His ways,

> and He is kind in all His acts.

[18]The Eternal One stays close to those who call on Him,

> those who pray sincerely.

[19]All *of you* who revere Him—God will satisfy your desires.

> He hears the cries *for help,* and He brings salvation.

[20]All *of you* who love God—He will watch out for you,

> but *total* destruction is *around the corner* for all the wicked.

[21]My lips will sing the praise of the Eternal One.

> Let every creature *join me and* praise the holy name of God—forever and always!

(continued from previous page)

idea of engaging others, we only look at those who fit our criteria. In fact, we're even willing to leave some out because we've labeled them in such a way that God *could not possibly* mean to extend His invitation to them as well. After all, if we belong to the club, how can someone we wouldn't want to be friends with or who didn't respect our faith also belong?

Could it be that the Eternal One isn't interested in clubs and exclusivity? Even here in the period when Israel feels isolated, God is looking beyond the chosen few. Could it be that He opens His arms so wide that all can enter in if they choose to come "until everyone on earth who has ears to hear knows Your valiant acts"? His mercy extends to all creation! From the very beginning, God's plan was to save all who would respond. "All of you who revere Him—God will satisfy your desires." Is that not great—that we are included instead of being left outside the family of God?

PSALM 146

¹Praise the Eternal One!

 Praise the Eternal One, O my soul;
²I will praise the Eternal One for as long as I live.

    I will sing praises to my God as long as breath fills my lungs and blood
       flows through my veins.

³Do not put your trust in *the rulers of this world—kings and* princes.

    Do not expect any rescue from mortal men.
⁴As soon as their breath leaves them, they return to the earth;

    on that day, all of them perish—*their dreams,* their plans, *and their*
      memories.

⁵Blessed are those whose help comes from the God of Jacob,

    whose hope is *centered* in the Eternal One, their God—
⁶Who created the heavens, the earth,

    the seas, and all that lives within them;
Who *stays true and* remains faithful forever;

    ⁷who works justice for those who are pressed down *by the world,*
    providing food for those who are hungry.

The Eternal One frees those who are imprisoned;

    ⁸He makes the blind see.
The Eternal One lifts up those whose backs are bent *in labor*;

    He cherishes those who do what is right.
⁹The Eternal One looks after those who journey in a land not their own;

    He takes care of the orphan and the widow,
    but He frustrates the wicked along their way.

¹⁰The Eternal One will reign *today, tomorrow, and* forever.

    People of Zion, your God *will rule forever* over all generations.
 Praise the Eternal One!

PSALM 147

¹Praise the Eternal One!
 It is good to sing praises to our God,
    for praise is beautiful and pleasant.
²The Eternal One, *Architect of earth,* is building Jerusalem,
    finding the lost, gathering Israel's outcasts.
³He binds their wounds,
    heals the sorrows of their hearts.

PSALM 147 | **Trusting God with Our Dreams.** We are so predictable. When in a room crowded with people, we normally give our attention to the most famous, the most powerful, the most beautiful, and the smartest—in that order. More often than not, the nicest, kindest, most loyal people are overlooked. But not by God. "He takes no pleasure in the raw strength of horses; He finds no joy in the speed of the sprinter. But the Eternal One does take pleasure in those who worship Him." This is great news. Those of us who are not famous, wealthy, powerful, good-looking, or particularly smart have a chance to get close to God.

So what does this really mean for us ordinary folks? The psalmist gives a list of what makes God so great and powerful as creator, sustainer, and judge. Just imagine the most powerful force in the universe, the architect of creation, is interested in us. First, we must praise Him. Then we must trust Him with our dreams and our future.

What's your biggest dream? Can you make it possible? Can you be the architect of your own future and bring about all you want simply because you desire it to be so? By yourself, on your own, the answer is probably no. But with God who is putting you before all the important or beautiful people—with the One who formed the very essence of earth and sky and stars and seas and who knew you before you ever entered or left your mother's womb—with God, everything is possible!

God makes your impossibles possible! It's time to think positively about the dream entrusted to you . . . for with God on your side, there's nothing in this world to stop you!

⁴He counts all the stars *within His hands,*
  carefully fixing their number
  and giving them names.
⁵Our Lord is great. *Nothing is impossible* with His overwhelming power.
  He is *loving, compassionate, and* wise beyond all measure.
⁶The Eternal One will lift up the lowly
  but throw down the wicked to the earth.

⁷*Open your mouths* with thanks! Sing praises to the Eternal One!
  Strum the harp *in unending praise* to our God
⁸Who blankets the heavens with clouds,
  sends rain to water the *thirsty* earth,
  and pulls up each blade of grass upon the mountainside.
⁹He opens His hands to feed all the animals
  and *scatters seed* to nestlings when they cry.
¹⁰He takes no pleasure in the *raw* strength of horses;
  He finds no joy in the speed of the sprinter.
¹¹But the Eternal One does take pleasure in those who worship Him,
  those who invest hope in His unfailing love.

¹²O Jerusalem, praise the Eternal One!
  O Zion, praise your God!
¹³For His *divine* power reinforces your city gates,
  blesses your children in the womb.
¹⁴He establishes peace within your borders,
  fills your *markets* with hearty golden wheat.
¹⁵His command ripples across the earth;
  His word runs out on swift feet.
¹⁶He blankets *the earth* in wooly snow,
  scattering frost like ashes *over the land.*
¹⁷He throws down hail like stones *falling from a mountain.*
  Can any withstand His wintry blast?
¹⁸But He dispatches His word, and the thaw begins;
  at His command, the spring winds blow, *gently* stirring the waters
    back to life.
¹⁹He brings Jacob in on His plan, *declaring His word*—
  His statutes and His teachings to Israel.

²⁰He has not treated any other nation in such a way;
>
> they live unaware of His commands.
> Praise the Eternal One!

PSALM 148

¹Praise the Eternal One!

All you in the heavens, praise the Eternal;

> praise Him from the highest places!

²All you, His messengers and His armies *in heaven*:

> praise Him!

³Sun, moon, and all you brilliant stars above:

> praise Him!

⁴Highest heavens and *all* you waters above the heavens:

> praise Him!

⁵Let all things *join together in a concert of* praise to the name of the
>
> Eternal One,
>
> for He gave the command and they were created.

⁶He put them in their places *to stay* forever—

> He declared it so, and it is final.

⁷Everything on earth, *join in and* praise the Eternal;

> sea monsters and *creatures of* the deep,

⁸Lightning and hail, snow and foggy mists,

> violent winds all respond to His command.

⁹Mountains and hills,

> fruit trees and cedar forests,

¹⁰All you animals both wild and tame,

> reptiles and birds who take flight:
>
> *praise the Eternal One.*

¹¹All kings and all nations,

> princes and all judges of the earth,

¹²*All people*, young men and women,
old men and children alike,
praise the Eternal One.

¹³Let them *all* praise the name of the Eternal One!
For His name stands alone above all others.
His glory shines greater than anything above or below.
¹⁴He has made His people strong;
He is the praise of all who are godly,
the praise of the children of Israel, those whom He holds close.
Praise the Eternal One!

PSALM 149

¹Praise the Eternal One!
Write new songs; sing them to Him *with all your might*!
Gather with His faithful followers in *joyful* praise;
²Let *all of* Israel celebrate their Maker, *their God, their friend;*
let the children of Zion find great joy in their *true* King.
³So *let the music begin*; praise His name—dance and sing
to *the rhythm of* the tambourine, and *to the tune of* the harp.
⁴For the Eternal One *is listening,* and nothing pleases Him more than His
people;
He raises up the poor and endows them with His salvation.
⁵Let His faithful followers erupt in praise,
singing triumphantly *wherever they are,* even as they lie down *for sleep*
in the evening.
⁶With the name of God and praise in their mouths,
with a two-edged sword in their hands,
⁷Let them take revenge on all nations *who deny God.*
Let them punish the peoples.
⁸Kings and nobles will be locked up,
and their freedom will be bound in iron shackles.

⁹This judgment against them, decreed *by a holy God,* will be carried out.
  It's an honor for all His faithful followers *to serve Him.*
 Praise the Eternal One!

PSALM 150

¹Praise the Eternal One!
 Praise the True God inside His temple.
    Praise Him beneath massive skies, *under moonlit stars and rising sun.*
²Praise Him for His powerful acts, *redeeming His people, cradling the
    universe in His hands.*
    Praise Him for His greatness that surpasses *our time and
    understanding.*

PSALM 150 **Joyfully in His Presence.** This book of 150 unique songs or poems comes to an end. About half of them have been about worshiping God for what He has done. There are many about paying evil people back for their wickedness. Most are corporate songs, but some are personal. Several caution about our speech, some teach discipline, some help raise children, but all are a word from God. At the heart of each is our service to a great God who deserves our praise.

Praise by its very nature evokes emotion. If you give praise to anyone, it comes from the heart, it fills the other person with joy, and it makes everyone

³⁻⁴Praise Him with the blast of trumpets *high into the heavens,*
    and praise Him with harps and lyres
    and *the rhythm of the* tambourines *skillfully played by those who love*
        and fear the Eternal.
Praise Him with singing and dancing;
    praise Him with flutes and strings *of all kinds*!
⁵Praise Him with crashing cymbals,
    loud clashing cymbals!
⁶*No one should be left out;* Let every man and every beast—
    every creature that has the breath *of the Eternal*—praise the
        Eternal One!
Praise the Eternal One!

---

who hears it glad. Magnify that experience and take it to the mountaintops on a crystal-clear morning or under a blanket of stars in the evening calm and feel the excitement mount. Fill a gathering with loving voices singing God's praise in unison and it's infectious. The place becomes one of unspeakable joy.

No matter how long you live, you may never fully appreciate all that God has done to bring you closer to Himself. His love for all that He created goes far beyond any experience we can ever imagine. If you want just a taste of what it's like to be joyfully in His presence, though, turn your heart to praise and raise your voice to God's ear! To Him belongs the power and the glory forever and ever!